THE NEW MIDDLE AGES

BONNIE WHEELER, *Series Editor*

The New Middle Ages is a series dedicated to [...] [...] studies of medieval cultures, with particular emphasis on recuperating women's history and on feminist and gender analyses. This peer-reviewed series includes both scholarly monographs and essay collections.

PUBLISHED BY PALGRAVE:

Women in the Medieval Islamic World: Power, Patronage, and Piety
  edited by Gavin R. G. Hambly

The Ethics of Nature in the Middle Ages: On Boccaccio's Poetaphysics
  by Gregory B. Stone

Presence and Presentation: Women in the Chinese Literati Tradition
  by Sherry J. Mou

The Lost Love Letters of Heloise and Abelard: Perceptions of Dialogue in Twelfth-Century France
  by Constant J. Mews

Understanding Scholastic Thought with Foucault
  by Philipp W. Rosemann

For Her Good Estate: The Life of Elizabeth de Burgh
  by Frances A. Underhill

Constructions of Widowhood and Virginity in the Middle Ages
  edited by Cindy L. Carlson and Angela Jane Weisl

Motherhood and Mothering in Anglo-Saxon England
  by Mary Dockray-Miller

Listening to Heloise: The Voice of a Twelfth-Century Woman
  edited by Bonnie Wheeler

The Postcolonial Middle Ages
  edited by Jeffrey Jerome Cohen

Chaucer's Pardoner and Gender Theory: Bodies of Discourse
  by Robert S. Sturges

Crossing the Bridge: Comparative Essays on Medieval European and Heian Japanese Women Writers
  edited by Barbara Stevenson and Cynthia Ho

Engaging Words: The Culture of Reading in the Later Middle Ages
  by Laurel Amtower

Robes and Honor: The Medieval World of Investiture
  edited by Stewart Gordon

Representing Rape in Medieval and Early Modern Literature
  edited by Elizabeth Robertson and Christine M. Rose

Same Sex Love and Desire Among Women in the Middle Ages
  edited by Francesca Canadé Sautman and Pamela Sheingorn

Sight and Embodiment in the Middle Ages: Ocular Desires
  by Suzannah Biernoff

Listen, Daughter: The Speculum Virginum and the Formation of Religious Women in the Middle Ages
  edited by Constant J. Mews

Science, the Singular, and the Question of Theology
  by Richard A. Lee, Jr.

Gender in Debate from the Early Middle Ages to the Renaissance
  edited by Thelma S. Fenster and Clare A. Lees

Malory's Morte Darthur: Remaking Arthurian Tradition
  by Catherine Batt

The Vernacular Spirit: Essays on Medieval Religious Literature
  edited by Renate Blumenfeld-Kosinski, Duncan Robertson, and Nancy Warren

Popular Piety and Art in the Late Middle Ages: Image Worship and Idolatry in England 1350–1500
  by Kathleen Kamerick

Absent Narratives, Manuscript Textuality, and Literary Structure in Late Medieval England
by Elizabeth Scala

Creating Community with Food and Drink in Merovingian Gaul
by Bonnie Effros

Representations of Early Byzantine Empresses: Image and Empire
by Anne McClanan

Encountering Medieval Textiles and Dress: Objects, Texts, Images
edited by Désirée G. Koslin and Janet Snyder

Eleanor of Aquitaine: Lord and Lady
edited by Bonnie Wheeler and John Carmi Parsons

Isabel La Católica, Queen of Castile: Critical Essays
edited by David A. Boruchoff

Homoeroticism and Chivalry: Discourses of Male Same-Sex Desire in the Fourteenth Century
by Richard Zeikowitz

Portraits of Medieval Women: Family, Marriage, and Politics in England 1225–1350
by Linda E. Mitchell

Eloquent Virgins: From Thecla to Joan of Arc
by Maud Burnett McInerney

The Persistence of Medievalism: Narrative Adventures in Contemporary Culture
by Angela Jane Weisl

Capetian Women
edited by Kathleen Nolan

Joan of Arc and Spirituality
edited by Ann W. Astell and Bonnie Wheeler

The Texture of Society: Medieval Women in the Southern Low Countries
edited by Ellen E. Kittell and Mary A. Suydam

Charlemagne's Mustache: And Other Cultural Clusters of a Dark Age
by Paul Edward Dutton

Troubled Vision: Gender, Sexuality, and Sight in Medieval Text and Image
edited by Emma Campbell and Robert Mills

Queering Medieval Genres
by Tison Pugh

Sacred Place in Early Medieval Neoplatonism
by L. Michael Harrington

The Middle Ages at Work
edited by Kellie Robertson and Michael Uebel

Chaucer's Jobs
by David R. Carlson

Medievalism and Orientalism: Three Essays on Literature, Architecture and Cultural Identity
by John M. Ganim

Queer Love in the Middle Ages
by Anna Klosowska Roberts

Performing Women: Sex, Gender and the Medieval Iberian Lyric
by Denise K. Filios

Necessary Conjunctions: The Social Self in Medieval England
by David Gary Shaw

Visual Culture and the German Middle Ages
edited by Kathryn Starkey and Horst Wenzel

Medieval Paradigms: Essays in Honor of Jeremy duQuesnay Adams, Volumes 1 and 2
edited by Stephanie Hayes-Healy

False Fables and Exemplary Truth: Poetics and Reception of a Medieval Mode
by Elizabeth Allen

Sacred and Secular in Medieval and Early Modern Cultures
edited by Lawrence Besserman

Tolkien's Modern Middle Ages
edited by Jane Chance and Alfred K. Siewers

TOLKIEN'S MODERN MIDDLE AGES

Edited by

Jane Chance and Alfred K. Siewers

TOLKIEN'S MODERN MIDDLE AGES
© Jane Chance and Alfred K. Siewers, 2005.
Softcover reprint of the hardcover 1st edition 2005 978-1-4039-6973-6

All rights reserved. No part of this book may be used or reproduced in any manner whatsoever without written permission except in the case of brief quotations embodied in critical articles or reviews.

First published in 2005 by
PALGRAVE MACMILLAN™
175 Fifth Avenue, New York, N.Y. 10010 and
Houndmills, Basingstoke, Hampshire, England RG21 6XS
Companies and representatives throughout the world.

PALGRAVE MACMILLAN is the global academic imprint of the Palgrave Macmillan division of St. Martin's Press, LLC and of Palgrave Macmillan Ltd. Macmillan® is a registered trademark in the United States, United Kingdom and other countries. Palgrave is a registered trademark in the European Union and other countries.

ISBN 978-0-230-61679-0   ISBN 978-0-230-62004-9 (eBook)
DOI 10.1007/978-0-230-62004-9

Library of Congress Cataloging-in-Publication Data

Chance, Jane, 1945–
    Tolkien's modern Middle Ages / by Jane Chance.
        p. cm.—(New Middle Ages)
    Includes bibliographical references (p.) and index.
    ISBN 978-1-4039-6973-6 (alk. paper)
      1. Tolkien, J. R. R. (John Ronald Reuel), 1892–1973—Criticism and interpretation. 2. Tolkien, J. R. R. (John Ronald Reuel), 1892–1973—Knowledge—History. 3. Literature and history—England—History—20th century. 4. Fantasy fiction, English—History and criticism. 5. Medievalism—England—History—20th century. 6. Postmodernism (Literature)—England. 7. Middle Earth (Imaginary place) 8. Middle Ages in literature. 9. History in literature. I. Title. II. New Middle Ages (Palgrave Macmillan (Firm))

PR6039.O32Z6224 2005
828'.91209—dc22   2005051027

A catalogue record for this book is available from the British Library.

Design by Newgen Imaging Systems (P) Ltd., Chennai, India.

First edition: November 2005
10 9 8 7 6 5 4 3 2 1

Transferred to digital printing in 2006.

For John and Tracy, Ben, Rachel, Matthew, and Peter, and for Olesya and Nicholas, and Father Mark

CONTENTS

List of Illustrations ix

Preface and Acknowledgments xi

Abbreviations xiii

1. Introduction: Tolkien's Modern Medievalism 1
   Jane Chance and Alfred K. Siewers

Part One Recontextualizing the Medieval in Postmodern Middle-Earth

2. A Postmodern Medievalist? 17
   Verlyn Flieger

3. The Medievalist('s) Fiction: Textuality and Historicity as Aspects of Tolkien's Medievalist Cultural Theory in a Postmodernist Context 29
   Gergely Nagy

4. Tolkien, *Dustsceawung*, and the Gnomic Tense: Is Timelessness Medieval or Victorian? 43
   John R. Holmes

Part Two Retreating to a Timeless Past: Middle-Earth and Victorian Medievalism

5. The Reanimation of Antiquity and the Resistance to History: Macpherson–Scott–Tolkien 61
   John Hunter

6. Archaism, Nostalgia, and Tennysonian War in *The Lord of the Rings* 77
   Andrew Lynch

CONTENTS

7. Pastoralia and Perfectability in
   William Morris and J.R.R. Tolkien 93
   Chester N. Scoville

8. English, Welsh, and Elvish: Language, Loss, and Cultural
   Recovery in J.R.R. Tolkien's *The Lord of the Rings* 105
   Deidre Dawson

Part Three   Confronting Modern Ideologies in Middle-Earth: War, Ecology, Race, and Gender

9. Fantastic Medievalism and the Great War in
   J.R.R. Tolkien's *The Lord of the Rings* 123
   Rebekah Long

10. Tolkien's Cosmic-Christian Ecology: The
    Medieval Underpinnings 139
    Alfred K. Siewers

11. Fear of Difference, Fear of Death: The *Sigelwara*,
    Tolkien's Swertings, and Racial Difference 155
    Brian McFadden

12. Tolkien and the Other: Race and Gender in Middle-Earth 171
    Jane Chance

Part Four   Visualizing Medievalism: Middle-Earth in Art and Film

13. Similar but not Similar: Appropriate Anachronism in
    My Paintings of Middle-Earth 189
    Ted Nasmith

14. Tolkien in New Zealand: Man, Myth, and Movie 205
    Michael N. Stanton

Works Cited 213

List of Contributors 229

Index 233

LIST OF ILLUSTRATIONS

13.1	Ted Nasmith, *An Unexpected Morning Visit* [detail, Gandalf by Bilbo's door], 1990	190
13.2	Ted Nasmith, Proposed Hotel-Office-Commercial Complex, Peoples Republic of China, ca. 1997	191
13.3	Ted Nasmith, *The Unexpected Party*, 1972	192
13.4	Ted Nasmith, *Rivendell*, 1984	193
13.5	Ted Nasmith, *The Riders of Rohan*, 1998	194
13.6	Ted Nasmith, *First Sight of Ithilien*, 2001	194
13.7	Ted Nasmith, *Portrait of Two Ferraris*, ca. 1999	196
13.8	Ted Nasmith, *Minas Tirith at Dawn*, 1989	197
13.9	Ted Nasmith, *At the Court of the Fountain*, 1990	198
13.10	Ted Nasmith, *Eärendil Searches Tirion*, 1998	199
13.11	Anne Washington, War Mausoleum, Verdun, France, ca. 1958	200
13.12	Ted Nasmith, *Barad-Dûr*, 1975	201

PREFACE AND ACKNOWLEDGMENTS

To address the issue of Tolkien's modernity and medievalism, a small band of leading Tolkien scholars assembled at a symposium at Bucknell University in the spring of 2003 organized by Alfred K. Siewers and then proceeded, with the aid of Jane Chance, to organize on the same topic sessions of the respected Tolkien symposium at the annual International Medieval Conference at Kalamazoo in 2004. Since 2001, these Tolkien conference sessions have been recognized as the premier North American academic forum for the field and have been the source of several scholarly books. It is from essays culled from both events that the current collection originates, along with another essay, from the symposium on "J. R. R. Tolkien, Fantasist and Medievalist," organized at the University of Vermont by Christopher Vaccaro. We remain indebted to Paul Szarmach and the other faculty of the Medieval Institute at Western University who have continued to encourage our presence and our intellectual contribution to medieval studies in general at the annual conferences.

Our gratitude to our universities is large and heartfelt: to Bucknell University (especially the English Department, Humanities Institute, and the College of Arts and Sciences, in particular Jim Rice, Eugenia Gerdes, John Rickard, Greg Clingham and Beth Cunningham) for funding the initial symposium and subsequent staffing and other needs in compiling the collection and preparing it for publication. And to the Rice University English Department we are grateful for mailings and for the aid by English Department editorial assistant Terry Munisteri until the end of the 2003–04 fiscal year. Terry has facilitated the publication of several books on Tolkien since 2000 by means of her careful editing of style and her knowledge of the various book and article styling manuals. Thanks also to Bucknell editorial assistants Sean Martin and Scott Gibson and to freelance indexer Blythe Woolsten for her excellent work.

The edition of *The Lord of the Rings* used throughout is the one-volume second edition from 1966, published in London by George Allen and Unwin in 1968, and again, by HarperCollins in 1993, and reset, with a note on the text by Douglas A. Anderson, by HarperCollins and Houghton Mifflin in 1994. References to *The Lord of the Rings* (henceforth *LR* in the text) appear within parentheses and indicate book, chapter, and page numbers—*The Fellowship of the Ring (FR)* being volume 1; *The Two Towers (TT)* being volume 2; and *The Return of the King (RK)* being volume 3.

Permission to reprint Ted Nasmith's illustrations for *The Lord of the Rings* in his essay has been granted by Houghton Mifflin. The illustration "At the Court of the Fountain" is reprinted by permission of HarperCollins Ltd., © Ted Nasmith, 1990.

Note: Tolkien prefers certain spellings that are used where appropriate in this study—for example, Dwarves (not Dwarfs), Middle-earth, not Middle Earth, Faërie, King of Faery (in "Smith of Wootton Major"), fairy-stories, sub-creation (not subcreation), and so forth; we capitalize the names of his species for consistency.

ABBREVIATIONS

"Beowulf"   "Beowulf: The Monsters and the Critics." *Proceedings of the British Academy* 22 (1936): 245–95. Repr. in: *An Anthology of "Beowulf" Criticism*. Ed. Lewis E. Nicholson. Notre Dame, IN: University of Notre Dame Press, 1963; *The "Beowulf" Poet*. Ed. Donald K. Fry. Englewood Cliffs, NJ: Prentice Hall, 1968; *The Monsters and the Critics and Other Essays*. Ed. Christopher Tolkien, 5–48. London: George Allen and Unwin, 1983; *Modern Critical Interpretations: "Beowulf."* Ed. Harold Bloom, 5–31. New York and Philadelphia: Chelsea House, 1987; *Interpretations of "Beowulf": A Critical Anthology*. Ed. R. Fulk, 14–44. Bloomington and Indianapolis: Indiana University Press, 1991; *"Beowulf": A Verse Translation*. Trans. Seamus Heaney. Ed. Daniel Donoghue, 103–30. *Norton Critical Editions*. New York: W. W. Norton, 2002.

FGH   J.R.R. Tolkien. *Farmer Giles of Ham*. London: Allen and Unwin, 1949; Boston: Houghton Mifflin, 1950.

FR   J.R.R. Tolkien. *Fellowship of the Ring*. Vol. 1 of *LR*.

H   J.R.R. Tolkien. *The Hobbit; Or There and Back Again*. London: George Allen and Unwin, 1937, 1951; Boston: Houghton Mifflin, 1938, 1958; New York: Ballantine, 1966. 2nd edn. New York: Ballantine, 1965; London: George Allen and Unwin, 1978; repr. Unwin Hyman, 1987.

"Homecoming"   J.R.R. Tolkien. "The Homecoming of Beorhtnoth Beorhthelm's Son." *Essays and Studies by Members of the English Association*, n.s., 6 (1953): 1–18. Repr. in *The Tolkien Reader*, 1–18. New York: Ballantine, 1966.

Letters   J.R.R. Tolkien. *The Letters of J. R. R. Tolkien: A Selection*. Ed. Humphrey Carpenter with assistance from Christopher Tolkien. London: George Allen and Unwin, 1981; Boston and New York: Houghton Mifflin, 1981;

	London: HarperCollins, 1995; New York: Houghton Mifflin, 2000.
LR	J.R.R. Tolkien. *The Lord of the Rings*. 3 vols.: *The Fellowship of the Ring*, *The Two Towers*, and *The Return of the King*. Rev. edn. London: George Allen and Unwin, 1966; Boston: Houghton Mifflin, 1967. First published in a single vol. 1968; London: HarperCollins, 1993. Reset edn., HarperCollins, 1994; Boston: Houghton Mifflin, 1994.
"*Monsters*"	J.R.R. Tolkien. *"The Monsters and the Critics" and Other Essays*. Ed. Christopher Tolkien. London: George Allen and Unwin, 1983; Boston: Houghton Mifflin, 1984.
"OFS"	J.R.R. Tolkien. "On Fairy-Stories." In *Essays Presented to Charles Williams*. Ed. C.S. Lewis. London: Oxford University Press, 1947. Repr. Grand Rapids, Mich.: William B. Eerdmans, 1966, 38–89. Rev. and repr. in *Tree and Leaf*. London: Allen and Unwin, 1964; Boston: Houghton Mifflin, 1965. Repr. in *The Tolkien Reader*. New York: Ballantine, 1966; *Tree and Leaf Including the Poem Mythopoeia*. London: Unwin Hyman, 1988; Boston: Houghton Mifflin, 1989.
PG	*Patrologia Graeca*. Ed. J.P. Migne et al. Paris, 1857–.
RK	J.R.R. Tolkien. *The Return of the King*. Vol. 3 of *LR*.
Silm	J.R.R. Tolkien. *The Silmarillion*. Ed. Christopher Tolkien. London: George Allen and Unwin, 1977. Boston, New York: Houghton Mifflin, 1977; New York: Ballantine, 1981. Repr. London: HarperCollins, 1994. 2nd edn. Boston: Houghton Mifflin, 2001.
TR	J.R.R. Tolkien. *The Tolkien Reader*. New York: Ballantine, 1966.
TL	J.R.R. Tolkien. *Tree and Leaf*. London: Allen & Unwin, 1964; Boston: Houghton Mifflin, 1965; rev. edn. *Tree and Leaf Including the Poem Mythopoeia*. London: Unwin Hyman, 1988; Boston: Houghton Mifflin, 1989.
TT	J.R.R. Tolkien. *Two Towers*. Vol. 2 of *LR*.

CHAPTER 1

INTRODUCTION: TOLKIEN'S MODERN MEDIEVALISM

Jane Chance and Alfred K. Siewers

The phenomenal success of J.R.R. Tolkien's *The Lord of The Rings*—first published in 1954–55 in England and 1954–56 in the United States, and adapted by Peter Jackson into trilogy film medium in 2001–03—has astounded its critics and gratified its fans and students. Tolkien's narratives in general continue today to engage and energize readers globally across a wide political and cultural spectrum, from the postmodern counterculture to Christian traditionalists. The context for this success in the author's professional medievalism has, however, continued to elude scholars. They agree that this modern epic-romance fantasy draws on Tolkien's personal and professional engagement with medieval texts and religion to present narratives from a premodern, traditional past. That consensus does not in itself explain why *The Lord of the Rings* has attracted such widespread attention.

This collection, *Tolkien's Modern Middle Ages*, poses several important questions related to this issue, for both Tolkien readers and scholars: What are the ways in which Tolkien's art translated and readapted medieval themes in relation to twentieth-century experience? How seriously should we take his own disclaimers against having done so in a direct way? Why and how does his fantasy engage right-wing and left-wing opponents of globalization today, and how does the medievalistic past in Tolkien's fantasy involve (much like the territory of the Arthurian realms) such very different readers and social readings across that spectrum? What explains the ongoing appeal of this modernist approach in the literary and cinematic imaginations of a postmodern era? And, finally, is the effect of Tolkien's medievalism ultimately more escapist or empowering in its engagement of readers with the "modern Middle Ages"?

The studies herein provide an opportunity to develop further the direct connections between Tolkien's adaptation of medieval traditions and the influence of his work on disparate modern audiences, rather than emphasizing (as Tolkien critics often do) the medieval and the modern as almost separate categories of discussion. Tolkien's yoking of the medieval with modern issues in his fantasy elicits connections that are postmodern in nature. And these postmodern connections require a more serious acknowledgment of the political role of medievalism as a response to modernism than scholarship has provided to date. Indeed, medievalism bears real social implications, primarily a looking to the past for a vision of more "organic" alternatives to modern institutions and systems of political and ethical value. This kind of backward look often confounds modern abstract categories of political ideology. The approach of this collection thus depends both on acknowledgment of the intellectual categories of "medieval" and "modern" as often artificial constructions of scholarship and on creation of a dialogue among scholars addressing related issues. Tolkien's fiction, particularly *The Lord of the Rings*, offers an ideal canvas for debating these issues.

Although born at the end of the nineteenth century and dying nearly at the end of the twentieth century, Tolkien in his literary preoccupations has generally not been regarded or interpreted either as a modernist or a postmodernist. Brian Rosebury argues in *Tolkien: A Cultural Phenomenon* (2003; a reworking of *Tolkien: A Critical Assessment*, 1992) that Tolkien's fiction evidences—surprisingly, given criticism of Tolkien's alleged conservativism—"an attitude to work that is close to John Ruskin's, and not too remote from Marx's."[1] Rosebury's focus on the nineteenth-century background to Tolkien's "liberal temper" and "joyful" tolerance for diversity[2] stems from his suggestion that Tolkien celebrates values with no specific historical valence.[3] Such an argument opens the door to consideration of Tolkien's peculiar postmodernism. His ahistoricity can support politics of both conservatism and subversion, the latter by providing a background for criticizing elite interests in dynamic socioeconomic trends and patterns. In Tolkien's case, the trends and patterns relate to the growth of industrial capitalism and modern war-oriented nation states. Tolkien presents a coherently constructed vision of cultural tradition as mounted above the historical fray. By its very evocation he brings into question the validity of contemporary claims to power and their accompanying categorizations of identity.

Key to understanding Tolkien's modern medievalism is his emergence from a Victorian tradition of literary medievalists. In his recuperation and memorialization of a distant past, Tolkien fits into a line with earlier (mostly nineteenth century) writers and composers such as James Macpherson, Mary Shelley, Alfred Lord Tennyson, Sir Walter Scott, William Morris and the Pre-Raphaelites, and Richard Wagner. Their reimagination of medieval themes helped shape resistance and social responses to modernization, industrialization, and the development of modern gender and racial identities. And their audiences developed from their works a wide range of personal and political ideologies. In various ways in the works of all these authors, reflections on the past elicited literary fantasies that provided a space for imagining alternate social realities to what appeared to be an advancing and stark economic libertarianism, matched by an often equally stark abstract utopianism. Indeed the reception of their art was subject to these same trends: Wagner's works could ultimately serve the purposes of later fascist ideology, Morris's could connect with the prospect of revolutionary tyranny as it would emerge in Russia, Tennyson's works could prop up British imperialism. Such appropriation by those in power illustrates the ambiguities often inherent in these writers' efforts. Thus, many readers ultimately might more easily ignore the social or political criticism of the modern inherent in such works, as was the case with Mary Shelley's *Frankenstein*, and instead accept them as popular escapist fantasy.

But Tolkien, one of the last of this line, also shared a literary culture in England defined as modernistic that influenced (but to some extent also remained distinct from) the fantasy of his "modern Middle Ages." The literary term "modernism," a style of writing popular between the first two world wars, is characterized by the experimental. It has been defined in varying ways by specific proponents, by T.E. Hulme, for example, as generally associated with classicism, that is, with "dry hardness." By this phrase Hulme meant a type of finitude, or the limitation of the individual, as he calls it in his famous essay "Romanticism and Classicism," written in 1913–14 and published in *Speculations* in 1924, posthumously. Through order and restraint placed on the individual it is possible to control human excess and depravity. But institutional regulation, in controlling depravity, also mandates sameness.

Cultural difference receives varying weight among modernist writers but might well be propounded as playing a significant role in contemporary events whose analogues are worked into their fiction. According to Vicki Mahaffey, writing on "Modernist Theory and Criticism" in *The Johns Hopkins Guide to Literary Theory and Criticism* (1994), the "different premium accorded to ethnic, social, religious, and sexual differences by writers who agreed on the limited nature of the individual, however, explains how the offensive tirades of Wyndham Lewis and the brilliant feminism of Woolf, the anti-Semitic propaganda of Pound and the Jewish hero of Joyce's *Ulysses* could stem from the same 'classical root.' "[4]

In addition to the controversial issues of racism and feminism that were aired during the period leading up to World War II, modernism also depended upon a form of narrative unity that operated independent of plot and through allusion, one defined by T.S. Eliot in "Ulysses, Order and Myth" (1923) as the "mythical method" used by W.B. Yeats. According to Mahaffey, myths such as that of Helen of Troy or Ulysses could be deployed by modernist writers through a system of allusion: "The mythical method works not through narrative but through allusion to different mythical narratives that, when fleshed out and juxtaposed, illuminate both the text in which they appear and each other in surprising and often revisionary ways."[5] In this light, Tolkien's own fantastic works, which allude to a system of mythology about Middle-earth he had invented mainly in his unfinished *Silmarillion*, can be recognized as also modernist: Modernist, yet also a critique through medievalism of the modern that again is ultimately postmodernist. The scholars represented in this volume take up the challenge of such a dynamic (and potentially paradoxical) interpretation of Tolkien's ongoing success, drawing upon expertise in a variety of literary fields and theoretical approaches.

The timing of this volume is propitious: It has been two decades since the appearance of the only major book collection to have focused on the relationship between J.R.R. Tolkien's fantasy and issues of modern culture, namely *J. R. R. Tolkien, This Far Land* (1983), edited by Robert Giddings.[6] However this collection has been denigrated by many academics writing about Tolkien, its attention to contemporary issues in the reading of his fantasy was important in its day for riveting attention on the accessibility of *The Lord of the Rings* and its existence as a litmus for popular culture. In the meantime, the field of serious Tolkien studies has grown tremendously, together with a surge of new attention to his works of fantasy. Medieval scholars use Tolkien studies to attract students to their discipline. Viewers of the new *Lord of the Rings* movies have turned to academic studies for elucidation. Both trends highlight the need for a new collection to examine the engagement of popular culture with his works—including the political subtext.

Since the appearance of the Giddings collection, other works, among them, Tom Shippey's *J. R. R. Tolkien: Author of the Century* (2001), Verlyn Flieger's revised edition of *Splintered Light: Logos and Language in Tolkien's World* (2002), and Jane Chance's edited collection *Tolkien the Medievalist* (2002, 2003), have begun to place Tolkien in a modernist literary context.[7] The revised *The Lord of the Rings: The Mythology of Power* (2001) by Chance and a series of recent and forthcoming essays by Gergely Nagy have plumbed the relationship of his fantasy to the 1960s counterculture and postmodern issues such as queer, reader response, and poststructural theory.[8] Likewise, individual essays and books, notably the work of Patrick Curry, have explored the relation of Tolkien's fantasy to modern issues and movements such as environmentalism and ecological activism.[9] Yet, there has been no single recent volume collecting and extending the approach begun in the Giddings collection across such developments in the past generation of scholarship, and into the more global and multicultural context that has become the norm for scholarly discourse on the Middle Ages.

Reflecting on the depth and breadth of scholarship in this volume, two aspects stand out: First, the degree to which Tolkien's creative meditation on premodern literary traditions enables an engagement with the Other that is distinctively resistant to the modern tendency to distinguish self through differentiation from the Other in narrative. In combining a self-reflective engagement with the Other with his own absolute sense of Christian values, Tolkien in *The Lord of the Rings* echoes premodern and traditional texts important to his own scholarship that nevertheless conceal subversive undermeanings. His own scholarship on Chaucer's *Canterbury Tales*—particularly "The Reeve's Tale"—illumines what recent revisionist historicist work has defined as the whole collection's Bakhtinian dialogic nature[10] Second, however, in that combination of subversion yet engagement with a traditional past, Tolkien's fantasy provides a template for considering ways in which to change and reconnect cultural and political coalitions today to deal with issues ranging from the causes of terrorism to climate change, by showing ways of removing related "culture wars" from simple modern polarities of right versus left. As the acclaimed Tolkien artist Ted Nasmith notes in his essay in this collection, just as notions of the sublime did for earlier eras, Tolkien's reintegration of mythos and logos in the theory and practice of fantasy has implications for the way in which we visualize narratives about ourselves and our society in the twenty-first century.

The essays in *Tolkien's Modern Middle Ages* respond to questions involving Tolkien's own connectedness to the past and the ways in which his work has, in a sense, anticipated and accommodated the future and its issues. The primary questions addressed—as reflected in the section titles organizing them—ask how Tolkien can be considered "postmodern"; how Tolkien reworked pre-twentieth-century medievalisms; how Tolkien incorporates, projects, and adapts modern issues and ideologies; how he has affected modern and contemporary fantasy writers and artists; and, most importantly over all, how he has made the medieval modern if not modernist.

The foundational idea of this collection and what might be termed Tolkien's portmanteau postmodernism is developed in the first section, "Recontextualizing the Medieval in Postmodern Middle-earth," in three important theoretical essays. Verlyn Flieger in "A Postmodern Medievalist?" questions even the application of medievalism in its conventional sense to Tolkien's work, given the way in which his fantasy world is, in fact, a conglomerate of many periods, a kind of textual Portmeirion drawing bits and pieces from various time periods and cultures ranging from ancient Babylon to nineteenth-century England. The only specifically medieval culture represented in Middle-earth, in Flieger's view, is that of Rohan. The Shire ruled by Sharkey is a model of late-nineteenth-century industrialism. Tolkien's world is no more "medieval" than it is anything else, and to characterize it as such, she concludes, is to unfairly narrow the scope of his imagination.

In contrast to Flieger, Gergely Nagy enters the debate on Tolkien's postmodernism by theorizing in a postmodern way Tolkien's concern for real world-history and historicity outside the real world (that is, outside what Tolkien refers to as the "primary world"). In "The Medievalist('s) Fiction: Textuality and Historicity as Aspects of Tolkien's Medievalist Cultural Theory in a Postmodernist Context," Nagy investigates the aspect of historicity in relation to textuality in Tolkien's approach. Following medieval interpreters of ancient and biblical texts, Tolkien apparently considered the history and provenance of a text part of, indeed partly constitutive of, its meaning. The textuality and historicity that his writings thus thematize oppose the unhistoricity of much postmodern(ist) thinking about literature and culture. At the same time, Tolkien's medievalism becomes preeminently meaningful if examined with the help of some of the concepts from these theories. Paradoxically, Tolkien's work is unhistorical in its presentation of a fantasy world that implicitly responds to the modern world from a timeless standpoint, and yet is historicized in its presentation and formation of a distinctive genre.

Nagy teases out this artful interlacing of modernist allusiveness and postmodernist ahistoricity by examining the facets through which Tolkien presents his history in several interconnected strands (literary and cultural history in speaking about *Beowulf* and fairy-stories; cosmogonic, mythological, and historiographic in his Middle-earth writings). The narrator, the narrative scope, the implied audience, the supposed authenticity of the account, and the source from which it obtains this authenticity are the most important of the relevant facets as Nagy identifies them. Within their framework, textuality also becomes central, in that Tolkien presents history through documents that tell of it and thus in their production, reception, and transmission construct it. These textual facets are used to fragment "unified history" and to break it down into the various viewpoints of authors, editors, translators, and other users of the text.

In contrast to both Flieger and Nagy, John R. Holmes theorizes the technique of Tolkien's medieval Victorianism by means of philological analysis of his use of an Anglo-Saxon technique in his fiction. In "Tolkien, *Dustsceawung*, and the Gnomic Tense: Is Timelessness Medieval or Victorian?" Holmes examines how Tolkien depends on the Old English literary technique of *dustsceawung*, "contemplation of dust," in his fiction and verse, as distinguished from the classical elegiac mode. This *dustsceawung* motif in Old English literature is just one example of a pervasive "polychronic" viewpoint in Old English narrative, in which present images contain shells of their past and seeds of their future. Indeed, a secret of English grammar, both ancient and modern, is that the so-called present tense, named after its analogue in Latin, rarely is used to express a present meaning. It is a timeless form of "be" that is always used in Old English gnomic passages, and this is another Old English/Norse motif that Tolkien adapts for his retrospective fantasy critique of, and reflection on, modernity.

Following Holmes's theoretical introduction to Tolkien's Victorian medievalism, the second part of the collection develops specific parallels to medievalism in eighteenth- and nineteenth-century English historical fiction. In "Retreating to a Timeless Past: Middle-earth in Victorian Medievalism," four essays examine his relationship with the seminal medievalist-fantasy works of James Macpherson, Sir Walter Scott, Alfred Lord Tennyson, and William Morris. Macpherson's pioneering Ossian poems in the eighteenth century, in particular, enjoyed enormous popularity and influence. Their reimagining of ancient Celtic bardic traditions exemplified notions of the sublime and exposed fissures in the emerging Cartesian worldview of the modern West, thereby highlighting the potential of post-Enlightenment fantasy literature.

John Hunter, in "The Reanimation of Antiquity and the Resistance to History: Macpherson—Scott—Tolkien," examines the way in which *The Lord of the Rings* functions as a literary union of two strands of modern pseudomedieval historical fiction. Tolkien's writing partakes both of the realistic (and ironic) stance of Scott's reinvention of the Middle Ages in novelistic form and of Macpherson's effort to fashion historical fiction as an escape from deterministic historical reality. Tolkien's interweaving of fantasy and realist approaches to historicism enables his narrative to include a sophisticated encoding of historical change and loss together with the type of fantasy wish-fulfillment that drives quest romances from medieval times to modern Hollywood films. Source studies of Tolkien's work in relation to medieval texts, while helpful, have tended to obscure this structural "generic duality" in the narrative. Tolkien's fantasy can be read as anticipating postmodern reshaping of historical fiction, with a Macphersonian escapist element.

Andrew Lynch, writing on "Archaism, Nostalgia, and Tennysonian War in *The Lord of the Rings*," notes how Tolkien hinted that his epic might have been generally influenced by his dreadful experience in the Great War. Yet the novel's war narrative is surprisingly different in image repertoire, diction, and general ambience from writing normally associated with

World War I. Its rhetoric resembles more than anything else the moralized warfare of Victorian medievalist literature and, especially, Alfred Lord Tennyson's rhetoric in *The Idylls of the King*. Tennyson provides a similar case of a writer who abhorred actual war but nevertheless made it a "high" subject in moral terms. Tolkien likewise allows his good characters to fight a glamorous "medieval" war of volunteers and pledged fellowship, while the bad side is "modern," with its nameless conscripts and industrialized war machinery that are associated with the desolate landscape of the trenches. Above all, Tolkien's rhetoric of "good" war looks very Tennysonian in its breadth of symbolic applications—presented as a cleansing of the environment, for example, as it is in the end chapter titled "The *Scouring* of the Shire," and therefore as a quotidian restoration of social order and of traditional right. Such applications contributed to Tennyson's influence on social concerns of subsequent Pre-Raphaelite art and texts, as the next essay testifies.

In "Pastoralia and Perfectibility in William Morris and J.R.R. Tolkien," Chester N. Scoville examines the influence of Pre-Raphaelite Morris on Tolkien and his Shire. Scoville strongly forges a link between these two authors and their use of medieval imagery and ideas in relation to modern issues in an essay that recognizes Tolkien as a reader of Morris during his formative years. In their constructions of fantasy utopias, Tolkien, a believer in Christianity and therefore in a fallen world, tempers his pastoralism with an awareness of the imperfectibility of life and of society, while Morris, a lapsed Anglican and a committed socialist, dedicates his vision to an ideologically idealized pastoral society. Tolkien felt obliged, for the same reason, to place his pastoral society in the past (indeed in an imaginary prehistory), while Morris felt equally obliged to place his in a postrevolutionary future. Morris had developed a utopian vision from such backward-looking fantasy in opposition to modern industrialization. A comparison of their "ideal" pastoral societies provides a good base for then moving on to examine ways in which Tolkien's engagement with nineteenth-century medievalism responded to the stark twentieth-century issues of his lifetime.

Awareness of language itself also formed a major avenue for Tolkien's response. In the last essay in this section, Deidre Dawson, in "English, Welsh, and Elvish: Language, Loss, and Recovery in Tolkien's *Lord of the Rings*," parallels the central role language played in the development of Tolkien's fantasy with that in the development of Macpherson's pioneering medievalist fiction. Macpherson wrote modern versions of purportedly ancient Celtic legends composed in Old Gaelic; Tolkien wrote a mythology to correspond to Elvish languages based on his knowledge of early Celtic and Finnish languages. Macpherson and Tolkien each wrote highly successful works in a nearly extinct genre, the epic. Most significantly, both *Ossian* and *The Lord of the Rings* resist linguistic and cultural imperialism through their revival or reconstruction of ancient languages and cultures that had either disappeared, or were fast disappearing, in the face of modern industrialization and early forms of globalization. These two works seek to reconstruct a mythical past for an increasingly modernizing Scotland and England respectively. *The Poems of Ossian* and *The Lord of the Rings* together mediate between a highly commercial, industrial, and individualistic age and a perceived human need in the modern world for a cultural landscape engaged with the natural world and reflective of the diversity of its life, including human cultures.

The third section of the collection, "Confronting Modern Ideologies in Middle-earth: War, Ecology, Race, and Gender," begins by extending discussion of Tolkien's retrospective reflection on language and identity to his fantasy response to modern warfare. In "Fantastic Medievalism and the Great War in Tolkien's *The Lord of the Rings*," Rebekah Long argues that Tolkien understands violence (especially in modern totalizing forms of mass warfare) as involving a linguistic phenomenon of confrontation, embodying the internal corrosive repercussions of that language problem. Her essay examines Tolkien's project in tandem with David Jones's *In Parenthesis*, with special attention to the ways in which each post–World War I text echoes Chaucer's *Knight's Tale* to speak to the horror of the Great War. Long's essay reveals how Tolkien's epic (as amplified also by recent film adaptations) ironically has been co-opted in modern political debate by those seeking abstract ideological justifications for warfare. Long concludes that such misappropriations absurdly reduce *The Lord of the Rings* to a contest of "good" versus "evil," ignoring the work's relentless, probing exploration of the deleterious effects of violence as a reflection of language. Tolkien in his actual narrative fundamentally and radically moves the Wittgensteinian "grammar" of violence out of frameworks that historicize, contextualize, or displace violence into a medieval past. In his pseudohistorical fantasy, violence paradoxically resists such contextualizing, by erupting into the present with a resounding forcefulness.

Alfred K. Siewers, in "Tolkien's Cosmic-Christian Ecology: The Medieval Underpinnings," examines how Tolkien's lifelong engagement with Celtic otherworldly narrative traditions provides a basis for understanding ecologically centered aspects of Tolkien's fantasy. As a textbook case for recovering alternative traditions from the Western past, these otherworldly narrative traditions in Tolkien form a basis for cutting-edge (and unlikely) multicultural coalitions in the twenty-first century. Specifically, the essay traces how views of nature in a cosmic Incarnational strain of early-medieval Christian asceticism influenced early Irish and Welsh monastic literary cultures, whose otherworldly stories helped provide Tolkien with a narrative pattern of "overlay landscape" with which to critique modern objectifying views of nature. Such premodern cosmologies, bridging the gap between classical and Christian worldviews in the late Roman and early medieval eras, can serve an oddly similar culture-crossing function today, judging from popular engagement globally with the recent film adaptations of *The Lord of the Rings*.

In "Fear of Difference, Fear of Death: The *Sigelwara*, Tolkien's Swertings, and Racial Difference," Brian McFadden examines how Tolkien has been criticized either for ignoring persons of color or for depicting them in a manner consistent with negative stereotypes, typical of Edwardian England's popular prejudices. However, McFadden argues that Tolkien's depiction of dark-skinned Swertings or Southrons was shaped by his reading of Latin and Old English descriptions of the Sigelwara, or Ethiopians, who are depicted in medieval texts as distant or unknown, but not necessarily hostile in intent toward outsiders. In Tolkien's fantasy epic, the Easterlings and Southrons are said to have been deceived by Sauron, rather than being villains. However, they still are not allowed to migrate to the lands of the "good guys." Sam begins to identify with a fallen Southron, and his identification with the Southron soldier is mixed with the former's own homesickness for his ethnically pure Shire. Tolkien's work thus reflects a dialogue of racial mores of both his time and of the time that he studied, in the process tending to subvert normative early-twentieth-century Western categories of race.

Finally, Jane Chance ends the third part, on the dialogue between Tolkien's globally best-selling fantasy and modern issues, with an epilogue to the literary portion of the collection. In "Tolkien and the Other: Race and Gender in Middle-earth," Chance provides a modern and postmodern analysis of Tolkien's treatment of alterity and difference. As a genre, fantasy has only recently been defined as more than escapist; it is also subversive in its mission to change the reader as well as profound in its ability to convey social criticism. Chance notes that Tolkien in both his Anglo-Saxon scholarship and the fantasy of *The Lord of the Rings* reveals his abhorrence of the deliberate isolation of and prejudice against those who differ from the hegemonic norm, in race, nationality, culture, class, age, or gender. And Tolkien's fantasy is, indeed, subversive in its portrayal of heroes as antiheroes—hairy-footed aging Halflings, a dirt-caked Ranger, a rebellious niece who wants to protect her uncle and king, among others. Through his elevation of such figures to heroic stature, Tolkien provides a means for Everyman to use his (or her) small, inferior abilities to aid others, out of a love and loyalty that are lifted out of medieval heroic poems.

The essays in the fourth and last section, "Visualizing Medievalism: Middle-earth in Art and Film," deal with the interaction between Tolkien's medievalized texts and new written and visual art that has been influenced by them. First is Ted Nasmith, in "Similar but Not Similar: Appropriate Anachronism in My Paintings of Middle-earth," who discusses and illustrates the relation between Tolkien's texts and Nasmith's own award-winning visual images. In the process Nasmith looks at Tolkien's own artwork and the interaction between modern interpretation of fantasy literature and visual texts such as those of the Hudson River landscape school. The visual artist's own creative reflections on Tolkien's fantasy texts further mirror medieval and modern, namely, the creative and artistic reception of Tolkien's work in conjunction with modern concerns.

In the last essay in the collection, "Tolkien in New Zealand: Man, Myth, and Movie," Michael N. Stanton returns us to the nineteenth century while pointing us forward into a future where visual representation in film (and digital visualization) allows for the delineation of utopian ideals like Tolkien's as well as for a commentary on the modern and contemporary. Stanton concludes that, while Tolkien had no direct connection with New Zealand, the place proved both an excellent backdrop for Peter Jackson's films of *The Lord of the Rings* and the nexus of a meaningful literary coincidence. Another English writer who *is* associated with New Zealand, Samuel Butler (1835–1902), author of *Erewhon*, anticipated Tolkien in his dislike and fear of mechanical and technological progress, and Tolkien cited Butler's disapproval admiringly. In Tolkien's world, Saruman and his works are the representatives of the dehumanization implicit in this kind of progress. Unfortunately, in Stanton's view, Jackson's films did not carry the theme to its logical conclusion, or indeed to any conclusion at all, leaving out, for example, the disturbing "Scouring of the Shire" episode as a sacrifice to popular narrative tastes.

Stanton's concluding essay brings us round again to the way in which Tolkien's worldview functions in fantasy as a kind of variant narrative of modern traditionalism, akin to E.F. Schumacher's work in economics.[11] This worldview demands more serious attention, given the potential for such narratives to reach across growing cultural fissures around the world. "Culture wars" rip through the world's "one remaining superpower" and "clashes of civilizations" debilitate humanity's capacity to deal with accelerating global crises involving resources, technology, health, and human rights, suggesting the urgency of the search for alternative social narratives.

In the end, this collection of essays demonstrates that concepts of historicity and textuality in Tolkien's fantasy form a distinctive bridge between medieval culture and postmodernist intellectual life. His medievalized fantasy illustrates how texts and stories (ultimately, fictions) work in our cultural history to produce complex signifying systems of mythology, ideology and history, and how we ourselves use these systems to produce theories of meaning. In the process, reading Tolkien with fresh scholarly views, we can understand better how traditions themselves can, paradoxically, subvert.

Put another way, the open-ended expression of absolute values may summon forth a powerfully dialogic, rather than objectifying, relationship with reality. This is the type of energy that Mikhail Bakhtin explicated in the literary fantasy of another conservative Christian traditionalist, Fyodor Dostoevsky.[12] Tolkien's fantasy functions philosophically, in our twenty-first century popular milieu, as a form of imaginative traditionalism akin in some respects to Dostoevsky's pioneering postmodernism but in the context of the Victorian medievalism and interwar culture of Tolkien's Europe. In resisting and subverting categorizations in its characterizations, themes, and genre of narrative, Tolkien's work is both medieval and modern, profoundly neither, but subversive of both. Drawing on deep traditions, often darkly pessimistic, his fantasy nonetheless within these very qualities holds open the prospect of alternatives to current culture wars, the possibility of reimagining better global futures to come.

Notes

1. Brian Rosebury, *Tolkien: A Cultural Phenomenon* (London: Palgrave Macmillan, 2003), 161.
2. Rosebury, *Cultural Phenomenon*, 166.
3. Rosebury, *Cultural Phenomenon*, 159.
4. Vicki Mahaffey, "Modernist Theory and Criticism," in *The Johns Hopkins Guide to Literary Theory and Criticism*, ed. Michael Groden and Martin Kreiswirth (Baltimore and London: Johns Hopkins University Press, 1994), 513. For other treatments of modernism, see, for example, Michael Levenson, ed., *The Cambridge Guide to Modernism* (Cambridge: Cambridge University Press, 1999), which looks at modernism in relation to different genres (novel, poetry, and drama) and media (visual arts, film), and in terms of cultural politics, economy, and gender. It also contains a fine chronology of modernist authors beginning in 1890 with James George Frazer's *The Golden Bough* (as well as with William Morris's *News from Nowhere* and Otto Bismarck's dismissal) and continuing on with other examples of modernist literature, culture, and politics through 1939 and James Joyce's *Finnegans Wake*, T.S. Eliot's *The Family Reunion*, Jean Renoir's *The Rules of the Game*, and World War II's beginning (vii–xvii). J. R. R. Tolkien does not appear on the list.
5. Mahaffey, "Modernist Theory," 514.
6. See Robert Giddings, ed., *J. R. R. Tolkien: This Far Land* (London: Vision Press; Totowa, NJ: Barnes & Noble Books, 1983), particularly the ridiculed essay by Brenda Partridge about Tolkien's latent homosexuality and misogyny, "No Sex Please—We're Hobbits: The Construction of Female Sexuality in *The Lord of the Rings*," pp. 179–98.
7. See T[homas] A. Shippey, *J. R. R. Tolkien, Author of the Century* (London: HarperCollins, 2000; Boston, MA: Houghton Mifflin, 2001); and also his "Tolkien as a Post-War Writer," *Mythlore: A Journal of J. R. R. Tolkien, C. S. Lewis,*

Charles Williams, and the Genres of Myth and Fantasy Studies (1996): 84–93, which examines Tolkien's links with George Orwell and other writers of this period;Verlyn Flieger, *A Question of Time:J. R. R.Tolkien's Road to Faerie* (Kent, OH: Kent State, 1997), on his relation to modern writers and artists; and Jane Chance, ed., *Tolkien the Medievalist* (London: Routledge, 2002), especially the first part, on the modern contexts of Tolkien's scholarship (including Nazism and war), 13–92.
8. See Jane Chance, *The Lord of the Rings: The Mythology of Power* (New York: Twayne/Macmillan, 1992; rev. edn. Lexington: University Press of Kentucky, 2001); and Gergely Nagy, for example, "The Great Chain of Reading: (Inter-)Textual Relations and the Technique of Mythopoesis in the Túrin Story," in Chance, *Tolkien the Medievalist*, pp. 239–58; and a poststructural reading of Gollum, "The 'Lost' Subject of Middle-earth: Elements and Motifs of Subject Constitution in the Figure of Gollum in J. R. R.Tolkien's *The Lord of the Rings*," forthcoming.
9. These include the essays in K.J. Battarbee, ed., *Scholarship and Fantasy: Proceedings of the Tolkien Phenomenon, May 1992, Turku, Finland, Anglicana Turkuensia* no. 12 (Turku: University of Turku, 1993), including work on issues such as violence and fantasy, speculative fiction and ideology, and technology and subcreation. Patrick Curry's *Defending Middle-earth:Tolkien, Myth and Modernity* (New York: St. Martin's, 1997) reflects on Tolkien and late-twentieth-century issues from an activist ecological perspective.
10. See Jane Chance, "Subversive Fantasist: Tolkien on Class Difference," in *Proceedings of the Conference on "The Lord of the Rings, 1954–2004: Scholarship in Honor of Richard E. Blackwelder," October 21–23, 2004*, ed.Wayne Hammond and Christina Scull (Milwaukee: Marquette University Press, 2005).
11. See E.F. Schumacher, *Small is Beautiful: Economics as if People Mattered* (London: Blond and Briggs, 1989); and *A Guide for the Perplexed* (New York: Harper & Row, 1979).Although the popular writings of this mid-twentieth-century German refugee in England specifically discuss economic problems in Buddhist and Gandhian terms, Schumacher, a British government economist, was a button-down convert to Catholicism whose social ideas arguably come the closest of any modern political economist to those found in Tolkien's correspondence and fantasy. Interestingly, Schumacher felt that using Buddhist rather than Catholic terminology would ensure a larger audience for his "appropriate technology" ideas in the postmodern era. Schumacher thus parallels in polemics Tolkien's view in literature of the efficacy of non-Catholic narratives to transmit traditional Christian values in a "post-Christian"West. Tolkien scholar Joseph Pearce recently wrote a sequel to Schumacher's original counterculture bestseller entitled *Small is Still Beautiful* (New York and London: HarperCollins, 2001), with a foreword by the author's daughter, Barbara Wood Schumacher.
12. See Richard Pevear's explication of Bakhtin's point, in the foreword to Dostoevsky's *Notes from Underground*, trans Richard Pevear and Larissa Volokhonsky (NewYork:Vintage Books, 1993), xvi–xx [vii–xxiii].

PART ONE

RECONTEXTUALIZING THE MEDIEVAL IN
POSTMODERN MIDDLE-EARTH

CHAPTER 2

A POSTMODERN MEDIEVALIST?

Verlyn Flieger

The fifty years' passage since the first publication of The Lord of the Rings *has allowed a view of Tolkien's work in deeper and clearer perspective, providing sufficient distance to see him less as a writer in the medieval mode, and more as an author with a medieval background writing in and to his own twentieth century.*

Like so many words we take for granted, the word "medieval" can mean different things to different people and in different contexts. If we say, "The stained glass is medieval," that evokes one image. If we say, "The plumbing is medieval," that evokes quite another. Just so, in the context of the work of J.R.R. Tolkien, and in particular of *The Lord of the Rings*, we should be both cautious and careful about what we mean by *medieval* and where and how we apply it to so rich and various a work. Tolkien's book is something of a chameleon; it will take on whatever literary hue best blends with its readers' assumptions. If you want fantasy, it is fantasy, replete with wizards, dungeons, dragons, and fantastical invented creatures such as Hobbits. If you want an epic, it is an epic, with battles galore, banners flying and swords flashing, not to mention axes, spears, and bows and arrows. If your taste is for romance, this is a classic journey into faery lands forlorn, and you can hear the horns of elfland faintly blowing. If your preferred genre is fairy tale, that is what you get: a brave and modest little hero, a magical ring of invisibility, supernatural helpers, spells, and incantations. If you see the book from any one of a number of the conventional medieval literary perspectives, you can find material in the text to support your view.

I am my own worst example, for over the course of nearly fifty years I have seen it as all of the above and more. When I first discovered *The Lord of the Rings* in the winter of 1957, before I ever knew who J.R.R. Tolkien was, what he taught, or where he taught it, I was struck by what seemed to me then its strongly medieval flavor. I had recently taken a course in translating *Beowulf*, and the correspondences I saw between the Anglo-Saxon language, customs, architecture, and verse forms—especially the verse forms—occurring in that poem and those of the culture of Rohan were unmistakable. A decade and a half later, as part of a course in modern fantasy I began to teach *The Lord of the Rings*. I made it my purpose in life to educate the untutored general reader in the medieval and mythic aspects of Tolkien's work, its epic and romance and fairy-tale underpinnings.

Thus, the Rohirrim were simply Anglo-Saxons transplanted straight from *Beowulf* to Middle-earth; Isengard and Mordor were obviously Celtic wastelands; Gandalf was a combination Merlin/Odin figure; Sting recalled Excalibur, and Narsil/Anduril recalled Gram, the broken and reforged sword of the Völsungs. Boromir was an epic hero; Aragorn, a healing king; while Éowyn's crush on him was a clear echo of Thomas Malory's Maid of Astolat and her infatuation with Lancelot. The Woses of Druadan forest were typical medieval Wild Men; and my Frodo staggered under the combined burden of being a fairy-tale hero, a Miraculous Child, and a fertility figure. I was not wrong. But I was only partly right.

What I was not seeing, because at the time it did not suit my purpose, was the demonstrably nonmedieval forest that surrounded without obscuring these undeniably medieval trees: the great stone city of Gondor; the nostalgic Shire of Tolkien's own Warwickshire childhood with its Hardyesque inhabitants good and bad; the 1920s reference slipped in with the hyphenate Sackville-Bagginses, carrying echoes of Vita Sackville-West and the modernist literary lights of Bloomsbury. (Okay, this last is a joke, but it is a modern joke, and it puts a spin on the Sackville-Bagginses that no medieval author would recognize.) Nor was I sufficiently willing to acknowledge that Isengard was a twentieth-century military-industrial complex, or that Saruman used some ominously modern political rhetoric, or that there was a perceptible whiff of Nazi-like annexation in the takeover of the Shire by Sharkey and his gang. And when Tolkien's *Letters* was published in 1981, I read with considerable surprise what he wrote to a correspondent, Rhona Beare, in 1958, "The Númenorians of Gondor [are]. . .best pictured in Egyptian terms."[1] He illustrated this with a sketch that depicts something remarkably like the high-peaked, white war crown of Upper Egypt under the pharaohs. That is one I suspect few readers imagined when they first tried to picture Gondor.

Nonetheless, such eclecticism is typical of Tolkien's sweeping approach to history and to the cultures of his Middle-earth. His Elves may use longbows, and his Dwarves protect themselves with chain mail and fight with axes, but Sarumann's Orcs make use of explosives, and something very close to flamethrowers is used against the Ents at Isengard. To underscore this and make sure we get the point that Saruman is waging a mechanized war, Tolkien has Pippin vividly describe one of the most horrific deaths in *The Lord of the Rings*, that of the "very tall handsome Ent" Beechbone at the Battle of Isengard, who "got caught in a spray of some liquid fire and burned like a torch: a horrible sight."[2] To be sure, both explosives and liquid fire were used in the ancient world by both Greeks and Romans, and was part of the technology of the Byzantine Empire. Nevertheless, neither is part of the common conception of what constitutes the Middle Ages in art, literature, or history.

To most modern readers the spray of liquid fire would evoke recognizably modern technology, and typically destructive technology at that. The effect achieved in the scene Pippin describes is shockingly realistic, deriving as it surely does not wholly from Tolkien's knowledge of history but also from his personal knowledge of World War I, where flamethrowers were used against human targets for the first time. There is a bizarre hybrid touch here, a deliberate mix of the realistic and the fantastic, each supporting the other. This inhuman weapon is used on a *tree*, something made of wood and therefore conventionally suitable for burning, but a tree that at the same time is a *person*, a "tall handsome" sentient being with a proper name, for whom burning "like a torch" is a hideous death. The combination adds both dreadful realism and weird fantasy to the scene; hence, Pippin's feeling comment that it is "a horrible sight."

When all these elements, not just collectively unmedieval but chronologically disparate among themselves, are acknowledged as being part of the fabric of *The Lord of the Rings* it becomes more difficult to characterize the book as being of any period except its own, the Third Age of Tolkien's distinctive Middle-earth. Even the thematic elements we most confidently label "medieval"—the doomed-warrior heroism, the quest, the sacrifice, even the great Ring itself—have correspondences in the mythologies of the ancient world that antedate the Middle Ages and transcend their medieval versions to be at once more archaic and more modern. A contemporary, retro-pre-Raphaelite, nouveau William Morris kind of fascination with medievalism may have had some hand in beguiling us into a tendency to lump all aspects of Tolkien's Middle-earth together under the umbrellaterm "medieval" or "pseudo-medieval."

It is my belief that Tolkien would have disapproved of such lumping. As evidence, I offer that same 1958 letter to Rhona Beare wherein, speaking in terms of costume, he stated unequivocally, "The Rohirrim were not 'mediaeval,' in our sense. The styles of the Bayeux Tapestry...fit them well enough" (*Letters*, 280–81). Granted, we do not know exactly the precise sense in which Beare was using the term (perhaps asking what kind of battle dress the Men of Rohan wore), but we can infer from Tolkien's denial that he was correcting her. Given that the language, customs, and culture of the Rohirrim are not just generalized medieval Anglo-Saxon but are particularized and localized as Mercian,[3] and that the central kingdom of medieval Anglo-Saxon England was known as Mercia, we might legitimately ask what he meant by "our sense" of medieval.

Tolkien gives a fair answer in the same letter, where he calls Pauline Baynes's illustrated knights in *Farmer Giles of Ham* "King-Arthurish," explaining that he means by that term, "belonging to our 'mythological' Middle Ages which blends unhistorically styles and details ranging over 500 years, and most of which did not of course exist in the Dark Ages of c. 500 A.D." (*Letters*, 280). At the very least, he seems to be suggesting, we ought to subdivide "medieval" into "early," "middle" and "late" or even "high." The "ish" suffix pejoratively appended to "King Arthur" suggests that he meant to refer to the kind of historically mixed treatment the Arthur story has received from some of its modern retellers and illustrators, a vague pastiche of styles and times, a Middle Ages not just mythologized but stretched and pulled into some sort of "one size fits all" blanket concept. Perhaps in calling *The Lord of the Rings* "medieval," not just Rhona Beare but other readers as well are unhistorically blending styles and details ranging over five hundred years. Or more.

I would say yes, we are doing just that. I would go even further to maintain that, in addition, we are confusing the author with the work to the detriment of both. Because we know that Tolkien was a scholar of medieval literature and language, because we have his learned essays on two of the great medieval poems, *Beowulf* and *Sir Gawain and the Green Knight* (poems themselves possibly separated by more than Tolkien's "500 years"), as well as his great essay "On Fairy-Stories," we assume that he must necessarily have written his fiction in the same mode in which he studied and taught. We are partly right. He did say on more than one occasion that his typical response to reading a myth or a fairy story was to try to write something of his own in the same mode.

Thus, Tolkien wrote in Modern English language and Old English alliterative meter a "Fall of Arthur." Thus, he wrote a Völsung cycle based on poems in the Icelandic Elder *Edda*, again using modern English but cast in fornyrðislag, a meter used in the Eddic poems. His last published story,

Smith of Wootton Major, is a "medieval" fairy story in the truest sense of that term. Yes, there is a clearly "medieval" (in the most general sense) flavor to certain aspects of *The Lord of the Rings*. Yet even in that massive work, he was not *always* re-creating a particular past in subject matter or style or tone. He was no more stuck in the Middle Ages than he was stuck in the twentieth century, and to be fair to him and his work, we have to see him situated in both.

Let us start with subject matter. Tolkien's book prominently features a quest, described by some enthusiasts as an "anti-Grail" quest, though that only tells what it is not, not what it is. But the book's closest analogue to the "Tale of the Sankgreal" in Sir Thomas Malory's great Arthurian work (published in 1485, and that is Renaissance, not by any stretch the Middle Ages) is the journey of Sam and Frodo in Mordor, which is different in important respects from that paradigmatic quest. Tolkien's quest (we should probably call it "journey") features ordinary people, not knights, as does Malory's; his heroes fight reality, not visions; they are beset with mud, dust, thirst, hunger, and despair rather than the Grail quest's demonic temptations that vanish in a puff of smoke. The only temptation Frodo has to battle is the one he carries with him—the Ring.

Certainly Tolkien's book has aspects of romance in the medieval tradition of Chrétien de Troyes and Marie de France, standard plots in which lovers separated by cruel circumstances are forced to go through a series of trials before being reunited. Still, it must be acknowledged that what romance there is exists largely by implication in the barely hinted-at love story of Aragorn and Arwen and their long wait to be together. So submerged is this in the larger story that the appearance of Arwen at the end of the action and her marriage with Aragorn may come as a surprise to many reading the book for the first time. The details of their romance are almost totally buried in the narrative proper, and the full treatment of the story is relegated to the appendix. Moreover, that particular romance motif has a distinctly modern analogue in Tolkien's own life, his guardian-enforced three-year separation from Edith Bratt.

Then there is style. Tolkien's book is cast in two distinct prose styles. One is the high or epic style. It is conventionally medieval in the pre-Raphaelite or William Morris sense of the word, but it borrows also from Malory, with paratactic constructions hung on a string of "ands." Here is an example: "And so they [Éowyn and Faramir] stood on the walls of the City of Gondor, and a great wind rose and blew, and their hair, raven and golden, streamed out mingling in the air. And the Shadow departed, and the Sun was unveiled, and the light leaped forth; and the waters of Anduin shone like silver, and in all the houses of the city men sang for the joy that welled up in their hearts from what source they could not tell" (*LR* 6.5, 941–42).

There are epic inversions like "Very bright was that sword" (*LR* 2.4, 269), declamations such as "Aragorn son of Arathorn was going to war upon the marches" (*LR* 2.4, 269), and archaisms such as "Forth the Three Hunters!" (*LR* 3.1, 410). This is the kind of writing the critics always single out for derision when they talk about Tolkien's style.

The other is the "low" style, or ordinary English (which the critics never seem to notice). In the narrative itself this is called the Common Speech and is used for the nonepic portions of the story (by far the major portion) and, in particular, for the Hobbit episodes and the actual speech of the Hobbits. Of the two styles, call them high and low or epic and common, the Common Speech is the dominant one and sets the tone for the entire book. It is hard to imagine anyone in a medieval work saying, "I shall have to brush up my toes," as Merry remarks to Pippin after their escape from the Orcs in book 3 (*LR* 3.3, 448). Or anyone, even in thought, referring to another character as "old Strider," as Pippin does after his capture by the Uruk-Hai (*LR* 3.3, 434). Or describing a forest as, "frightfully tree-ish," as Merry characterizes Fangorn (*LR* 3.4, 451). Nor can I imagine a medieval writer—even Chaucer in "The Reeve's Tale"—having characters talk like Tolkien's Orcs: "You've no guts outside your own sties," sneers Ugluk to Grishnakh (*LR* 3.3, 436); "I'll put red maggot-holes in your belly," Shagrat snarls to Snaga (*LR* 6.1, 885). And the anonymous soldier and tracker orcs who follow Sam and Frodo in Mordor are capable of such nonmedieval locutions as "Nar!" and "Garn" and "I'll stick you if you don't shut it [your mouth] down!" (*LR* 6.2, 904).

This kind of gutter language is more typical of John Osborne than it is of John Gower. Nevertheless, the exchanges among the Orcs, rough-edged, rude, and colloquial-laden as they are, present some of the most immediate and realistic passages of conversation in the book. The Orc dialogues—quarrelsome, contentious, and abusive—have the ring of authentic speech. This is how some strata of the hoi polloi talk among themselves. Somewhere, somehow (at a guess, in the war), Tolkien, with his ear attuned to languages of all kinds, overheard real people using such salty vernacular, appropriated it to his invented world, and made it into a sort of Tolkienian Vulgate, a direct translation of the Black Speech.

Finally and most important of all, there is tone, manifest in the attitude of the author toward the narrative. Tolkien's tone, his attitude toward his narrative and characters, is more complex and multivalent than it first appears. *The Lord of the Rings* subverts (we might even say deconstructs) itself by *looking* like a medieval, or pseudomedieval, or imitatively medieval fantasy epic/romance/fairy tale, while in specific places in the narrative *sounding like*—in spirit, in character, and (most important but least noticed) in tone—a surprisingly contemporary twentieth-century novel, very much in and typical of its time. And here Tolkien is not only not medieval; he is emphatically modern or—dare I say it?—postmodern.

Even its adherents often find it difficult to say, succinctly, just what postmodernism is, but one of its hallmarks is the intentional questioning of strategies of representation. On the literary plane this is called metanarrative and characterizes a level at which the narrative refers to or reflects on itself, deconstructs itself, or interrogates itself. John Fowles's *The French Lieutenant's Woman* (published, let us not forget, in 1969, fifteen years after *The Lord of the Rings*) is a classic example of this technique. Having considered and rejected the possibility of suicide for his heroine, Sarah, Fowles's narrator, who is and is not himself, inquires portentously at the close of chapter 12, "Who is Sarah? Out of what shadows does she come?"[4] The mystery thus set up is solved only with the introduction of a deeper mystery, that of the imagination, as Fowles opens the following chapter by answering literally his own rhetorical question: "I do not know. This story I am telling is all imagination. These characters I create never existed outside my own mind. If I have pretended until now to know my characters' minds and innermost thoughts, it is because I am writing in. . .a convention universally accepted at the time of my story."[5] Fowles has not just set up a mystery; he has set up his audience as well. We have been forcibly ejected from the story and made to feel a little foolish in the process. We may even be a bit abashed, as if we have been caught doing something we should not do—believing in the story, participating in the fiction.

Not content with this, Fowles goes on to use his authorial power to play with our minds. The time of his story—that is, the time in which the story is set—is 1867. So he is writing a Victorian novel. But the time of the story, as he very well knows is also the time when he is writing it, the middle sixties of the twentieth century, and further, of course, whatever time after that a reader is engaged in reading it. What convention, then, is "universally accepted" and at what time? Fowles is reminding us that it is we who accept the conventions and allow them to operate, and by that reminder he is intentionally breaking the willing suspension of disbelief so beloved of Coleridge. He forces us as readers to see that the "time" of the story is any time it collaborates in the reader-text bargain that is the re-creative reading process, and that we as readers are in league with the author in whatever he does.

Fowles was hot stuff in the late sixties, when *The Lord of the Rings*, considered "popular" in the negative sense, was being hooted at by the critical heirs of Edmund Wilson,[6] scorned as "boys' adventure" with no sex, and its swift demise predicted on that basis. How times have changed. The "boys' adventure" has been steadily in print for fifty years, enjoyed by readers of all ages, with the demand displaying no signs of a slacking-off.

Defying the predictions, *The Lord of the Rings*, far from being a short-lived phenomenon in the literary landscape, is an enduring and important twentieth-century landmark. In addition, critical attitudes have slowly come round to the recognition that Tolkien was when he wrote and is now as modern an author as his contemporaries. The critics are starting to see what has always been there.

Evidence of Tolkien's postmodernity is both obvious and unobtrusive in *The Lord of the Rings*. Like the purloined letter, it is in such plain sight that it is easy to overlook. The most critically interesting, theory-oriented passage in the book is also one of the quietest, calling no attention to itself yet accomplishing much the same thing as does Fowles in the passage from *The French Lieutenant's Woman* quoted above. The only difference is that Tolkien does it better, using greater narrative skill, more authorial subtlety, and more courtesy toward his reader. The passage in question is from *The Two Towers*, book 4, and it records the conversation between Sam and Frodo on the Stairs of Cirith Ungol. As an episode, it is structurally unnecessary, contributing nothing to plot or character. Indeed, it is a kind of "time out" from the action, a breathing space for its exhausted characters, and is used by Tolkien as a "time out" from the whole fictive process. It says a great deal about Tolkien's own awareness of literary conventions and how their spotlight can be turned on the reader as easily as on the fiction.

Stranded by Gollum at the very entrance to Mordor, and enjoying a brief respite from their ordeal, Frodo and Sam wander into distinctly postmodern territory by idly (at first) kicking around the self-reflexive idea that they are in a story. Sam remarks that stories are not nearly as much fun to be in as they are to read about. He wonders what kind of story he and Frodo are in and how it will end. Note that Tolkien, unlike Fowles, has not broken through the confines of his narrative. We are still within the Secondary World. This kind of imaginative speculation is right in character for Sam, who, as we have been told repeatedly, loves stories and is always talking about them. Here he talks himself through one of his favorites, the story of Beren and Lúthien, only to realize as he gets to the end that it is not the end, for that story goes on into another story, that of Eärendil. It is at this point that Sam finally comes to the realization that he and Frodo are part of the same ongoing story, that they are, in fact, in the Silmarillion.

This is an interesting conceit, but it is hardly anything new, or it would not be if Sam, or Tolkien, did not take the concept to the next level. Sam says he wants to be in a tale "put into words" that is "told by the fireside" (and by implication told by someone other than Sam) or, even better, *read* out of "a great big book with red and black letters, years and years afterwards. And people will say: 'Let's hear about Frodo and the Ring!' And they'll say: 'Yes, that's one of my favourite stories. Frodo was very brave, wasn't he, dad?' 'Yes, my boy, the famousest of the hobbits, and that's saying a lot.'" Sam's little flight of fancy cheers the doomed and despairing Frodo, who laughs in genuine enjoyment and declares, "Why Sam. . .to hear you makes me as merry as if the story was already written" (*LR* 4.8, 697).

Tolkien is here being postmodern with a vengeance, cocking a knowing eye at his reader as if to say, "If you haven't got it yet, here it is." For the story *is* already written. And it *is* read out of a book, the very book we are holding in our hands as Frodo speaks—perhaps even, if the reader chances to have the Collector's Edition, a great big book with red and black letters. At the same time, it has not yet been written because Sam and Frodo are in the middle of their adventure and it is not yet over, nor do they know how it will come out. By forcing the reader to be in two places at once, inside the story on the stairs with Sam and Frodo and outside the story reading the already-written book that puts them there, Tolkien enters the world of postmodern theory (and quantum physics, to which postmodern theory, especially Werner Heisenberg's indeterminacy principle, owes a great deal).

That scene on the Stairs of Cirith Ungol is itself an image of postmodern indeterminacy. Sam and Frodo are poised on the threshold of Mordor, neither in nor out. The reader is in precisely the same position, neither wholly in the narrative (for we have been reminded that we are reading a book) nor wholly outside it (for as long as we are reading it, the book we are reading has not yet been finished). Tolkien's deft handling of this whole episode is the measure of his skill and modernity as a writer. For where Fowles blatantly and rather crudely has his narrator reflect on his own process of narration, Tolkien far more subtly has his characters reflect on their own function as characters. Where Fowles intentionally and abruptly breaks the illusion to kick his readers away from the narrative and shock them into self-consciousness, Tolkien intentionally but unobtrusively allows Frodo and Sam to conduct his readers outside the narrative before they have noticed the transition and to usher them into readerly self-awareness before they realize it.

This is not as innovative a technique as it might seem. It was used by the *Beowulf* poet twelve hundred or so years ago when, as a scop singing of Beowulf's victory over Grendel, he sang of the scop who sang of Beowulf's victory over Grendel. The poem (and, indeed, the poet) is thus as self-reflexive and self-referential as is John Fowles or J.R.R. Tolkien. Well then, is the *Beowulf* poet anachronistically postmodern? Or is the technique actually surprisingly medieval? What exactly do these terms refer to? And how should we use them? It seems clear that, for a start, we should use them more cautiously and with a fuller awareness of their resonance than we have heretofore.

My last example not only examines Tolkien's influence on an author usually regarded as an exemplar of postmodern technique, but also one who, like Tolkien, was a scholar and teacher of medieval literature. I mean John Gardner, the author of *Grendel*, one of the most metatextual works to come out of the late twentieth century. Sam's final speech in that conversation on the Stairs of Cirith Ungol is the link. Musing on the nature of story, he reflects, "Why, even Gollum might be good in a tale. . .and he used to like tales himself once, by his own account. I wonder if he thinks he's the hero or the villain?" And then Tolkien rams the conceit home. " 'Gollum!' [Sam] called. 'Would you like to be the hero?' " (*LR* 6.8, 697). The direct address brings out the obvious but generally unstated truth that we are all the heroes of our own stories, and that it is only the point of view that privileges one hero over another. In 1971, Gardner took Gollum and made him (by way of his medieval/postmodern equivalent) the hero of his own story in *Grendel*, and not just the hero but the narrator as well.

In Gardner's hands this once-medieval monster becomes Sam's postmodern stepchild and Gollum's foster brother. No longer the inarticulate, shadowy monster villain of the tale of *Beowulf*, Grendel becomes the highly articulate, self-pitying, self-mocking, self-dramatizing, hyper-self-conscious hero of his own tale, told in his own words. Giving him the starring role in his own story is Gardner's inevitable and predictable postmodern answer to the challenge of Sam's question, "Gollum! Would you like to be the hero?" The answer is obvious. Of course he would. In fact, he probably thinks he is. And Frodo and Sam are supporting players in his story, only elevated to starring roles by a shift in perspective, like Tom Stoppard's Rosencrantz and Guildenstern.

Gardner's Grendel and Tolkien's Gollum, however, both owe a debt to the Grendel of the original poem. Gardner's character owes it directly; Tolkien's, more obliquely but no less plainly, as his second edition revisions to the Gollum chapter of *The Hobbit* reveal.[7] Moreover, our understanding of the "medieval" Grendel is inevitably colored by our familiarity with his twentieth-century avatars. We read him by their light. Such a round dance, with characters reflecting one another and giving voice to one another, shows a continuity of literature and literary themes that transcends periods, terms, and labels.

What this all means is that we must abandon our preconceptions and start seeing and reading Tolkien as we have always seen and read Fowles and Gardner and their peers—as a man of his time. We must take him out of the medieval box in which he has languished for too long and set him solidly in the context of the twentieth century that shaped him and produced his work. We will have to abandon our conventional understanding of words like *medieval* and *postmodern* and, instead, start regarding Tolkien afresh and as he is and has always been.

Tolkien himself had a word for this necessary process. He called it "Recovery," and he declared it to be one of the essential uses of fairy-story. In "On Fairy-Stories" he defined Recovery as the regaining of a clear view, "so that the things seen clearly may be freed from the drab blur of triteness or familiarity." This drab blur of triteness, the familiarity that takes things for granted, Tolkien sees as the product of a kind of appropriation of things seen but not looked at. "We say we know them," he goes on. "They have become like the things which once attracted us by their glitter, or their colour, or their shape, and we laid hands on them, and then locked them in our hoard, acquired them, and acquiring, ceased to look at them."[8]

It is exactly this, I suggest, that we have done with and to Tolkien for the past fifty years. We have said we "know" him and his work, which attracts us so powerfully by its glitter and color and shape. And assuming that we "know" both, we have then all too often laid hands on them and locked them in our hoard and ceased to look at either. (I do not mean we have ceased to read; but "reading" and "looking at" are not necessarily the same thing.) We have appropriated Tolkien, pronounced his work to be "medieval," and continued for too long to read both book and author by that light. It is time for a change.

Now that we have the advantage of fifty years of hindsight, we can put *The Lord of the Rings* in clearer perspective. We can look at it from a distance that, far from lending enchantment, removes it and allows us to more easily see Tolkien in his time—as an essentially modern author using all the authorial tools and techniques available from whatever period—writing to and for and about any audience from his own time and beyond it that can appreciate his story.

Notes

1. J.R.R. Tolkien, *The Letters of J. R. R. Tolkien*, ed. Humphrey Carpenter with Christopher Tolkien (Boston: Houghton Mifflin Company, 1981), 281 (hereafter cited in text and notes as *Letters*).
2. J.R.R. Tolkien, *The Lord of the Rings*, one-volume edn. (Boston: Houghton Mifflin, 1994), 554 (hereafter cited in text and notes as *LR*).
3. See Shippey's discussion of cultural parallels in *J. R. R. Tolkien: Author of the Century*. (London: HarperCollins Publishers, 2000), 91–92.
4. John Fowles, *The French Lieutenant's Woman* (Boston: Little, Brown and Company, 1969), 94.
5. Fowles, *French Lieutenant's Woman*, 95.

6. See Edmund Wilson, "Oo Those Awful Orcs!" *Nation* 182, April 14, 1956, 12–13.
7. See Bonniejean Christensen's article "Gollum's Character Transformation in *The Hobbit*," in *A Tolkien Compass*, ed. Jared Lobdell, 2nd edn. (Chicago: Open Court, 2003), 7–26.
8. J. R. R. Tolkien, "On Fairy-Stories," in *The Monsters and The Critics and Other Essays*, ed. Christopher Tolkien (London: George Allen & Unwin, 1983), 146 [107–61].

CHAPTER 3

THE MEDIEVALIST('S) FICTION: TEXTUALITY AND HISTORICITY AS ASPECTS OF TOLKIEN'S MEDIEVALIST CULTURAL THEORY IN A POSTMODERNIST CONTEXT

Gergely Nagy

> *Following medieval interpreters of texts, Tolkien conceived of the meaning of writing as partly defined by its history and provenance. Paradoxically, his work is unhistorical in presenting a fantasy world timelessly apart from modernity, yet historicized by its framework in a way that counters many postmodernist ahistorical views of culture and text.*

That contemporary literary theory should disregard Tolkien seems at first sight perfectly normal. The revival of medieval or even antique narrative traditions, generic features, and thematic elements that Tolkien's work exhibits and tries to affect does not make for a text that would appeal readily to the theoretician: it operates models of reading, frameworks, and presuppositions that no longer form a part of the basic apparatus of readers (not even of critics), and thus it creates a text that would seem to be a "curiosity" rather than a serious problem for interpretation. The models and sources Tolkien uses are in this sense "classical";[1] such texts generally do not draw much praise today. You cannot write classics in a context where people believe that classics do not function any more, in a context that requires something very different from literature it values.

Not only that: Tolkien's fiction also makes use of other theoretically unpopular devices such as a radical importance assigned to the idea of history; a theologically coded hierarchy in the fictional world; and an archaizing language that supposedly does not conform to contemporary expectations about either accessibility or the "problematization of signification" (and the conventions of representation attached to this language). Tolkien presents his work as fictional history; but we do not believe in history any more. Tolkien's world is theologically explained; but we know God is dead (presumably even in "better" fiction). Tolkien's language is heavily stylized and conventionalized, using the style and rhetorics of representational strategies we know to be outdated, invalid, and problematic (which all such strategies are).

But what Tolkien does with these unpopular concepts is something important and unique. He presents history as manifesting in (and thus constructed by) texts, written by authors and used by receivers embedded in the fictional culture(s) created by these very texts. He problematizes all explanations of the world, including history and theology, through the aspects of the *text* that he brings to the front; his historically and theologically focused representation in the fiction (and of the fiction) is thus all but uncritical. Tolkien is, in fact, theoretically interesting exactly at the points where he looks, at first sight, schematic, outdated, and hopelessly conservative.

It is time, therefore, that Tolkien's love for the medieval, the archaic, and the out-of-date should be seen from a different perspective and become the starting point for a theoretically grounded postmodernist appreciation. The strong and audible voice he assigns to the past, to history (not surprising in the work of a medievalist), coexists with his voicing of characteristically contemporary concerns (like his preoccupation with and depiction of power);[2] and his adaptation of elements from medieval literary and cultural history only makes this more pronounced. His stress on the *text* and the *history* of the text do not only play at a medieval verisimilitude: they bring into play elements of the medieval text and medieval culture that bear on both the way we see and interpret the world and the language we use to write about it. Tolkien uses medieval models in a way that problematizes modern questions, postmodern concerns; the image of the text he presents and its inalienable historicity reinterpret medieval manuscript culture and its unquestioned (if it is in fact unquestioned) representations of the world. Actually, these representational frameworks are transposed into a postmodern context and turned into devices that we can use to articulate postmodern problematizations. These two facets of a paradigm Tolkien sets up in his academic work about *Beowulf* and fairy-stories, and the way he uses these in his fiction, will be the starting point of this essay's survey of the points of connection between Tolkien's fiction and postmodernist critical/theoretical concerns. A discussion of these will enable us to go on to some other theoretically significant motifs that Tolkien also foregrounds, most notably the subject positions connected to the production of texts and of meanings in the story and the theological discourse his fiction uses. It will become apparent that Tolkien's fiction is, in fact, medieval; but it is also a medievalist's modern text that necessarily has to be read (or, to claim less, *can* be read) with modern assumptions.

The conception of a historically evolving complex of motifs and stories, coming to the interpreter through specific (textual) versions, is set up by Tolkien in his famous essay on *Beowulf*.[3] The lecture urges the awareness of this background and the looking at the poem as a poem. The "ancient and largely traditional material" ("Beowulf," 9), the elements in it that the poet (re)uses "in the making of a new thing" ("Beowulf," 25), including the pagan stories, the pagan monsters, even pagan (but preserved) ethical conceptions (like Tolkien's beloved "Northern courage" ["Beowulf," 19]), are all secondary to their *handling* by the poet: the activity of the author is by Tolkien seen as central.[4] The poet "has used [heroic legends] afresh in an original function, giving us not just one more, but. . .a measure and *interpretation* of them all" ("Beowulf," 16; my emphasis); this interpretive relationship to the material is made possible by the poet's position, the "moment of poise," his being removed from the material ("Beowulf," 21). The fact that the poet is a Christian using the pagan elements with a new function means that, while preserving the legendary material (like the tower-building man in the allegory), he also makes new *meaning* out of it ("looking out to the sea" becomes a metaphor for meaning).

Critical practice, Tolkien argues, cannot disregard this difference of background and poem. The quarrying of the material (mythological, historical, or of whatever origin) blurs our sight as to *Beowulf* as art; the poem is indeed more important than the history of the material. Still, that history is there and has to be reckoned with. The individual poem is part of a tradition and is itself a complex "new thing," incorporating, preserving, and rewriting previous materials (which themselves can be poems, stories, or texts). As for the poet, historicity and the version that makes historically "other" material available are also for us of supreme importance.

In "On Fairy-Stories,"[5] Tolkien also has something to say about this historical complexity. Fairy-stories come from many sources and many traditions, but they always make up the "here and now," the text that we read at the moment. There is not much use in comparativism to discover "meaning" (as with *Beowulf*): that only means we use stories "not as they were meant to be used" ("OFS," 45). Tolkien nevertheless devotes a section to "Origins," and he argues that it is the specificity, "the unclassifiable individual details of the story" ("OFS," 46), that count. The interrelationships of the various versions are metaphorized by the "Tree of Tales" and its study explicitly likened to philology ("OFS," 46); and the extensive "pool" of background material that is also there with fairy-stories becomes the "Cauldron" into which elements, "ingredients," are dropped ("OFS," 47, 52–54). From this is taken the "soup": "by 'the soup'," Tolkien writes, "I mean the story as it is served up by its author and teller and by 'the bones,' its sources or material" ("OFS," 47)—the stress is on the individual integrity of any specific version. Individual authors draw on this "pool" of elements ("OFS," 47–49);[6] in the metaphor, they become the "Cooks" ("OFS," 55) who serve up the story for us. Their choice is of course not entirely arbitrary: the elements they make use of and thus preserve are again (as in the case of *Beowulf*) used for their literary effect. "The things that are there must often have been retained (or inserted) because the oral narrators, instinctively or consciously, felt their literary 'significance' " ("OFS," 57). Iwan Rhys Morus emphasizes rightly that Tolkien always assigns great importance to "individual authorship" over the inheritance, the pool.[7] It is always the soup that we eat, and rarely the entire contents of the cauldron—never the cauldron itself.

The version's partaking in a historically determined tradition is, as we see, an important aspect of Tolkien's analysis of *Beowulf* and fairy-stories and of the critical practice he proposes. The difference of the poet's handling, the unique meaning of the poem, can only become articulated against such a historical background. We can only see this text as something significantly different if we are aware of what it is different from. But the authors' awareness of this difference (and connectedness) is also important: as Elizabeth Scala summarizes, "The cultural conception of originality that underwrites [medieval literary practice]"[8] is exactly this sense of connectedness, which manifests both conceptually and materially in medieval manuscript textuality. "Even as medieval authors reference other sources of authority for their works, medieval narratives 'reference' other stories."[9] Originality in this sense means a "clear documentation of textual origins,"[10] a need for a specific sort of authentication. But on a more general theoretical level, the very conception of textuality becomes different in a manuscript culture, since the text proves to be a much more unstable and final construct than it is in modernity. Such a culture is, in fact, a space of variance, where the texts themselves are plural and heterogeneous, resembling more the (post)modern hypertext than the modern standard of the printed text.[11] The (perhaps implicit) suggestions in Tolkien's paradigms for cultural and literary history can be contextualized in these more recent approaches to medieval textual and literary culture: manuscript context studies, the concern with the essential variance and its consequences on authentication and representation practices, can provide frameworks in which to see Tolkien's own fiction and texts. In other words, medieval literary practice operates a very characteristic discourse of representation; Tolkien adapts this discourse, linking his work to medieval models. His postmodernity, however, is exactly in the way this discourse is problematized in his texts.

In the context of Tolkien's own fiction, medievalism thus has two senses: first, Tolkien mirrors medieval representational discourse and with it medieval textual phenomena; second, this very mirroring necessitates medievalist stances of criticism by the thematization of elements that have become central in "postmodern medievalism." The importance of the individual variant is put into the center of attention by Tolkien's emphasis on *textuality*, the role of which is primarily that of structuring the corpus. Tolkien's texts consistently construct and maintain a "fiction of the text" (the text of Bilbo, of Frodo, of Dírhavel, of Pengoloð, or of simply an unknown author): Middle-earth is presented through a fictitious textuality bringing into play the medieval conceptions of the text. This leads to the creation of the corpus as a *philological corpus*, one that, in fact, shows many of the characteristics of medieval manuscript textuality: it has nearly exclusively variants, versions, of the same text, of the same story, from which it is the editor's task to produce a "standard." But there is no standard, no "real" version in the multitude of variants: Tolkien's writing, as medieval writing, is in this variance,[12] which the publication of *The History of Middle-earth* has amply demonstrated. Philological depth is signaled by relationships between (often fictitious) texts instead of stories. The 1977 edition of *The Silmarillion*, edited by Christopher Tolkien, is thus a good representative of this aspect of Tolkien's writings and also of the critical stances it invites. Christopher Tolkien (himself a supremely competent philologist) demonstrated in it how an *edition* is in fact a *rewriting*, "composed of bits and pieces borrowed from manuscripts of various periods."[13] The radical plurality of the corpus and its failure to produce a final, fixed version (expected from an author in what Bernard Cerquiglini calls "textuary modernity")[14] open up the concept of the "text" into a characteristically medieval space of variants without a standard; but a postmodern conception of the text, a space for the interaction of elements and meanings, also comes into play. Manuscript textuality is a metaphor for this: Tolkien does not "regress" to the medieval; he uses it and comments on it.

This stress on textuality also deepens the representation of culture by highlighting the various implied cultural positions and roles. The different author positions in the fictional texts (like Bilbo's roles as original author, translator, compiler or adaptor or Frodo's as author) inscribe different sorts of relationships toward texts and their contents into the textual world, expanding the "philological" fiction into a "cultural" one: culture, Tolkien seems to imply, comes into being and is maintained exactly in these acts of handing on and authoring. The texts' layers, reflecting various uses, make available a variety of voices, from the past and present of the imagined world, even if only in the very moment of their being silenced by the editor, their noninclusion, excerpting, and anthologizing.[15]

But authors usually read before they write; these positions are also receiver and interpreter positions. The voice and activity of the scribe, the interpolator, and the editor come out in this fiction in a way that is very much like the way their real medieval equivalents' voice and activity can be heard and glimpsed in manuscript variants and their textual reworkings. We saw in the *Beowulf* essay how Tolkien sees clearly the necessary interpretive nature of the poet's handling of the traditions he uses ("Beowulf," 16): we see what and how authors understand from what and how they use. Tolkien, in fact, generalizes the role of interpretation: even though authors are responsible for producing representations, the heroes whose deeds form the story (the subject of the representation) also have to use stories, and they are thus also in receiver, interpreter positions. Aragorn and Arwen in *The Lord of the Rings* replay the story of Beren and Lúthien; Aragorn consciously uses that story to pattern his own life and actions. John A. Calabrese summarizes well several other such instances of the uses of the past and stories;[16] and as Alexandra Bolintineanu points out, even the smallest heroes, the Hobbits, do this.[17] Heroes in *The Lord of the Rings* often "enact legends by performing in the fictional present deeds that will provide legendary material for future generations";[18] but the Hobbits's taking their own lives *as* stories seems to come from Bilbo, whose conception of everything as either already narrated or yet to be narrated (preferably by himself) is apparently contagious, at least with Hobbits. Pippin and Merry always carefully think of their story as one to be remembered and told to Bilbo for writing up (see *LR* 3.3, 480; 3.4, 482; 5.10, 926; 6.4, 992); and Pippin, hearing the eagles' coming at the Morannon before he faints, conceives this as a parallel to Bilbo's (already written) story: " 'Bilbo!' [his thought] said. 'But no! That came in his *tale*, long long ago. This is my *tale*, and it is ended now' " (*LR* 5.10, 874; my emphasis). We see Frodo (or the fictitious author/narrator of the book) writing the figure of Sam at Cirith Ungol in a way that brings into play old stories to make sense of and assign meaning to Sam,[19] and earlier, in a dialogue on literary theory (discussed so well in the present volume by Verlyn Flieger), Frodo and Sam "picture their present ordeals not just as past but as *formally narrated past, as historical text*."[20] In these, medieval relationships to the reception, production, and transmission of texts become similar to a postmodern view of representation, the writing and reading of the world and history as a text.

By the differentiation of such positions and the projection of a textual history into the world of Middle-earth, Tolkien makes *historicity* another key aspect, really another side of textuality. Both in his academic work and his fiction he supplies an awareness that the text (or elements in it) is past, speaks from another position; and that changes and determines its meaning. The very succession of texts itself is historical, but this historicity itself is also made a theme when it is *history* that is presented in texts: the ways history is written, handled, and used. The various textual traits, through which Tolkien assigns historicity to his writings mark different types of history. In *The Silmarillion*, the teller, the source and its authority, the narrative scope, and the implied audience of a text clearly separate the cosmogonic (the "Ainulindalë"), the mythological (the early parts of the "Quenta Silmarillion"), and the historiographic texts (the later "Quenta" and onward)—all within the fiction of Bilbo's imaginary compilation made from "all the sources available to him in Rivendell, both living and written" (*LR* prologue, 14). Elvish sources as "living history" show how history in Middle-earth is for a significant extent remembrance; Elrond at the Council thematizes this pointedly when he answers Frodo's unbelieving question: "my memory reaches back even to the Elder Days. . . . I have seen three ages in the West of the world, and many defeats, and many fruitless victories" (*LR* 2.2, 237). But even Elvish texts are only seen through our versions of the "Silmarillion": history is remembrance, but it necessarily becomes recorded remembrance, a text.

These aspects of historicity also function to "spread" stories, meanings, and their uses in the context of (differentiated) cultures. The source of a narrative (and consequently, its authority) defines previous versions and the ultimate reference point: "What has. . .been declared [in the Ainulindalë] is come from the Valar themselves, with whom the Eldalië spoke in the land of Valinor" (*Silm*, 12). Later on, only intermediate Elvish sources or even only Mannish ones (like the *Narn i Hîn Húrin*: see *Silm* 243 and 427, or presumably the sources of Númenorean history) can be hypothesized. The text of *The Silmarillion* itself is compendious: interpolations, fragments, different traditions are compiled in it (as in the chapter "Of the Sindar," or "Of Beleriand and Its Realms") by Bilbo's activity as translator/editor (mirrored in Christopher Tolkien's editing the 1977 *Silmarillion* from the manuscript versions, later made into the twelve volumes of *The History of Middle-earth*). The work and voice of various (sorts of) authors, various traditions of many cultures, go into Bilbo's book. The narrative scope of texts changes accordingly: from the theological horizon (the cosmogony of the "Ainulindalë") it shifts to specific areas and cultures (Arda generally, Valinor, Beleriand; Sindarin, Mannish, and Númenorean), as these proliferate and fragment the original unified history to that of smaller groups and at the same time import into the narrative the viewpoints of specific authors, tellers, and cultures. Universal history is not possible any more; local, personal "micro-histories" are written. When a place name in Valinor and the name of the White Tree in Túna are given in Sindarin (*Silm*, 32, 62), the text necessarily implies a Sindarin-speaking audience and some uses it can make of these names. The authorial concerns and purposes marked by these textual facets strengthen an awareness of the historical difference and its significance in Tolkien's texts—both for the reader and for Bilbo and other fictitious users. Sam uses the "Fall of Gil-galad" (what he knows of it) differently than do Bilbo or Aragorn. The incorporation of texts is, in fact, the incorporation of historical aspects of culture, even in cases where there is no original and the included historically different "other" is simply a fiction. As far as we know, Tolkien never wrote or even started a fuller "Fall of Gil-galad," but as in *The Silmarillion*, the fiction of the compiler's text not only implies but also offers insight into lost traditions.[21] In the accumulation of material in thirteenth-century compilations, precisely the difference of the various sources and incorporated materials functioned as the principle grounding meaning.[22] The point of Vincent de Beauvais's *Speculum maius* is to collect different sources and arrange them into an encyclopedic account of the whole. A great number of medieval and antique texts survive only in scraps other authors quote. The *ordinatio* of a compilation is the compiler's responsibility (as is the purpose of the work), while the *auctores* are answerable for whatever is said in the material.[23] Such works juxtapose fragments of texts for some well-articulated purpose (which belongs to the compiler); their meaning, as that of *Beowulf*, is grounded in the differences of their elements but ultimately derives from their handling. Cerquiglini also claims that "the medieval manuscript in form, and probably in function, was an anthology, a collection.... The codex was the open space of confrontation, a gesture that brought together."[24] Tolkien's own work fictionalizes itself as exactly such a philological corpus, taking on its dynamics and eliciting similar critical activity (editions, learned commentary, and criticism). At the same time, it offers a space where two conceptions of texts, authorities, and representations can be examined.

While on the basis of medieval analogues this historical awareness is used to suggest and layer meaning, much postmodern thinking about texts tends to disregard exactly this historicity. In interpreting literary works of art, Tolkien is not concerned with the "origin" of the material (as seen in the *Beowulf* essay) but with the way the origin is incorporated and used, always grounding his assertions about this use not in the author but in the text. This way of "close reading" could align him with the New Critics of the 1930s—but it is exactly the historical facet that differentiates him from this notably unhistorical way of reading.[25] The emphasis on authors and their voices also brings up considerations that Roland Barthes's "dead" author and Michel Foucault's author, really a "function" of the text, also disregard.[26]

Postmodern texts appear to exist (and always to have existed) in a timeless present:"There is no other time than that of the enunciation and every text is eternally written *here and now*."[27] Barthes's conception of the classical text (of which the reader realizes that "it is impossible today to write like that")[28] is based exactly on the inability of the reader to tolerate other, past types of writing. But for Tolkien, as Tom Shippey puts it, a text "was not just the words on the page one happened to be reading, it was also the whole history of how the words got there—a history, in many of the works he devoted his life to studying, of misunderstanding or downright error."[29] Tolkien, in fact, brings texts and their history back to interpretation—*this* is the real "return" to philology.

The writing and interpreting of texts are in Tolkien complex cultural activities, the processes of meaning production; medieval strategies of writing and reading the past can also serve as parallels here. As Janet Coleman writes, writing is representation for medieval historiographers (an account of the world, of events, and of experience is "primary signification");[30] for them, "the past came to be observed as *fixed in a text* whose *interpretation* in the present brought to light discontinuities between how it is now and how it was then."[31] The historical discourse about the world and its inhabitants is necessarily bound up with interpretation, the gauging of representation, and the perception of the difference: the production of meaning.

While Tolkien's fictitious past(s) in his fictitious texts, interpreted by his imagined and implied authors and readers, utilize(s) medieval strategies of relating to texts and their pastness, with this they also foreground characteristically postmodern ideas. The concept of the text and the relationships between texts and what they stand for form the horizons in which such problematizations work. The essential plurality and unfixedness produced by the versions in medieval manuscript textuality and in Tolkien offer us the text as a space of free play, where modification (the writing of further variants or adaptation) and interpretation (glossing, commenting, translating, editing, and compiling) yield new meanings, but which is also a space for quotations, borrowed and appropriated elements. The textual units from various origins, interacting with each other, make the "soup" truly intertextual. One is reminded of Roland Barthes's words about the text: "A text is not a line of words, releasing a single 'theological' meaning (the 'message' of the Author-God), but a multi-dimensional space in which a variety of writings, none of them original, blend and clash. The text is a tissue of quotations drawn from the innumerable centers of culture."[32] As we have seen, recent studies in the manuscript context of medieval literature argue that manuscript textuality is exactly such a space.[33]

Peter Lombard's *Sentences*, made up entirely of quotations, would be another parallel, but at the same time it also thematizes another important aspect, the theological codedness of representations. Compiled with a pedagogical aim, the *Sentences* makes texts interact and produces commentary (a standard school exercise) to elucidate meaning; but more importantly, the central role of theology in medieval culture (and therefore in its signifying system) also points out that in Tolkien's world the ultimate horizon of explanation is also theological. As in what Yuri Lotman calls the "medieval world model,"[34] where every element of the world is a sign referring to the creator, every detail and event of Eä refers back to Ilúvatar's plan, the ultimate pattern of meaning (the Music of the Ainur). "No theme may be played that hath not its uttermost source in me, nor can any alter the music in my despite," says the creator (*Silm*, 6): the "meaning" cannot be changed and remains to be discovered. Subjects have to read and understand the world; and Tolkien's creation of Middle-earth in emphatically textual terms highlights the status of linguistic representations as based on a final guarantee of meaning, whether real (as inside the fiction or for the medievals) or fictitious. The problematization and interrogation of representation are decidedly central notions of the postmodern; Tolkien's approach is again special in its coming to the problem by using medieval culture as a metaphoric vehicle.

The representation of the world and its history in textual terms has more consequences concerning writing and especially the writing of history. If the world appears as a text (as indeed it does in a pansemiotic medieval world model), history is again only one representation: indeed, the events and facts of the "outside world" do not form a "story" at all. As Hayden White and others (most notably, of course, New Historicist scholars) have argued, the writing of history is significantly similar to the writing of fiction;[35] its narrative element necessarily reflects the author's concerns, positions, and presuppositions. Only facts and events can be documented and referenced: a story has to be constructed to offer a space for telling "what happened." The need for such a construction of story then signals history as a discourse not radically different from fiction; it is its cultural use that is specific. We have seen how Tolkien places great weight on the differentiation of such cultural uses, turning his concern with representation into the (again typically postmodern mode of) metafiction, history into metahistory.

What we see Tolkien adapting from his medieval models (conceptualized in what he says of *Beowulf* and fairy-stories) are the various discourses that make up a complex signifying system. Theology, mythology, and history are all among the discourses gathered together; textuality, authorship, and interpretation are concepts centrally important in this system. By using medieval models and paradigms as vehicles through which our own stances can be articulated and defined, Tolkien points out problems that are at the heart of much postmodern thinking about culture and literature.

The theorists' disregard for him is therefore surprising: his handling of these problems is interesting, relevant, and significant. For Tolkien and his sensitive reader, the Middle Ages as a model can say much about our problems and how we approach them. In presenting the Middle Ages in much authentic conceptual detail, Tolkien also actualizes the medieval; and thus he produces a postmodern (representation of the) Middle Ages. Postmodernism might be defined (admittedly with a goodly amount of simplification) as a distrust of language, and therefore a (sometimes paranoiac) hyperreflexive relationship to it. But while many postmodern theorists lament our imprisonment in language and the maze of representations, without a direct link to what is "real," Tolkien delights in language and shows that, even knowing it is all we have, we should be aware how much, in fact, we have with it.

Notes

My thanks are due to Jane Chance, Theodore J. Sherman, and Tom Shippey for the opportunity to use various materials I refer to in this essay. Jane Chance and Alfred Siewers, as editors of this volume, deserve especial thanks for their patience with this Niggle-like contributor.

1. See Roland Barthes, "From Work to Text," trans. S. Heath, in *Modern Literary Theory: A Reader*, ed. Philip Rice and Patricia Waugh (London: Edward Arnold, 1992), 166–72 (especially 171).
2. As T.A. Shippey argues, in *J. R. R. Tolkien, Author of the Century* (Boston: Houghton Mifflin, 2001), the depiction and problematization of power in *The Lord of the Rings* is, in fact, a very modern one, which would not have been possible in the Middle Ages (115–17). See also Jane Chance's Foucauldian reading of Tolkien's representation of power in *The Lord of the Rings: The Mythology of Power*, rev. edn. (Lexington: University of Kentucky Press, 2001), 20–25 (I am grateful to Professor Shippey and Professor Chance for supplying me with a copy of these books). In a paper read at the sixth conference of the Hungarian Society for the Study of English (HUSSE 6, Debrecen, Hungary, January 2003), "Sauron and the Sign: From Mythological Sign to Mythological Subject," I also thematized this aspect of Tolkien's representation of power.
3. J.R.R. Tolkien, "Beowulf: The Monsters and the Critics," In *Modern Critical Interpretations: "Beowulf,"* ed. Harold Bloom (New York and Philadelphia: Chelsea House, 1987), 5–31 (hereafter cited in text and notes as "Beowulf").
4. Tolkien makes the very explicit statement, "Also [*Beowulf*] is by an author, and is a thing in itself," in an earlier version of the essay: the "Beowulf and the Critics" A-text; see J. R. R. Tolkien, *Beowulf and the Critics*, ed. Michael D. C. Drout (Medieval and Renaissance Texts and Studies 248. Tempe: Arizona Center for Medieval and Renaissance Studies, 2002), 37.
5. J.R.R. Tolkien, "On Fairy-Stories," in *The Tolkien Reader* (New York: Ballantine, 1966) (hereafter cited in text and notes as "OFS").

6. Even in discussing the historical provenance of fairy-stories, evolution/invention, and inheritance and diffusion, the basic figure of Tolkien's argument is the storyteller-inventor ("OFS," 47).
7. See Iwan Rhys Morus, " 'Uprooting the Golden Bough': J. R. R. Tolkien's Response to Nineteenth-Century Folklore and Comparative Mythology," *Mallorn* 27 (1990): 8.
8. Elizabeth Scala, *Absent Narratives, Manuscript Textuality, and Literary Structure in Late Medieval England*, New Middle Ages (New York: Palgrave Macmillan, 2002), xviii.
9. Scala, *Absent Narratives*, xvii–xviii.
10. Scala, *Absent Narratives*, 3.
11. See Bernard Cerquiglini, *In Praise of the Variant: A Critical History of Philology*, trans. Betsy Wing (Baltimore: Johns Hopkins University Press, 1999), especially 79–82 (on hypertext as the possible authentic representation of medieval textuality).
12. Cerquiglini, *In Praise of the Variant*, 77–78; and further, 37–38.
13. Cerquiglini, *In Praise of the Variant*, 50. Cerquiglini is, of course, speaking about how a Lachmannian-Parisian philology, in search of the "archetype" that is behind all (corrupt) manuscripts, in fact gives us a text that is nowhere attested; but the applicability of this to Tolkien is, I think, remarkable.
14. Cerquiglini, *In Praise of the Variant*, 1–12.
15. See my study of instances of this effect by the activity of the fictitious and real editors in the 1977 *Silmarillion*: "The Adapted Text: The Lost Poetry of Beleriand," *Tolkien Studies* 1 (2004): 21–41.
16. John A. Calabrese, "Continuity with the Past: Mythic Time in Tolkien's *The Lord of the Rings*," in *The Fantastic in World Literature and the Arts. Selected Essays from the 5th International Conference on the Fantastic in the Arts*, ed. Donald E. Morse (Contributions to the Study of Science Fiction and Fantasy 28, New York, Westport, CT., London: Greenwood Press, 1987), 31–45.
17. Alexandra Bolintineanu, " 'On the Borders of Old Stories': Enacting the Past in *Beowulf* and *The Lord of the Rings*," in *Tolkien and the Invention of Myth: A Reader*, ed. Jane Chance (Lexington: University of Kentucky Press, 2004), 267–68.
18. Bolintineanu, " 'On the Borders of Old Stories'," 265.
19. See my "Samu és a szilmarilok" [Sam and the Silmarils] *Lassi Laurië* (Hungarian Tolkien Society) 2, no. 2 (2003): 8–10. I hope to publish an enlarged English version of this article in the future.
20. Bolintineanu, "On the Borders of Old Stories," 267; my emphases.
21. See my "The Adapted Text," passim, and especially 36.
22. See Alastair J. Minnis, *Medieval Theory of Authorship: Scholastic Literary Attitudes in the Later Middle Ages*, 2nd edn. (Aldershot: Wildwood House, 1988), 145, 158.
23. Minnis, *Medieval Theory of Authorship*, 192.
24. Cerquiglini, *In Praise of the Variant*, 28.

25. See also Michael Drout's remarks in the introduction to *Beowulf and the Critics*, 20–22.
26. Roland Barthes, "The Death of the Author," in *Modern Literary Theory: A Reader*, ed. Rice and Waugh, 114–18; and Michel Foucault, "What Is an Author?" trans. Josue V. Harari, in *Contemporary Literary Criticism: Literary and Cultural Studies*, ed. Robert Con Davis and Ronald Schleifer, 2nd edn. (New York: Longman, 1989), 262–75.
27. Barthes, "Death of the Author," 116.
28. Barthes, "From Work to Text," 171. See also his *S/Z*, trans. Richard Miller (New York: Hill and Wang, 1974), chap. I, where he elaborates on the concepts of the "readerly" and the "writerly" texts.
29. Tom Shippey, "Light-elves, Dark-elves and Others: Tolkien's Elvish Problem," *Tolkien Studies* 1 (2004): 11.
30. Janet Coleman, *Ancient and Medieval Memories: Studies in the Reconstruction of the Past* (Cambridge: Cambridge University Press, 1992), 289–90; see also 279, 283. Coleman is talking about twelfth-century historiography at this point.
31. Coleman, *Ancient and Medieval Memories*, 287; my emphases.
32. Barthes, "Death of the Author," 116.
33. See Cerquiglini, *In Praise of the Variant*, 34–45; it is the essential variance, the "surplus of text, language, and meaning" (45), that the modern edition erases.
34. See Yuri Lotman, "Problems in the typology of culture," in *Soviet Semiotics: An Anthology*, ed. Daniel P. Lucid (Baltimore, MD: Johns Hopkins University Press, 1977), 213–21.
35. Hayden White, *Metahistory: The Historical Imagination in Nineteenth-Century Europe* (Baltimore, MD: Johns Hopkins University Press, 1973). New Historicist critics, such as Jeffrey Cox and Larry J. Reynolds, "[reject] the idea of 'History' as a directly accessible, unitary past" (Cox and Reynolds, eds., *New Historical Literary Study: Essays on Reproducing Texts* [Princeton, NJ: Princeton University Press, 1993], 1). See also Robin Headlam Wells, Glenn Burgess, and Rowland Wymer, eds., *Neo-Historicism: Studies in Renaissance Literature, History, and Politics* (Cambridge, UK: Brewer, 2000).

CHAPTER 4

TOLKIEN, *DUSTSCEAWUNG*, AND THE GNOMIC TENSE: IS TIMELESSNESS MEDIEVAL OR VICTORIAN?

John R. Holmes

Tolkien's writing hinges on the Old English literary technique of dustsceawung, *"contemplation of dust," distinct from classical elegiac style. This technique reflects an emphasis in Anglo-Saxon culture on how present images contain shells of their past and seeds of their future. Tolkien used this motif as an implicit critique of modernity in his medievalist fantasy.*

Now that there is a whole century between me and the 1800s, I am starting to think that maybe those Romantics and Victorians got more right than I had given them credit for. Certainly, the nineteenth-century vision of medievalism was flawed, and thankfully Tolkien set it right. But as I settled down to write, I kept seeing more and more what the nineteenth century got *right* about the Middle Ages and the great intellectual and emotional debt that Tolkien owed to nineteenth-century medieval scholarship, for the Romantics were rescuers when it came to the Middle Ages, especially its art and literature. Both in Germany and England Romantics redeemed the idea of the Middle Ages from the scorn heaped upon it by the enlightenment and imitated the poetry of the medieval romances— which was, after all, the reason they were called Romantics.

Nor did the Victorians get it all wrong, either. Even Tennyson, for all his tinkerings with the Arthurian legendarium in *Idylls of the King*, for which some Arthurophiles will never forgive him, nevertheless benefited by the great progress in Anglo-Saxon studies in his day and wrote a fine, sensitive translation of the Old English *Battle of Brunanburh*. Tolkien's source critics have long ago identified Tolkien's debt to Victorian poet and novelist William Morris's imaginative projections into the Northern past. It is true that readers of Tolkien, including me, have tended to remember his 1939 Andrew Lang lecture as ridiculing nineteenth-century manglings of the fairy-story, but that memory is not entirely accurate. Tolkien reports Andrew Lang's pique, not his own, at Victorian fairy-stories (though the particular book by Lang that Tolkien quotes is technically Edwardian), but then he quickly adds, "But the business began, as I have said, long before the nineteenth century, and long ago achieved tiresomeness."[1] For the rest of the lecture "On Fairy Stories," the negative examples are typically from the sixteenth century (Shakespeare and Drayton), not the nineteenth. The only place I could find in which Tolkien mentions nineteenth-century literature in general, he calls it "the great nineteenth century," without, as far as I could tell, any sense of irony.[2]

It is, then, in this context of a defense, however token and puny, of the nineteenth-century's conception both of the Middle Ages and the fairy-story that I wish to identify two points of divergence between Tolkien's conception of medievalism and that of his nineteenth-century predecessors. Both points have to do with implications in Old English literature about the perception of time. Tom Shippey has demonstrated how much Tolkien's depiction of elves owes to difficulties reconciling temporal discrepancies between British and Danish stories of elves, the notion that time either stands still or moves too quickly in Elf-land.[3] Verlyn Flieger, in a book-length study of Tolkien's notions of time, made the bold statement that Tolkien's lecture "On Fairy Stories" was not so much about fairies *or* stories as about *time*.[4] Yet the diverging notions of time in which I am interested here are not those between human and elvish but any of three dichotomies: Christian and pagan, Germanic and classical, or, most to the point of this forum, Victorian and Tolkienian. I would like to explore a notion of time that Victorians (and latter-day Victorianists) seem to think that they invented, and that classicists attribute to classical thought and yet that Tolkien finds not only central to Northern (that is, Germanic) thought but also to his own fiction as well. That treatment of time takes the form of a lament for an irretrievable past, which the Greeks and Romans called "elegiac," but which will be considered here under an Old English name for it, *dustsceawung*, the "contemplation of dust."

If *dustsceawung* is indeed a subgenre of elegy, the classicist could still argue that its source is classical or, in Tolkien's terms, "Southern." Nineteenth-century medievalists, because of their classical training, invariably seized on a Latin term and spoke of the *ubi sunt* motif, from the Latin phrase *ubi sunt que ante nos fuerunt* ("Where are those who were before us?"). The medieval Latin lyrics that use the phrase—the earliest at least two centuries later than the Old English word—are said to derive from Boethius's discussion of the goddess *Fortuna* in *The Consolation of Philosophy*. And it is well known how popular Boethius was in the Old English period; surely the Old English poets cribbed the *ubi nunc* from Boethius, translated it to *Hwær com* in *The Wanderer* and other similar elegiac passages, which Aragorn quoted as an ancient Rohirric verse in the "King of the Golden Hall" chapter of *The Two Towers*. It would seem that the *dustsceawung* sentiment, which Tolkien presents as quintessentially Northern, originated with the man whom Edward Gibbon called "the last of the Romans whom Cato or Tully could have acknowledged for their countrymen."[5] Yet this Roman was an exact contemporary of the kings in *Beowulf*, insofar as they are historical, and the king whom Boethius served in Rome was himself "Northern," or perhaps Northeastern—the Ostrogoth Diedrich von Bern, or "Theodoric." The court in which Boethius served had as many Germanic as Italic influences, so his *ubi nunc* has an equal claim to either pedigree.

The Old English connection with Boethius, if not the general Germanic, was noted by the very first nineteenth-century commentator on the elegiac strain in Old English poetry; he specifically mentioned "The Ruin" and "The Wife's Lament." William Daniel Conybeare, the brother of one of Oxford's first professors of Anglo-Saxon, first used the term "elegy" for these two poems in 1826, and he identified "Elegiac" as one of eight types of Old English poetry.[6] Conybeare also identified Alfred's translation of *The Metres of Boethius* as a source of the Old English elegy.[7] German scholars (and a few Americans) kept the term current throughout the nineteenth century, until Ernst Sieper's book-length study *Die altenglische Elegie* (1915). The word was still inseparably connected to those two poems including "The Husband's Message" in 1961 in R.F. Leslie's *Three Old English Elegies*.[8]

What was it about these three poems, and the many others identified by Siepers, that made philologists think of the Greek-derived word *elegy*? After all, even in Greek the word was ambiguous: the earliest Greek elegists, the seventh-century Callinus and Tyrtaeus, celebrated war and patriotism in elegiac meter, and the elegies of Mimnus and Theognis were love poems. Not until the third century, when Theocritus wrote funeral laments in elegiacs was the word associated with death and sorrow. And even then such funeral poems, and their imitations a century later by Bion and Moschus, were known to the Greeks not as "elegies" but "idylls," affirming Tennyson's nomenclature in *Idylls of the King*, which was indeed a lament for the passing of greatness. "Lamentation" is certainly not what Roman poets like Propertius and Ovid, who wrote elegies in bright and playful moods, meant by the word. But it *is* what the nineteenth-century Anglo-Saxonists meant by *elegy*: a poem expressing the sadness for the loss of heroes and a heroic world that may never return.

For Tolkien, the elegiac mode, so defined, was not just the province of a few isolated lyrics but the predominant mode of all great old Germanic poetry; indeed it was part and parcel of what Tolkien called "the Northern courage, the theory of courage, which is the great contribution of early Northern literature."[9] When he attempted to illustrate this Northern theory of courage, Tolkien pointed not only to the Old English *Battle of Maldon*, but also, albeit slightly, to Tennyson's "Charge of the Light Brigade."[10] The connection between this Northern theory of courage and the elegiac mode follows, I think, from Tolkien's argument, but perhaps requires explication. In venturing *elegy* as a generic label for *Beowulf*, though squirming at the ill fit of Greek words for Germanic things, Tolkien selects one of *Beowulf*'s elegiac lines—a frank narrative description of Beowulf's funeral pyre—as emblematic for the whole poem. "*Beowulf*," says Tolkien, "is not an 'epic,' not even a magnified 'lay.' No terms borrowed from Greek or other literatures exactly fit: there is no reason why they should. Though if we must have a term, we should choose rather 'elegy.' It is a heroic-elegiac poem; and in a sense all its first 3,136 lines are the prelude to a dirge: *him þa gegiredan Geata leoda ad ofer eorðan unwaclicne* [the Geatish people then prepared for him a splendid pyre on the ground]; one of the most moving ever written."[11] One term Tolkien didn't venture in place of "elegy" is our term *dustsceawung*, "contemplation of dust." Readers of Bruce Mitchell and Fred C. Robinson's introduction to the poem most associated with the elegiac mode, *The Ruin*, in their *A Guide to Old English*, might be surprised at Tolkien's avoidance of a word so useful for the mood he was trying to articulate. "In both their poetry and their prose," the *Guide* announces, "the Anglo-Saxons were very given to reflection on former civilizations and the people who built them, so much so that their language had a word for such meditation: *dustsceawung* 'contemplation of the dust.' "[12]

What Mitchell and Robinson do not observe is that while the *dustsceawung* motif is everywhere in Old English writing, *dustsceawung* the word is not. It is indeed significant that Old English has a word for the lament for past civilizations, but it is also significant that the word is used only once in the entire corpus of Anglo-Saxon texts. It is in one of the Blickling homilies, an undistinguished sermon on the end of the world, "þisses Middangeardes Ende Neah Is" [The end of this Middle-earth is near]. The unidentified homilist tells the story of a rich man who visited the grave of a friend, whose bones spoke to him, saying that he, too, would come to this. The homilist concluded: "*He þa swa geomor, & swa gnorngende, gewat from þære dustsceawunga & hine þa onwende from ealre þissa worlde begangum*" [He then, so sad and sorrowful, departed from the dust-spectacle, and turned himself away from all the affairs of the world].[13] A laudable response to *dustsceawung*, but not exactly the lament for a lost past that Tolkien had in mind. Nevertheless, if we can accept Mitchell and Robinson's extension of the term, we can use it as a marker for the Germanic sentiment so carefully articulated by Tolkien.

Yet if *dustsceawung* was not a common native English word, Old English did have a word for elegy, a gloss for the Latin word that appears in the very source Conybeare identified in 1826: Alfred's *Metres of Boethius*. The word is *sarcwiðe*, "sorrow-speech," or song of lament. Of the two roots in this compound, the second, *cwiðe*, is in the top 100 most-common words in the Old English poetic corpus—it is, to be precise, number 63, appearing, in various forms, 430 times. The other root, *sar*, is number 230, appearing 150 times. The title of this essay, then, ought to be "Tolkien's *sarcwiðe*" rather than "Tolkien's *dustsceawung*," were it not for a thematic advantage to the image of dust and its relation to Tolkien's thoughts about the human experience of time and eternity. In fact, Verlyn Flieger connected Tolkien's experience of a literal contemplation of dust with the nature of eternity.[14] That epiphany of Tolkien's, which will be explored in more detail later, widens the meaning of *dustsceawung*, but for now it is enough to connect it with the elegy. The distinction between elegy as simply a lament for the dead, and the northern elegiac mood as Tolkien evinced it, a brooding on the past and its implications for the present and the future, is worth keeping. *Dustsceawung* is just the right word for this second species of the elegiac.

The connection between his Northern "theory of courage" and the elegiac mood of the *dustsceawung* type, has to do with a perception of time that the Victorians thought to be modern, but that Tolkien knew to be ancient. In discussing echoes of Romanticism in Tolkien's verse, Joe R. Christopher attributes a more general elegiac mood to earlier nineteenth-century verse: "The Romantics had a tendency to tell of the passing of greatness or beauty: *The Fall of Hyperion, The Last of the Mohicans, The Last of the Barons*."[15] Yet the shift in the consciousness of time that was supposed by Victorianists to have occurred later in the nineteenth century, and involved contemplation not of the passing but the past*ness* of greatness or beauty—in a word, *dustsceawung*—was supposed to have been influenced by the rise of archaeology. Typical of this notion is George H. Ford's statement in the headnote on Tennyson in *The Norton Anthology of English Literature*: "Tennyson is the first major writer to express this awareness of the vast extent of geological time that has haunted human consciousness since Victorian scientists exposed the history of the earth's crust."[16] We see it as early as the speaker's reflection on "the process of the suns" in Tennyson's "Locksley Hall" (1842), or the theme (and the very title) of Browning's "Love Among the Ruins" (1855), inspired by his reading of his friend A.H. Layard's archaeological sensation, *Nineveh and Its Remains* (1849).[17]

Still, one need not contemplate dust on the spade or pickaxe of an excavator to be imbued with the sense of the vastness of time and to recreate imaginatively the daily life of those who left that dust. The Victorians may have dug into the dust they contemplated, but the original audience of the Old English elegy walked daily past barrows they knew to contain the dust and artifacts of ancient kings, and they needed no Boethius to bid them ask "*hwær cwom?*" or "*ubi sunt?*" The divines who calculated the age of the earth at a mere four thousand years were children of the enlightenment, not the Middle Ages. The Anglo-Saxon mind distinguished *eald* ("old") from *oreald* ("primeval"; *oreald* occurs in Alfred's *Boethius* and provided Tolkien with one of the names for Tom Bombadil).

So, if the Victorian expansion of time-consciousness was not unknown to the medieval mind, what does it have to do with the Northern Theory of Courage? Tolkien elaborated the theory most thoroughly in his famous essay, the 1936 British Academy lecture, "Beowulf: The Monsters and the Critics," yet defined it there succinctly as "the exaltation of undefeated will." The theme is fugitive in *The Battle of Maldon* and other Old English poems, says Tolkien, but "it is in *Beowulf* that a poet has devoted a whole poem to the theme."[18] Yet earlier we heard Tolkien assert, in a passage taken from the same lecture, that the whole poem is the "prelude to a dirge"—as if the *dustsceawung* at Beowulf's funeral pyre were the whole point of the poem. If we accept both of these statements simultaneously, then there must be a connection between the Northern courage and *dustsceawung*. And there is—once again, in the Northern perception of time.

In *Beowulf*, Tolkien says (just a few lines after his definition of the Northern Courage as "undefeated will"), we see "man at war with the hostile world, and his inevitable overthrow in Time."[19] It is Tolkien's ability to see this theme as a triumph of hope rather than as defeatism that allows him to modernize it in *The Lord of the Rings*. *Inevitable overthrow in time*: Byrhtnoth's and Byrhtwold's heartiness in facing a superior force in a battle they knew they would lose; Beowulf's sure knowledge of his own imminent death in the dragon fight; Théoden King's eagerness for the Battle of Helm's Deep despite the certainty of his people's destruction—all of these particular instances of the Northern Courage in *Maldon*, *Beowulf*, and *Lord of the Rings* are but manifestations of the general destiny of man: defeat by the powers of "chaos and unreason." The reason that a Northern hero like Byrhtwold, Beowulf, or Théoden could ride blithely to his destruction is that his mythology—even, if you prefer, his metaphysics—has told him that such is the destiny not only of Middle-earth, but even of Middle-earth's gods.

All of time is a prelude to, a preparation for, the end time, just as the first 3,136 lines of *Beowulf* (98.55 percent of the whole poem) are a prelude to the hero's funeral. That is what the Northern pagan metaphysic looks like, whether you are contrasting it with the Christian metaphysic or with the Southern pagan (that is, Greek and Roman; Tolkien studiously avoids the word "classical" in his British Academy lecture, since the North has its own classicism). What happens next in Tolkien's analysis strikes at one item that nineteenth-century medievalism really did get wrong: the contrast between Germanic mythology and Christianity. George Lyman Kittridge in 1888 and Francis Blackburn in 1897 emphasized cosmological differences between pagan and Christian in *Beowulf*. Tolkien in 1936—and even today it seems a little surprising—stressed the continuity in world view before and after the Christianizing of England.

This continuity accounts for a puzzling and much-quoted remark of Tolkien's in a letter to Amy Ronald in 1956: "I am a Christian, and indeed a Roman Catholic, so that I do not expect 'history' to be anything but a 'long defeat.' "[20] The quotations marks around "history" and "long defeat" are crucial for catching Tolkien's meaning, and in fact, for the most part, Tolkien's commentators have had no trouble at all catching his meaning: "history," that is, the human race's tenure in time, is doomed to end in the race's defeat. But such an ending is only tragic if temporal existence, the here-and-now Middle-earth, is all there is. Traditional comparisons of the Christian and the Norse teleology pitch the essentially comic vision of Christianity against the tragic vision of the North. But Tolkien's explication of the teleology of a reflective Englishman in that *Götterdämmerung* moment between pagan and Christian—in short, exactly the moment in which *Beowulf* was composed—suggests that the Christian vision changes the meaning and value of the tragic rather than eliminating it altogether. "A Christian was (and is) still like his forefathers a mortal hemmed in a hostile world. The monsters remained the enemies of mankind, the infantry of the old war, and became inevitably the enemies of the one God, *ece Drihten*, the eternal Captain of the new. Even so the vision of the war changes. For it begins to dissolve, even as the contest on the fields of Time thus takes on its largest aspect. The tragedy of the great temporal defeat remains for a while poignant, but ceases to be finally important."[21] In fact, precisely what makes the Christian author of *Beowulf* so effective, Tolkien suggests, is his appreciation for and sympathy with the pagan past—in a word, his *dustsceawung*. "As the poet looks back into the past, surveying the history of kings and warriors in the old traditions, he sees that all glory...ends in night.... We get in fact a poem from a pregnant moment of poise, looking back into the pit, by a man learned in old tales who was struggling, as it were, to get a general view of them all, perceiving their common tragedy of inevitable ruin, and yet feeling this more *poetically* because he was himself removed from the direct pressure of its despair."[22] The *Beowulf* poet feels the greatness, the glory, of the pagan civilization whose dust he contemplates, as the speaker in *The Ruin*, whether Christian or pagan (in terms of the *dustsceawung* theme, I do not think it matters), feels the past majesty of the British Romans when he surveys the remnants of their architecture.

Nowhere so much as in this theme of *dustsceawung* does Tolkien unite the two spheres of English studies, poetry and philology, *Lang' and Lit'*, as he calls them, whose estrangement he lamented and strove to eradicate his entire professional life; for just as the *Beowulf* poet casts his mind back to re-create the heroic age of the court of Heorot, so the Anglo-Saxonist contemplates dusty manuscripts, if not the very dust, to re-create imaginatively the world of the Old English writers. One of Tolkien's earliest works of criticism was, we could say, a *dustsceawung*: in the *Year's Work in English Studies* for 1924, he wrote, with equal measure of scholarship and imagination, on the perception of ancient Roman roads in Anglo-Saxon England.[23] And as Thomas Shippey has observed, it was in a bit of *dustsceawung* of Roman ruins in *Maxims II* that Tolkien first speculated in print on the Old English words *ent* and *orþanc*.[24]

It may be that reflection on the physical remnants of past greatness in England—the *sceawung* of England's *dust*, if you will—was part of what Tolkien's public school chum G.B. Smith meant by "what I dreamed and what we all agreed upon" in his last letter to Tolkien, from the trenches in France at the end of 1916. Thinking of the recent death in battle of their mutual friend Rob Gilson, and perhaps sensing his own imminent death, Smith hoped that Tolkien would live to "say the things I have tried to say long after I am not there to say them."[25] The things Smith had been trying to say included, it turns out, a *dustsceawung* of the Roman roads in Britain like Tolkien's later scholarly one, but in poetry. Only the year before he wrote his last letter to Tolkien, Smith published a poem echoing this ancient theme:

> This is the road the Romans made,
> This track half lost in the green hills,
> Or fading in a forest glade
> 'Mid violets and daffodils.[26]

Whatever the poetic merits of Smith's verse, Smith in this poem is doing precisely what Tolkien pictures the *Beowulf* poet as doing: casting his mind back to a heroic past implicit in what is now but dust.

It is in this context that the nineteenth- and twentieth-century critics who in Tolkien's mind slighted *Beowulf* by calling it "an historical document" were guilty not of misdirection so much as of lack of imagination. If by "historical document" the critics meant a text that projects the modern mind back to an earlier culture, then they were not so far from Tolkien's view as they may seem. But it is unlikely that many of them meant that. The "shadow of research" that Tolkien says "has lain upon criticism" had also lain upon history.[27] "Historical document" to the earliest *Beowulf* critics, excited by the rising Victorian tide of geology and biology, had come to suggest empirical evidence rather than imagination. Yet surely the historian's job is, like the elegiac poet's and the Tolkien-style critic's, to contemplate the dust of the heroes whose dust is presented for contemplation.

The dust of heroes, however, is not the only connotation for the image of *dustsceawung* in Tolkien. The idea of contemplating dust immediately suggests to the student of Tolkien's biography a "sudden vision" or "apperception" he related in a November 7–8, 1944 letter to his son Christopher.[28] During a half hour of Eucharistic adoration, Tolkien said, he "perceived or thought of" the light of God and a mote of dust suspended in it. The context of the adoration is significant, because it is by its very nature an act of contemplation. It consists of an exposition (the Old English word would be *sceawung*) of a consecrated host in a frame called a *monstrance* (from the Latin *monstrare*, "to show," a gloss for the Old English *sceawan*). In Roman Catholic worship, the faithful are encouraged to meditate on the real presence of the person of Jesus in the wafer of bread. This *breadsceawung*—a better word for "contemplation of bread" might be :"hlaf sceawung" because the Old English word *bread* meant "crumb"—reminds us that any pessimism involved in a Boethian contemplation of dust is either illusory or, at the very least, not the whole picture, for just as the Blickling homilist conjured images of talking bones only to remind his flock of a higher reality beyond them, the point of Eucharistic exposition is for the adorer to see more than a wafer of bread.

In this contemplative mood, Tolkien received (though he scrupulously avoids, even to his son, any claims of *revelation*—yet another word glossed by the Old English *sceawung*) an image of a mote of dust suspended in light. The relationship of the light to the dust was precisely the relationship of eternity to time, "a finite parallel to the Infinite," as Tolkien put it. In terms of Catholic doctrine, that's just what a sacrament is: a finite form (e.g., bread) that reveals (*sceawan* again) a higher reality (the body of Christ).

In the case of Tolkien's vision, the light (in its source, God; in the single ray, an angel) both holding and illuminating the mote (which Tolkien saw as himself, "or any other human person that I might think of with love"). Tolkien's imaginative projection of himself into the mote in the light beam parallels a similar self-projection in his critical essays, in which Jane Chance has found an analogue to the hero in his fiction.

Chance's opening chapter of *Tolkien's Art* suggests that *Beowulf: the Monsters and the Critics* presents the artist as hero, and that in his prefaces to *The Lord of the Rings* and *Tree and Leaf* Tolkien associates himself with both the artist and the hero.[29] In the context of the *dustsceawung* motif, such an association makes perfect sense. To be a hero in the Germanic world is to contemplate the artifacts, if not the dust, of the heroes who came before you. The heroic code is literally a covenant of heirlooms. The ties between a lord and his *thegn* are sealed by gifts, which are typically the residue of former heroes, each ring or sword or shirt of mail bearing the tale of former campaigns. We know two swords by name in *Beowulf*: the hero's own sword, Nægling, is said to be "ancient and grey"; Unferth's sword Hrunting is a family heirloom when he gives it to Beowulf; and the genealogy of the necklace Queen Wealtheow gives Beowulf is even more detailed. The unnamed sword that Beowulf retrieves from Grendel's mere is a source of wonder, and more contemplation, of the workmanship of giants long gone from Middle-earth. Of all the sword names in Tolkien's fiction—Glamdring, Orcrist, Sting, and Herugrim—the one most redolent of the ancient past— and in this case, the future as well—is Aragorn's *Andúril*, the Sword-That-Was-Broken and, it is hoped, the Sword-That-Shall-Be-Reforged.

But one sword that goes unnamed in *The Lord of the Rings* is the first sword to pierce anything substantial in any Ringwraith: indeed, when in the hands of Merry it strikes the Lord of the Nazgûl, in the penultimate book of the novel, it is the first reference to anything material in the Nazgûl, after countless references to black "shapes," "shadows," and "forms." First, in Chapter 8 of book I, Tom Bombadil had given the blade's genealogy, as is proper during any passing of swords in Northern literature: "Then he told them that these blades were forged many long years ago by Men of Westernesse: they were foes of the Dark Lord, but they were overcome by the evil king of Carn Dûm in the Land of Angmar."[30] Some seven hundred pages later, in "The Battle of Pelennor Fields" (5.6), Merry's sword, having found flesh and sinew beneath the insubstantial shadow of the Nazgûl Lord, disintegrates precisely as did the sword Beowulf snagged from the long-dead giants in Grendel's mere. Just as the *Beowulf* poet indulges in *dustsceawung* over the sword Beowulf uses to slay Grendel's mother—twice in the space of four lines the poet recalls the ancient giants who made the sword, calling it *ealdsweord eotenisc*, "ancient sword of giants" and *giganta geweorc*, "work of giants"—so Tolkien describes the melting away of the barrow-sword Merry receives from Tom Bombadil: "So passed the sword of the Barrow-downs, work of Westernesse. But glad would he have been to know its fate who wrought it slowly long ago in the North-kingdom when the Dúnedain were young, and chief among their foes was the dread realm of Angmar and its sorcerer king. No other blade, not though mightier hands had wielded it, would have dealt that foe a wound so bitter, cleaving the undead flesh, breaking the spell that knit his unseen sinews to his will."[31]

The *Beowulf* poet gives us a corresponding passage, in which Beowulf presents Hrothgar with the hilt of the melted sword, and Hrothgar's mind, in contemplating the dusty relic, casts back to the ancient giants who contended with God before the flood: "Hrothgar spoke, contemplated[32] the hilt, the old heirloom. On it was written the origins of ancient strife, when the flood, the rushing sea, slew the race of giants; they had lived fiercely; that people was estranged from the eternal Lord. The Ruler gave them final punishment for that in the whelming of the water. Thus on the sword guard of bright gold it was in runic letters clearly marked, set down and told, for whom that sword was first wrought, the choicest of blades, with its twisted hilt and snake decorations." Even without such runes, the sword as heirloom always mediates past, present, and future in the Northern imagination.

It is the knowledge of the deeds these great blades have done in the past that stands as a pledge of the deeds they will do in the future. But if such contemplation of the past is an essential task for the Northern warrior, it is no surprise that *dustsceawung* should be an essential part of that Northern warrior's poetry. Yet there is one way in which all Old English narrative poetry is imbued with this "Northern Theory of Time," if you will—in fact, it could be said that elegy comes naturally to Old English poetry because the language itself reflects the way in which the Anglo-Saxon mind finds the past and the future hidden in the present. What could be called a "polychronic" time sense can be seen both in the narratology of Old English poetry and in the tense system of its verbs.[33]

The narrative sense of this polychronic point of view has already been discussed at length as the *dustsceawung* motif, though the sense in which such contemplations also include the future is not always obvious. Sometimes it leaps out at the reader, however, as when the *Beowulf* poet, in the act of describing the very construction of Hrothgar's mead hall, tells us that the flames that will devour Heorot already wait within its wood.[34] But the grammatical sense of the polychronic can also be illustrated in translation, because modern English has the same tense structure as Old English, and as Tolkien observed in his O'Donnell lecture "English and Welsh," the "Old" in Old English is relative. "Old English and Old Welsh," he noted, "were not on a European basis old at all." And of the two, Tolkien continued,

Welsh was, in an evolutionary sense, the elder. "It resembled far more closely the movement of the Romance languages—for example, in the loss of a neutral gender; the early disappearance of declensions contrasted with the preservation of verbs of distinct personal inflections and a fairly elaborate system of tenses and moods."[35] What Tolkien is referring to is the Germanic innovation of streamlining the Indo-European tense system. In the indicative mood alone, Welsh, like most Indo-European languages, expressed present, imperfect, past, pluperfect, and future tenses. Old English, like Modern English, had only present and past. The horrible truth that students of Old English do not want to hear, especially those who one day hope to teach it, is this: *there is no future in Old English.*

Though it has no future tense, English (whether Old, Middle, or Modern) can express it quite easily by using other tenses with temporal words indicating the future.[36] Someone like Tolkien who had, as C.S. Lewis put it, "been inside language," would be alert to differences in the ways different languages signal temporal concepts.[37] The fourth chapter of Verlyn Flieger's *A Question of Time* articulates in great detail the differences between Elvish and human perceptions of time, and Flieger correlates these differences with the theoretical explorations of time sense by J.W. Dunne in *An Experiment with Time*. But there is also a similar dichotomy of time inherent, not in the twentieth-century English Tolkien learned in the waning years of the nineteenth century, but in the tenth-century Old English Tolkien learned in the early years of the twentieth century.

Tolkien discussed this dichotomy in his "English and Welsh" lecture. The Old English verb "to be," he observed, "had two distinct forms of the 'present.'"[38] Tolkien placed the word "present" in quotation marks because he knew another secret of English grammar: that the so-called present tense form rarely referred to the actual present. When it did, it was the distinct verb *seon*; when it did not, the verb was *beon*, the ancestor of all of our verbs of being that begin with *b*. English today lacks this useful distinction: when we say "It is raining," we mean, "right this moment"—that is, we are using the true present tense. But when we say "God is good," we don't mean that God happens to be behaving Himself at this moment, but stay tuned for an update. No, we have stumbled onto a way of speaking of eternal truths, like "God is good," or "Green is a color," or "Tolkien is a genius." Modern English allows an Arkansas law professor to quibble about what "is" means.

But that quibble would not be possible in Old English. Or rather, the distinction in the time sense would be clear. The "is" of "It is raining" was Old English *seon*, which had a true present form; the "is" of "Tolkien is a genius" would have been Old English *beon*, whose present form was never present in meaning but always one of three non-present senses. The first sense, of course, was future. The second sense is consuetudenal, that is, covering action over a prolonged period. The third sense can be called gnomic, proper to the expression of timeless truths. Tolkien observed that Welsh shared this distinction of *to be* verbs.[39]

The third sense of the Old English *beon*, the gnomic, deserves a closer look. So peppered is *Beowulf* with *gnomoi*, those succinct nuggets of folk wisdom spread throughout the poem, that we should not be surprised that there was in fact a special verb of being reserved for gnomic use. Moreover, we realize that Tolkien's fiction is itself gnomic, and that Tolkien strives perversely, as it seems to us, or at least counterintuitively, to make his Hobbit folk-sayings less streamlined and less quotable, not more. Eowyn/Dernhelm's "Where will wants not, a way opens" is certainly more cumbersome than the more familiar "Where there's a will there's a way," which the Orc taskmaster later perverts to "where there's a whip there's a will."[40] But on second thought we realize that if a proverb is a coin worn smooth by much handling across generations, then the smoothest coin of our age should be presented with unworn features in the unimaginably earlier Third Age—though the Hobbit proverbs were already spoken of as ancient family wisdom. Sam typically attributed them to Gamgee senior, the Old Gaffer, and the narrator of *The Hobbit* implies that their gnomoi are part of their survival equipment. Hobbits, the narrator tells us, "can move very quickly, and hide easily, and recover wonderfully from falls and bruises, and they have a fund of wisdom and wise sayings."[41]

It seems to be merely linguistic coincidence that the Greek word for a small bit of folk wisdom was twisted in relatively recent times into a name for mythic races like Tolkien's Elves, Dwarves, and Hobbits. The sixteenth-century alchemist Paracelsus coined the word "gnome" to refer to spirits of the earth (though later Paracelsians claimed that he was merely using an older terminology). Aside from translations of Paracelsus, the word "gnome" does not appear in English until 1712, in Alexander Pope's *Rape of the Lock*. Yet early in his conception of the various races of elves in Middle-earth, Tolkien used the term "gnomes" to refer to the Noldor, or Deep Elves, and Gnomish was a dialect of Elvish.[42] The connection was in the idea of wisdom, and the *gnomoi* of Tolkien's fiction comprise his treasury of Hobbit, Elvish, and Dwarvish wisdom. What makes this wisdom partake of the timelessness of elves is our construing Tolkien's *gnomoi* in, as it were, a gnomic tense. When Elrond says, "nothing is evil in the beginning," the "is" in the sentence should be translated as Tolkien translated Old English *bið* in the "English and Welsh" passage: "is (naturally, always, or habitually)."[43]

As Verlyn Flieger has shown in *A Question of Time*, Tolkien's conception of time in *Lord of the Rings* is the work of an undeniably modern mind. But there is also no mistaking the influence of much older apprehensions of time implied by three elements in Tolkien's fiction that Victorian medievalists would have recognized: the Old English motif of *dustsceawung*, a polychronic narrative voice, and a timeless gnomic tense.

Notes

1. J.R.R. Tolkien, *Tree and Leaf* (London: Allen & Unwin, 1964), 14 (hereafter cited in text and notes as *TL*).
2. J.R.R. Tolkien, "*The Monsters and the Critics*" *and Other Essays*, ed. Christopher Tolkien (London: George Allen and Unwin, 1983), 229 (hereafter cited as *Monsters*).
3. T.A. Shippey, *The Road to Middle-earth* (Boston: Houghton Mifflin, 1983), 46–47.
4. Verlyn Flieger, *A Question of Time: J. R. R. Tolkien's Road to Faërie* (Kent, Ohio: Kent State University Press, 1997), 2.
5. Edward Gibbon, *The Decline and Fall of the Roman Empire*, 2 vols. (New York: Modern Library, n.d.), 2: 468 (Chapter 39).
6. John Josias Conybeare, *Illustrations of Anglo-Saxon Poetry*, ed. William Daniel Conybeare (London: Harding and Lepard, 1826), lxxxi, 245, 250.
7. Conybeare, *Illustrations*, 260 ff.
8. Christian W.M. Grein, *Bibliothek der angelsächsischen Poesie*, vol. 1 (Göttingen: Georg H. Wigand, 1857); F. Dietrich, "Die Räthsel des Exeterbuchs," *Zeitschrift für deutsches Altertum und deutsche Literatur* 11 (1859): 452–53; Richard Paul Wülker, "Aus englischen Bibliotheken," *Anglia* 2 (1879): 374–87; J.H. Kirkland, "A Passage in the Anglo-Saxon Poem *The Ruin*," *American Journal of Philology* 7 (1886): 367–69; F. Hicketier, "*Klage der Frau, Botschaft des Gemahls, und Ruine*," *Anglia* 11 (1889), 363–68; Fritz Roeder, *Die Familie bei den Angelsachen: Eine kultur- und literarhistorischen Studie auf Grund gleichzeitiger Quellen.* Erster Haupteil: *Mann und Frau* (Halle: Niemeyer, 1899), 11–12; Ernst Sieper, *Die altenglische Elegie* (Strassburg: K.J. Trübner, 1915); Alois Brandl, "Venantius Fortunatus und die angelsächsischen Elegien *Wanderer* und *Ruine*," *Archiv* 139 (1919): 84; B.J. Timmer, "The Elegiac Mood in Old English Poetry," *English Studies* 24 (1942): 34–36; R.F. Leslie, *Three Old English Elegies* (Manchester, UK: Manchester University Press, 1961).
9. Tolkien, *Monsters*, 20.
10. J.R.R. Tolkien, *The Tolkien Reader* (New York: Ballantine, 1966), 25.
11. Tolkien, *Monsters*, 31.
12. Bruce Mitchell and Fred C. Robinson, *A Guide to Old English*, 6th edn. (Oxford: Blackwell Publishers, 2001), 253.
13. Richard Morris, ed., *The Blickling Homilies, with a Translation and Index of Words Together with the Blickling Glosses* (London: Early English Text Society, 1880), 113. Translation is Morris's, from the facing page (112).
14. Verlyn Flieger, *Splintered Light: Logos and Language in Tolkien's World*, 2nd edn. (Kent, Ohio: Kent State University Press, 2002), 1.

15. Joe R. Christopher, "Tolkien's Lyric Poetry." In *Tolkien's* Legendarium: *Essays on* The History of Middle-earth, ed. Verlyn Flieger and Carl F. Hostetter (Westport, CT: Greenwood Press, 2000), 145.
16. M.H. Abrams et al., *The Norton Antholgy of English Literature*, 6th edn. (New York: W.W. Norton, 1993), 2:1056.
17. Alfred, Lord Tennyson, "Locksley Hall," line 138. In *Poetry of the Victorian Period*, Jerome Hamilton Buckley and George Benjamin Woods, 3rd edn. (Glenview, Illinois: Scott, Foreman, and Company, 1965), 48.
18. Tolkien, *Monsters*, 18.
19. Tolkien, *Monsters*, 18.
20. J.R.R. Tolkien, *The Letters of J. R. R. Tolkien*, ed. Humphrey Carpenter with assistance from Christopher Tolkien (London: George Allen and Unwin, 1981), 255, letter 195 (hereafter *Letters*).
21. Tolkien, *Monsters*, 22.
22. Tolkien, *Monsters*, 23.
23. J. R. R. Tolkien, "Philology: General Works" in *The Year's Work in English Studies* 5 (1924): 26–65.
24. Shippey, *Road*, 100.
25. Humphrey Carpenter, *J.R.R. Tolkien: A Biography* (London: George Allen and Unwin; Boston: Houghton Mifflin, 1977), 94.
26. G[eoffrey] B[ache] S[mith], "Roman Roads," in *Oxford Poetry*, ed. G.D.H.C. and T.W.E. (Oxford: B.H. Blackwell, 1915), 60. The connection of this poem with Tolkien's professional antiquarianism originates, as with more of my ideas than I care to admit, in Tom Shippey's *Road to Middle Earth*, which reprints this passage on page 24.
27. Tolkien, *Monsters*, 14.
28. Tolkien, *Letters*, 99. As fundamental as this connection is to Tolkien readers, it escaped me in the first draft of this essay. I am grateful to the editors of this volume, not only for pointing out the missed opportunity for this context, but also for allowing me to reclaim it in revision.
29. Jane Chance, *Tolkien's Art: A Mythology for England*, rev. edn. (Lexington: University Press of Kentucky, 2001), 25.
30. J.R.R. Tolkien, *The Lord of the Rings*, 2nd edn., rev. (one-volume edn.) (Boston: Houghton Mifflin, 1994), 1.8, 142 (hereafter *LR*).
31. Fr[iedrich] Klaeber, *Beowulf and the Fight at Finnsburgh*, 3rd edn. (New York: D.C. Heath, 1950), 58–59 (lines 1559 and 1562); *LR* 5.6, 826.
32. Klaeber, *Beowulf and the Fight*, 63. The verb here translated (by me) as "contemplated" is in fact the second element of the *dustceawung* compound; R.K. Gordon's literal prose translation renders *hilt sceawode* as "beheld the hilt," though I think we are justified in preferring "contemplated." See R.K. Gordon, trans. *Anglo-Saxon Poetry* (London: J.M. Dent, 1926), 34.
33. For a more thorough discussion of grammar and time-sense in Old English (and other Germanic languages), consult Paul C. Bauschatz, *The Well and the Tree: World and Time in Early Germanic Culture* (Amherst: University of Massachusetts Press, 1982), particularly his discussion of tense in the fifth chapter, though he does not discuss the *seon/beon* distinction.

34. Klaeber, *Beowulf and the Fight*, 4.
35. Tolkien, *Monsters*, 177.
36. The usual means of expressing future in modern English is through a special category of verbs known as "modals," descendants of Old English verbs known as "preterit-present" because of the ambiguity of their tense structure (they began as preterit, or simple past forms, then were reinterpreted as present, adding a preterit suffix). By convention, and a rather shaky convention at that, we agree to use the combination "will" (or another modal) plus the present tense, to form the future. But the fact is that virtually any English verb form can be made to express a future meaning simply by adding a time word indicating future. **Present**: "Tomorrow I leave Kalamazoo." **Present Participle**: "Tomorrow I am leaving Kalamazoo." **Infinitive**: "I am to leave Kalamazoo tomorrow." The subjunctive can even use the past tense of the verb: "If I left Kalamazoo tomorrow, I'd miss it." Other verbs with future meaning: "I am going to leave Kalamazoo." "I intend to leave Kalamazoo." In addition to the modal *will* already cited, other modal verbs may create a future sense: "I *would* leave Kalamazoo." "I *shall* leave Kalamazoo." "I *should* leave Kalamazoo." "I *can* leave Kalamazoo." "I *could* leave Kalamazoo." "I *may* leave Kalamazoo." "I *might* leave Kalamazoo." And, of course, the imperative always calls for future action: "Leave Kalamazoo!" The leaving must always be logically after the command.
37. Carpenter, *Tolkien*, 138. The phrase is from Lewis's (unsigned) London *Times* obituary of Tolkien—a fact which eerily illustrates the paradoxes of time and eternity examined above: since the *Times* solicited the obit from Lewis, and then filed it away until Tolkien's death in 1973, Lewis, who had died more than a decade earlier, was in effect speaking from his grave.
38. Tolkien, *Monsters*, 186.
39. Because Welsh was Tolkien's inspiration for Sindarin, it would be tempting to construe his point as the English borrowing a more sophisticated time-sense from the Celts, an analogue for the temporal dissonance of man and elf. But when he says that "this system. . .is not found in any other Germanic language" (*Monsters* 186), Tolkien does *not* mean that it is necessarily derived from Welsh. After all, with its complex "pre-Germanic" tense system, Welsh would not need the *beon/seon* distinction. Rather, the point is that this peculiar construction appears in *both* languages, about the same time, and "on British soil" (*Monsters* 187). It is both British (i.e., Celtic) and English (i.e., Anglo-Saxon).
40. Tolkien, *LR* 5.3, 787; 6.2, 910.
41. J.R.R. Tolkien, *The Hobbit; or There and Back Again* (New York: Ballantine, 1966), 70.
42. J.R.R. Tolkien, *The Lays of Beleriand* (New York: Ballantine, 1994), 24, 32–33, 103, 112; *Letters*, 23, 31, and 318, nos. 17, 25, and 239.
43. Tolkien, *Monsters*, 186.

PART TWO

RETREATING TO A TIMELESS
PAST: MIDDLE-EARTH AND
VICTORIAN MEDIEVALISM

CHAPTER 5

THE REANIMATION OF ANTIQUITY AND THE RESISTANCE TO HISTORY: MACPHERSON–SCOTT–TOLKIEN

John Hunter

> *Tolkien's fantasy reflects two strands of modern pseudomedieval historical fiction: Sir Walter Scott's reinvention of the Middle Ages in novelistic form, and James Macpherson's effort to fashion historical fiction as an escape from deterministic reality. Thus Middle-earth anticipates postmodern historical fiction with a Macphersonian escapist twist.*

The Lord of the Rings is a text that presents itself, from beginning to end, as a history. The "legends" that the characters know are usually half-forgotten histories, needing only to be properly understood to reveal the determining power of the past on present events.[1] The novel provides the detail, context, and scholarly apparatus expected of a history and explicitly offers itself to be consumed as such. The prologue describes how both *The Hobbit* and *The Lord of the Rings* are extracts from Bilbo and Frodo's *Red Book of Westmarch* and indicates that the new Fourth Age of Middle-earth will be marked by the production, editing, and consumption of proper historical records, even in the heretofore amnesiac Shire.[2] Bilbo's idiosyncratic retirement project becomes Frodo's personal history of the War of the Ring and, finally, the official history of Gondor (after "much annotation and many corrections" at the hands of the scribes in Minas Tirith [*LR* prologue, 14]). More than this, the insular Third Age Hobbit culture of oral legend, in which nothing that happened outside the Shire was seen to matter very much, gives way to a Fourth Age Shire that has "several libraries that contained many historical books and records" (*LR* prologue, 14). A thousand pages later, Frodo's last speech in the novel urges Sam to "read things out of the Red Book, and keep alive the memory of the age that is gone, so that people will remember the Great Danger and so love their beloved land all the more" (*LR* 6.9, 1006). In between these poles, the characters make crucial use of the forgotten creatures, monuments, and histories of the past ages of Middle-earth to understand and solve the crisis in the present. History and its repressed traumas arrive, appropriately, with Gandalf's story of the One Ring in "The Shadow of the Past"; later, the siege of Minas Tirith is won only with the help of two "remnants of an older time" (*LR* 5.5, 813), the Woses (a marginal "primitive" culture barely surviving in the Third Age) and the "Shadow Host" of the dead (a spectral embodiment of Gondor's troubled past that redeems itself by rescuing the present).[3] The history that this novel records is imagined rather than factual, but this has not in any way distracted readers from the linguistic and cultural "authenticity" of Tolkien's world or the pleasures of historical fiction that it provides.[4]

Whatever one's opinion of the novel, understanding the appeal of *The Lord of the Rings* is not a question of investigating a naïve, uncomplicated turn away from the real and into the fantastic because the connection between real and imagined history is one of its central themes. When Tolkien states in his prologue that Hobbits were "more numerous formerly than they are today" (*LR* prologue, 1), he deliberately asserts a historical connection to present reality for his text that he just as deliberately refuses to elaborate in any histories of the Fourth Age.[5] To the dismay of his detractors, this refusal has proved to be one of the greatest sources of the novel's popularity, as generations of readers have been imaginatively supplying this missing connection ever since. Matching this claim in the novel is Tolkien's repeated assertion in his letters that his narratives are, in some vague sense, historical fact: "Always I had the sense of recording what was already 'there,' somewhere: not of 'inventing.'"[6] This claim has generated no small amount of comment and/or embarrassment among Tolkien scholars, and even those (like Tom Shippey) who face up to it intelligently have not fully explored its sources or implications.[7] The discomfort comes from the obvious self-contradiction contained within it. It claims a specifically historical truth for a work of fiction and sets out "to restore to England something like the body of lost legend which it must once have had,"[8] even though the "likeness" of the restoration is purely conjectural. Both critics and the reading public, however, have accepted this paradoxical claim and celebrated the "authenticity" that the fictional "historical" detail of *The Lord of the Rings* generates. And rather than undermining its historicism, it is Tolkien's desire to supplement history as we know it with a fictional history as we would wish it—coupled with the novel's explicit theme of historical emergence—that locates the novel firmly within the context of post-Enlightenment historical literature. Its procedures and pleasures are as familiar as its setting is remote. What follows can only be a sketch of this historical context and of the position of *The Lord of the Rings* within it, written with the goal of bringing the heretofore fragmentary references to the novel's roots in modern European literature together coherently. *The Lord of the Rings* is certainly a fantasy, but it is also a laboratory of historical fiction and a potent recent example of the modern West's techniques for reanimating its past.

Far from being unique or aberrant, Tolkien's historicism has a very canonical pedigree for both its technique and its goals, and the popular success that has accompanied it has equally strong precedents. This pedigree has little to do with the particulars of the novel's many mythic sources and allusions—source criticism is, in any case, a field in which Tolkien's writing is already well served—but comes rather from the eighteenth- and nineteenth-century project to harness mythology to the emerging national ideologies of the northern European nations. The two most relevant and influential examples of this tradition for Tolkien's purposes are James Macpherson's "Ossian" poems (1760–63) and the career of Sir Walter Scott (1771–1832). Rather than "sources" for Tolkien in a conscious sense, they are best understood as creators of the literary and historical tradition into which *The Lord of the Rings* fits, albeit in ways that have gone largely unnoticed. It is in this tradition that we find the modern sources of the desire to reanimate a nation's lost past through historical fictions and some early examples of the mass popularity that fictionalizing the past can achieve with readers (they were each as sensational or more in their own day as Tolkien has been in ours). The real uniqueness of *The Lord of the Rings* lies not in its formal archaisms or controversial popularity but in the remarkable extent to which it has been cut off from its place in the evolution of historical fiction by critics and general readers alike. Whatever the causes and implications of this separation, it is clear that analyzing it will tell us a great deal about postmodern culture's relationships to the "age that is gone."

Macpherson and the Nordic Renaissance

[Macpherson] exploits a large gap in Scottish prehistory to conjure up, Tolkien-like, a fantasy third-century Gaelic world with its own customs, traditions, and genealogies. And in order to underline the significance of his text. . .he supplies it with an extensive editorial apparatus of learned dissertations and scholarly footnotes.

—Howard Gaskill, *Ossian Revisited*

Several times in his letters, Tolkien mentions Elias Lönnrot's *Kalevala* as an inspiration to him in the creation of his mythology, and Tom Shippey and others have rightly named Lönnrot as one of the "philologist creators" with whom Tolkien can be identified.[9] Lönnrot published the *Kalevala* in 1835, claiming that it was an authentic Finnish epic poem that he had painstakingly transcribed from the oral poetry of the Karelia region. It caused a nationwide sensation. As Shippey goes on to relate, however, there was a problem: "Lönnrot's *Kalevala* is now viewed with suspicion by scholars, because Lönnrot, like Walter Scott with the Border Ballads, did not just collect and transcribe, but wrote, rewrote, and interpolated, so that you cannot tell what is by him and what is 'authentic.' Just the same, the date of publication of the *Kalevala* remains a national holiday in Finland, and the work has become a cornerstone of national culture."[10] The text's authenticity was defended for nationalistic reasons, even by those who knew better, because, as one folklore scholar puts it, "the forces of romanticism and nationalism were—and are—so powerful in Finland that what the people *believed* was—and is—more important than what was true."[11] Lönnrot's work thus provides a creative model for Tolkien and its reception foreshadows the analogous relation between Tolkien and his readers: Tolkien too wanted to "reconstruct" a tradition by inventing one, and his readers have correspondingly felt an authenticity and realism in the text that does not directly correspond to any historical reality. The difference between these two literary successes is one of degree, not of kind. Tolkien, to be sure, did not make public claims as strong or as specific as Lönnrot's, and this frees his readers from the need to repress the kind of contradictions that Lönnrot's admirers faced. In both cases, however, readers' desires and authorial intent caused them to enjoy a historical fiction as if it were historical fact.

The modern beginnings of this phenomenon lie in the eighteenth century as part of what is sometimes called "the Nordic Renaissance."[12] This movement, which manifested itself in both literary and scholarly writing, was a nationalistic reaction against two well-established ideas: (1) the Enlightenment's Cartesian commonplace that almost all mythology was worthless and irrational superstition and (2) the much older humanist assumption that the only founding cultures of which Europe could be proud were ancient Greece and Rome. It effectively began with Paul Henri Mallet's *Introduction à l'histoire de Danemarc* (1755–56), a multivolume history of Scandinavia that contained the first versions of Norse mythology from the *Eddas* to be made available to modern Europe. This was soon translated into several other languages and widely admired in intellectual circles for its celebration of early northern cultures.[13] The kernel of Mallet's appeal to northern Europeans was his claim that native northern cultures (that is, the Goths and Scandinavians) gave birth to the concept of the ineradicable natural liberty of mankind and imposed this idea, by conquest, on the decadent civilization of late Rome. As he puts it in his preface: "I should rather call [the north of Europe], the forge of those instruments which broke the fetters manufactured in the south. It was there those valiant nations were bred, who left their native climes to destroy tyrants and slaves in the south, and to teach men that nature [had] made them equal."[14] Greece and Rome may have given Western civilization its intellectual pedigree, but the natural liberty that so many Enlightenment thinkers celebrated was here identified as a specifically northern invention and the sign of a unique quality in northern cultures.

After Mallet's work, the nations north of the Alps could finally claim an empowering and ennobling myth of origins (albeit one that later contributed to theories of racial superiority). In the English context, this led to the fetishization of the language and culture of the Anglo-Saxons as the "authentic" early English people and, of course, to the academic study of Norse and Saxon cultures, which was Tolkien's profession. His desire "to restore to the English an epic tradition and present them with a mythology of their own" (*Letters*, 231) can thus be understood as a contemporary echo of the eighteenth- and nineteenth-century revival of indigenous northern myths of origin and their nationalist ideological uses. It is a strange-sounding motive for writing a novel to modern ears, but only because Tolkien's work has been so completely deracinated from this cultural context. No one finds the ideological functions of, say, Richard Wagner's operas or the Bayreuth Festival hard to understand, even though their debt to Mallet's ideas is just as easy to trace.

The second, more sensational component of this recovery of a northern mythic heritage was James Macpherson's "edited" works of the ancient Gaelic poet Ossian.[15] His two epic poems and collection of shorter pieces purported to be the work of a third-century Scottish bard and recounted the life and times of Fingal, King of Morven. Ever since they first appeared, the controversy about their authenticity has raged. Samuel Johnson famously dismissed them, but they swept all of Europe into a frenzy of imitation and attained a popularity that dwarfs the Tolkien phenomenon.[16] Readers of the caliber of Goethe, Herder, Hume, and Grimm were seduced into believing in their authenticity (for a time, at least); Mme de Staël called Ossian "the Homer of the North";[17] and he was the favourite poet of both Napoleon and Thomas Jefferson. The authenticity debate has been carried forward almost to the present, with the current consensus being that Macpherson invented much of what he presented as authentic, but that there was an ancient and genuine oral verse tradition in Scotland to which he had access. The more people realized that Macpherson had been dishonest, however, the less it seemed to matter because he showed his readers how history could be made conformable to their desires. As Bruce Lincoln puts it: "Macpherson's success stimulated those of other nations to seek their own lost myths, epics, and legends, and the *Nibelungenlied*, *Chanson de Roland*, and *Kalevala* are among the results. Even when Ossian was thoroughly discredited, the attitudes it helped shape remained unshaken."[18] Once the genie of literary nationalism was out of the bottle, nothing could contain it, and the "sublimity" and affective power of Macpherson's poetry made it irresistible. Mallet created the intellectual justification for the study of northern mythology, but it was not until Macpherson's poetry that there existed a literary form for nationalistic legends that could work in a modern context.

As Walter Scott astutely pointed out, the key elements in Macpherson's success were "a system of mythology, and a train of picturesque description and sentimental effusion, of which there is not the least trace in any Gaelic originals."[19] In other words, his appeal was based on the same combination of mythic/historical coherence and descriptive power for which *The Lord of the Rings* is justly admired. From Mallet to Tolkien "one can trace the Nordic and the Ossianic influence" in this desire to reanimate a lost (or never extant) national past and in the deliberate mingling of fiction and fact; after Mallet and Macpherson, "the European artist who wished to use old myth had, for the first time, a concrete and indigenous alternative to the ancient Mediterranean mythologies."[20] The immense popularity, the heated academic debate, and the international success that have attended *The Lord of the Rings* have all played out in the pattern that Macpherson's work established and that the Brothers Grimm and others continued.[21] Consciously or not, Tolkien's novel was resurrecting a long-established mode of writing that was closely associated with nationalism, but in a postwar environment that had good reason to suspect or repress national ambition, especially when it invoked the special value of the Germanic peoples. While its status as a "fantasy" novel has enabled *The Lord of the Rings* to separate itself from the more disquieting aspects of its pedigree, the historical pleasures that it creates for its readers are at once familiar and difficult to explain.[22]

Sir Walter Scott and Modern Historical Fiction

It has been my object to throw together. . .a variety of remarks, regarding popular superstitions, and legendary history, which, if not now collected, must soon have been totally forgotten. By such efforts, feeble as they are, I may contribute somewhat to the history of my native country; the peculiar features of whose manners and character are daily melting and dissolving into those of her sister and ally.

—Sir Walter Scott, *Minstrelsy of the Scottish Border*

Tolkien has a flair for verse, and there is no reason to suppose that he could not have written an Ossianic poem about Middle-earth had he so chosen. Yet he wrote what was, in effect, a self-consciously historical novel of Middle-earth, and this choice leads to the European historical novel (beginning with Scott) as the other salient tradition in which *The Lord of the Rings* must be situated. As an antiquarian, Scott manifests the same desire to preserve the last fragmentary remnants of a lost culture that animated Macpherson, and, as the passage above indicates, he anticipates Tolkien's description of his own historical project to an almost uncanny degree. Like Macpherson (although he was much more honest about his procedures), Scott had no qualms about smoothing out his traditional materials in order to make them more palatable to the reading public. He was interested in the Norse sagas made available by Mallet, and it was Scott who reviewed the Highland Society's report on the Ossian controversy to settle it once and for all; predictably, he concluded that the historical value of Macpherson's poems could not be assessed solely by their strict fidelity to originals.[23] "Romance and real history," he notes in his "Essay on Romance" in the *Encyclopedia Britannica* (sixth edition), "have the same common origin. It is the aim of the former to maintain as long as possible the mask of veracity."[24] Finally, Scott anticipated (albeit as a non-Englishman) Tolkien's famous lament about the relative scarcity of English legend and traditional literature as compared to other nations. As Scott puts it, "England, so often conquered, yet fated to receive an accession of strength from each new subjugation, cannot boast much of ancient literature of any kind."[25] It was precisely the same problem that Tolkien wished to address over a century later, and it was Scott who laid out the form for a literary response to this erasure of England's origins.

The first five Waverley novels are set in Scotland and center on the historical events of the seventeenth and eighteenth centuries that were most important for producing the nation as it was in Scott's own day. Their crucial conflict is traditional Scottish culture's valiant but futile attempt to maintain itself against the encroachments of the cosmopolitan modernity embodied by England. Tolkien's Elves and Ents face analogous cultural pressures, but this kind of direct analysis of how the past produces the contemporary present is precisely what Tolkien refused to do in his "historical" writing. It is only when Scott turned to write about premodern English history that his work becomes crucial for understanding Tolkien. When he did so, he had to face the same scarcity and remoteness of material and cultural remains that Tolkien later faced, and the novel he wrote in response was *Ivanhoe* (1819). It has always been one of Scott's most successful works. It sold prodigiously; Victor Hugo called it "*la véritable épopée de notre âge*";[26] and it spawned several successful stage adaptations, at least two operas, and several film and television adaptations. Like Macpherson and Tolkien, Scott loved to use the formal machinery of history in his fiction, and the preface, which takes the form of a letter from one fictional antiquary to another, explores the problems he faced in writing about the remote Middle Ages. In England, unlike Scotland, "civilization has been so long complete, that our ideas of our ancestors are only to be gleaned from musty records and chronicles," and an author wishing to write about traditional manners and customs can "only have the liberty of selecting his subject amidst the dust of antiquity, where nothing was to be found but dry, sapless, mouldering, and disjointed bones."[27] It is also hard, he continues, for modern readers to imagine how the liberty and comfort of contemporary England could have origins in the violence and ignorance of medieval culture (as Scott depicted it).[28] Whatever else it was, *Ivanhoe* was thus to be the novel that set Scott's pattern for how historical fiction was to deal with the scant sources and alienating strangeness of the distant past.

Reading back from *The Lord of the Rings*, *Ivanhoe* might be termed Scott's "Return of the King"—a novel about the secret return of Richard the Lion-Hearted to England from the Crusades and imprisonment in Austria and the resumption, after many chivalric adventures, of his public role and identity. The plot contains many features that critics have analyzed in *The Lord of the Rings*: rival ethnic and class groups that have to cooperate for a greater good; a concluding social arrangement that cannot accommodate everyone (in this case, the persecuted Jews); ordinary people who are capable of remarkable heroism; and a nation that has to accept a new social arrangement and a strong, lawful monarch after a period of confusion and neglect. The continuity of Scott's work with Mallet's is shown by the former's adoption of the notion (now thoroughly discredited) that Saxon culture was rooted in individual freedom and ancient liberties, in contrast to the excessively hierarchical Norman government.[29] Despite its remote historical setting, Gothic interludes, and exaggerated chivalric action, however, *Ivanhoe* is also, as Marilyn Butler has pointed out, the Scott novel that most directly responds to the events of his own historical moment: written in the shadow of the Peterloo Massacre, its dominant theme of ethnic antagonism resonates strongly with the open class warfare of its time, and its criticisms of thoughtless monarchs and rapacious nobles set against a lost Saxon culture of free individuals articulate the positions of nineteenth-century radicals and reformers without allowing their republican conclusions.[30] Just as *The Lord of the Rings* seems to echo the historical events of Tolkien's day without being an allegory for them,[31] *Ivanhoe* reanimates a remote and pleasurable "merry England" for a modern audience while maintaining a subtle but significant connection to modern life.

These are more than just fortuitous parallels, but their significance is only fully apparent in relation to the most marked differences between the two novels: *Ivanhoe*'s narrator maintains an ironic and frequently critical distance from the excesses of medieval culture, whereas *The Lord of the Rings* is without the least trace of ironic detachment from its subject matter. This is not just a function of the difference between a historical novel and a fantasy novel but an indicator of the two main traditions of historical representation that have come down from Scott's work. The first (now almost extinct as a popular form) is the realist tradition that Georg Lukács described, in which contemporary individuals are depicted as products of historical forces that are absolutely inescapable, whether or not they are beneficial.[32] The Saxons in *Ivanhoe*, for example, have to accept Angevin rule and a compromise with Norman culture, even though it means the end of their traditional way of life; fighting this change is represented as, at best, quixotic. The second (and much more popular) of these traditions fuses Scott's novel form to Macpherson's desires to make the past conformable to our fantasies and to allow an escape from history's impact rather than an accession to its inevitability. The alienating distance between the events of the past and the present is closed in this tradition, because its purpose is to remake the unpleasant aspects of the past into something completely unthreatening to the reader.

Examples of this second tradition are legion, from Scott's day to the present. The Civil War, for example, is the most traumatic and resonant event in United States history, and it duly provided the setting for two of the twentieth century's most important popular American novels, Thomas Dixon Jr.'s *The Clansman: An Historical Romance of the Ku Klux Klan* (1905) and Margaret Mitchell's *Gone With the Wind* (1936). Both of these best-selling works aimed not to represent the complexities and unavoidable consequences of the Confederacy's defeat and Reconstruction but rather the ideological illusions that a large section of the United States public (Northern and Southern) already held or were inspired to hold. The former imagines the Ku Klux Klan as a neomedieval order of chivalry successfully defending Southern female honor against the injustice of Reconstruction and the subhuman desires of African Americans for white women; the latter allows Scarlett O'Hara's defiant and amoral egotism to maintain her patrimony in the face of the Confederacy's defeat and transformation. The public loved them both, and their shared insistence that local or personal forces (often heroic honor or romantic love) can somehow inoculate us against sociohistorical change has been one of the most potent and seductive versions of history throughout the twentieth century. Perhaps the most salient success of this tradition of fantasized history, however, has been its importance in cinema, which is, as the director Atom Egoyan has noted, "by nature a very dubious way of presenting history."[33] It is no exaggeration to say that D. W. Griffith's *Birth of a Nation* (1915), which is an adaptation of *The Clansman,* invented feature-length narrative cinema.[34] The film version of *Gone With the Wind* (1939) remains one of the form's most instantly recognizable and durable icons. And the popularity of fantastic historical cinema shows no signs of abating: the most financially successful film of the past generation, James Cameron's *Titanic* (1997), cleverly manipulates this same terrain and can best be read as a "historical" film in which unpleasant historical forces, like wealth and class privilege, cannot ultimately overcome true love.

What makes *The Lord of the Rings* such a lightning rod for critical debate is that it successfully works in both of these traditions at once, and Peter Jackson's critically acclaimed and enormously popular film adaptations have only highlighted this generic duality. His films use the same blend of fantasy and historical allusion as do these previous blockbusters, and, as has been the case from Macpherson onward, the narrative fantasy is a product of "historical realism." Jackson's self-consciousness, however, shows how effectively his film (as well as Tolkien's novel) plays with both the realistic *and* the fantastic strains of historical fiction. Discussing his design philosophy for the film, Jackson notes "how authentic, genuinely authentic, [the novel] feels, so you start to believe that it could possibly be history." As a result, he goes on, "I didn't want fantasy movie Hollywood sort of style of design, I wanted something that felt authentic."[35] One of his chief designers relates that "it was always 'Ground this in reality. . . . We're making a historical film, we're not making a fantasy film.' To that end, we looked at a lot of historical influences. . . . What we wanted to create were alternative cultures that looked like they could come straight out of history, but you're never quite sure where they're from."[36] Rather than starting with a complex history and rewriting it as fantasy, Jackson (like Tolkien in his novel) starts with fantasy and rewrites it as a complex history. *The Lord of the Rings* contains the complexity, frustration, and ambiguity of realistic historical fiction *and* the fantasy wish fulfillment that drives quest romances, whether it is *The Faerie Queene* or *Pretty Woman.* Tolkien's detractors see only the stereotypical limitations of some of the characters and the unconvincing simplicity of Sauron's evil empire. These limitations are undoubtedly present, but so are passages with a sophisticated sense of historical change and loss that is characteristic of the Waverley novels at their most direct. Most historical fictions consciously or unconsciously choose one of these approaches to historicism. The achievement of *The Lord of the Rings* is to make simultaneous use of both.

In conclusion, I am arguing that *The Lord of the Rings*'s dramatization of how history can be discovered underneath legend and myth needs to be matched by a critical willingness to see it as a product of post-Enlightenment forms of historical fiction. Critics like Tom Shippey have energetically tried to prove that *The Lord of the Rings* is a novel outside the main traditions of twentieth-century fictions. This may be true in some senses, but to suggest (as he does) that it can best be contextualized in a group of novels that explore evil as an irreducible transhistorical phenomenon of human life is to relegate it to a far less interesting ghetto than some of its detractors do.[37] Others, most recently Brian Rosebury, have recognized the combination of historical realism and fantasy wish fulfillment in the novel, but without any appreciation of how closely Tolkien's use of both follows a well-worn path in European literature.[38] This deracination of the novel from some of its most obvious predecessors has been unintentionally abetted by source criticism, which has tended to focus on Tolkien's substantive, rather than formal, sources. If *The Lord of the Rings* is seen as a monad standing outside the mainstream of postwar British literature, it is because the realistic historical novel (in Scott's tradition) had ceased to be a vital literary form by Tolkien's day, and the determining influence of figures like Mallet and Macpherson on the forms of historical fiction is so little understood.

The Lord of the Rings is thus Tolkien's attempt to reanimate a lost past and claim a connection to present reality, but, unlike in the Waverley novels, in such a way that this reanimated world is in no way responsible for producing the present. He does away with an overtly historical setting but keeps historical claims and procedures in order to produce a better fantasy. To say this is in no way to slight the novel or its success; it is only to restate a procedure about which Tolkien is quite open throughout. He managed to be both Scott and Macpherson at once, the recorder of historical processes and the creator of a fantasy in which we can have at least a provisional moment of satisfaction and escape from those processes. By replacing Scott's historical setting with a simulacrum of history, Tolkien's novel illustrates (perhaps more clearly than any other contemporary text) how fascinated postmodern Western culture is with historical change, even as it resists understanding itself in traditional historical terms.[39] In keeping with the two traditions of historical fiction that it brings together, this leaves us with two possible conclusions. One is that this is only escapism and that, rather than the hard road from the past to a historical present, Tolkien instead provides the satisfactions of a fictionalized past history without the compromises and disappointments of brute historical facticity. This would make it a suitable popular classic for a postmodern age that, as Fredric Jameson puts it, has "forgotten how to think historically in the first place."[40] The other conclusion is to acknowledge *The Lord of the Rings*'s place as a prophetic anticipation of a postmodern cultural environment that produces historical fiction in ever-proliferating forms and modes (one thinks of Salman Rushdie's *Midnight's Children*, Don DeLillo's *Underworld*, Jeannette Winterson's *The Passion*, and many others). This, in turn, is part of a much wider revision of the category of history itself, one in which (as Hayden White and others have shown)[41] theories of narrative and fantasy have important roles to play. It would be foolish to banish either of these avenues for thought, but the tension between them guarantees that Tolkien's place in the literary academy will never be a peaceful one.

Notes

1. Previous essays have addressed Tolkien's historicism include Anders Stenstrom, "A Mythology? For England?" *Mythlore* 80 (1996): 310–14; Lionel Basney, "Myth, History, and Time in *The Lord of the Rings*," in *Tolkien: New Critical Perspectives*, ed. Neil D. Isaacs and Rose A. Zimbardo (Lexington: University Press of Kentucky, 1981), 8–18; and Barton R. Friedman, "Fabricating History: Narrative Strategy in *The Lord of the Rings*," *Clio* 2 (1973): 123–44. Basney's article speaks directly about the conversion of myth into history in the novel, but (like the others) does not explore its origins or implications. Gergely Nagy's "The Great Chain of Reading: (Inter) Textual Relations and the Technique of Mythopoesis in the Túrin Story," in *Tolkien the Medievalist*, ed. Jane Chance (London and New York: Routledge Ltd., 2002, 2003), 239–58, shows how Tolkien's writing creates its own internal context. See also J.R.R. Tolkien, *The Letters of J. R. R. Tolkien: A Selection*, ed. Humphrey Carpenter with assistance from Christopher Tolkien (Boston, MA: Houghton Mifflin, 2000), 207 (hereafter cited as *Letters*).
2. J.R.R. Tolkien, *The Fellowship of the Ring*. 2nd edn. (Boston, MA: Houghton Mifflin, 1993), 13–15. All references to *The Lord of the Rings* are to the second edition, hereafter cited as *LR*.
3. Examples from *Fellowship* alone would include the Old Forest (*LR* 1.7, 127–28), the ruins and remnants of Westernesse on the Barrow Downs (*LR* 1.9, 142–43) and at Weathertop (*LR* 1.11, 181), the ruins of the North Kingdom at the Last Bridge (*LR* 1.12, 196), Caradhras (*LR* 2.3, 282–83), the Balrog (*LR* 2.5, 321 and 2.7, 346–47), Lothlórien (*LR* 2.6, 340), and the Argonath (*LR* 2.9, 383). Frodo's traumatic vision, on the summit of Amon Hen (*LR*, 391) summarizes the present crisis to which they all lead.
4. See W.H. Auden, "The Quest Hero," from *Tolkien and the Critics: Essays on J. R. R. Tolkien's "The Lord of the Rings*," ed. Neil D. Isaacs and Rose A. Zimbardo (South Bend, IN: University of Notre Dame Press, 1968), 50–52. On Tolkien's creation of a fictional historical context for his own novel, see Gergely Nagy, "Saving the Myths: The Re-creation of Mythology in Plato and Tolkien," in *Tolkien and the Invention of Myth: A Reader*, ed. Jane Chance (Lexington and London: University of Kentucky Press, 2004), 81–100. For the modern context of fiction's relations with history, see Katie Trumpener,

Bardic Nationalism: The Romantic Novel and the British Empire (Princeton, NJ: Princeton University Press, 1997), 109–15; and Peter Hughes, "Narrative, Scene, and the Fictions of History," in *Contemporary Approaches to Narrative*, ed. Anthony Mortimer (Tübingen: Gunter Narr, 1984), 73–87.
5. In early versions of *Silm*, Tolkien linked his mythology to English legends much more directly. See Wayne G. Hammond and Christina Scull, "The History of Middle-earth," *VII* 12 (1995): 106–08. For more on Tolkien's indications that Middle-earth is our earth, see Paul Kocher, "Middle-earth: Imaginary World?" in *Tolkien: New Critical Perspectives*, ed. Neil D. Isaacs and Rose A. Zimbardo (Lexington: University Press of Kentucky, 1981), 121–32.
6. Tolkien, *Letters*, 145. A letter dated twenty years later (412–13) shows his sense of discovery undiminished.
7. Tom Shippey, *J. R. R. Tolkien, Author of the Century* (Boston, MA: Houghton Mifflin, 2000), xv, xxxiv, 231–44.
8. Shippey, *Tolkien*, 232.
9. See Tolkien, *Letters*, 144, 214, and Shippey, *Tolkien*, xxxiv.
10. Shippey, *Tolkien*, 8.
11. Alan Dundes, "Nationalistic Inferiority Complexes and the Fabrication of Fakelore: A Reconsideration of Ossian, the *Kinder- und Hausmärchen*, the *Kalevala*, and Paul Bunyan," in *Papers of the 8th Congress for the International Society for Folk Narrative Research, Bergen, June 12–17, 1984*, vol. 1, ed. Reimund Kvideland and Torunn Selberg (Bergen, Norway: International Society for Folk Narrative Research, 1984), 155–71, 161.
12. For an overview of this revival of ancient Nordic culture (and its consequences for contemporary nationalism), see Burton Feldman and Robert D. Richardson, *The Rise of Modern Mythology, 1680–1860* (Bloomington: Indiana University Press, 1972), 199–214; and Bruce Lincoln, *Theorizing Myth: Narrative, Ideology, and Scholarship* (Chicago, IL: University of Chicago Press, 1999), 47–75.
13. It was translated into English by Bishop Percy in 1770 and reissued with copious additions in 1847. See Feldman and Richardson, *Modern Mythology*, 200–01; and Lincoln, *Theorizing Myth*, 50–51.
14. M. Mallet, *Northern Antiquities; or, An Historical Account of the Manners, Customs, Religion, and Laws, Maritime Expeditions and Discoveries, Language and Literature of the Ancient Scandinavians, (Danes, Swedes, Norwegians, and Icelanders.) With Incidental Notices Respecting Our Saxon Ancestors*, trans. Bishop Percy, ed. I.A. Blackwell, 2nd edn. (London: Henry G. Bohn, 1847), 58.
15. These were *Fragments of Ancient Poetry* (1760), *Fingal: An Ancient Epic* (1762), and *Temora* (another complete epic, 1763). For a modern edition, see James Macpherson, *The Poems of Ossian and Related Works*, ed. Howard Gaskill, introd. by Fiona Stafford (Edinburgh: Edinburgh University Press, 1996).
16. The best accounts of the Ossian poems' phenomenal popularity are by Paul van Tieghem, *Le Préromantisme: Études d'histoire littéraire européenne* (Paris: F. Rieder, 1924), 208–85; and Howard Gaskill, "Ossian in Europe," *Canadian Review of Comparative Literature* 21, no. 4 (1994): 643–78.

17. Cited in Feldman and Richardson, *Modern Mythology*, 201.
18. Lincoln, *Theorizing Myth*, 51. See also Howard D. Weinbrot, *Britannia's Issue: The Rise of British Literature from Dryden to Ossian* (Cambridge, UK: Cambridge University Press, 1993), 528–56.
19. Sir Walter Scott, "Review of Report of the Committee of the Highland Society of Scotland and *The Poems of Ossian*," *Edinburgh Quarterly* 6 (1805): 446.
20. Feldman and Richardson, *Modern Mythology*, 202. As W.W. Robson observes, "The more posthumous Tolkien material is published, the more it looks like Ossian." W.W. Robson, *A Prologue to English Literature* (Totowa, NJ: Barnes & Noble, 1986), 234.
21. On the Brothers Grimm, see John M. Ellis, *One Fairy Story Too Many: The Brothers Grimm and Their Tales* (Chicago, IL: University of Chicago Press, 1986).
22. While several critics have pointed out the connections between Tolkien and Macpherson, they have yet to be productively discussed in Tolkien scholarship. Brian Rosebury raises the possibility, but, by confining himself to a stylistic comparison, utterly misses its real importance in *Tolkien: A Cultural Phenomenon* (New York: Palgrave Macmillan, 2003), 3, 225.
23. Scott, "Review of Report," 460–62.
24. Sir Walter Scott, "An Essay on Romance," in *Essays on Chivalry, Romance, and the Drama* (1834; repr. Freeport, NY: Books for Libraries Press, 1972), 134–35.
25. Scott, "Essay on Romance," 203.
26. Quoted in E. Preston Dargan, "Scott and the French Romantics," *PMLA* 49 (1934): 605.
27. Sir Walter Scott, *Ivanhoe*, ed. Graham Tulloch (London: Penguin, 2000), 6–7.
28. Scott, *Ivanhoe*, 7.
29. Scott, *Ivanhoe*, xviii.
30. Marilyn Butler, *Romantics, Rebels, and Reactionaries: English Literature and Its Background, 1760–1830* (Oxford: Oxford University Press, 1981), 138–50.
31. Shippey, *Tolkien*, 164–71.
32. Georg Lukács, *The Historical Novel*, trans. Hannah Mitchell and Stanley Mitchell (Harmondsworth, UK: Penguin, 1969), 15–99.
33. Stephen Kinzer, "Movie on Armenians Rekindles Flame over Turkish Past," *New York Times*, January 20, 2004, sec. E.
34. See Raymond A. Cook, *Thomas Dixon* (New York: Twayne, 1974), 109–23.
35. Peter Jackson, "Designing Middle-earth," disc 3, *The Lord of the Rings: The Fellowship of the Ring*, Platinum Series, ext. ed. DVD (New Line Home Entertainment, 2002).
36. Daniel Falconer in Peter Jackson, "Weta Workshop," disc 3, *The Lord of the Rings: The Fellowship of the Ring* DVD.
37. Shippey, *Tolkien*, 116–20. Shippey makes an unconvincing attempt to show how Tolkien could be characterized as a modernist writer (313–15). On Tolkien's antimodernist characteristics, see Jed Esty, *A Shrinking Island: Modernism and National Culture in England* (Princeton, NJ: Princeton University Press, 2004), 118–23.

38. Rosebury, *Tolkien Phenomenon*, 11–60, especially 32–34.
39. On postmodernity and history (especially historical fiction), see Amy J. Elias, *Sublime Desire: History and Post-1960s Fiction* (Baltimore, MD: Johns Hopkins University Press, 2001), 1–99; and Elisabeth Wesseling, *Writing History as a Prophet: Postmodernist Innovations of the Historical Novel* (Philadelphia, PA: John Benjamins, 1991), 117–91.
40. Fredric Jameson, *Postmodernism, or, The Cultural Logic of Late Capitalism* (Durham, NC: Duke University Press), ix.
41. For an introduction to these issues, see Hayden White, *The Content of the Form: Narrative Discourse and Historical Representation* (Baltimore: Johns Hopkins, 1987).

CHAPTER 6

ARCHAISM, NOSTALGIA, AND TENNYSONIAN WAR IN *THE LORD OF THE RINGS*

Andrew Lynch

> *Despite Tolkien's personal experience of modern war, his fantasy epic is surprisingly different in image, diction, and ambience from literature associated with World War I. Its war rhetoric resembles more than anything else the moralized combat of Victorian medievalist literature.*

Through his long-running *Idylls of the King*, whose composition stretched from the 1830s to the 1880s, Alfred Tennyson became a major influence on the Victorian shift toward the symbolic in medievalist representations of warfare. Seeing his own era as morally superior to Geoffrey of Monmouth's or Malory's, Tennyson committed himself to capturing the true "spirit" or "ideal" of Arthurian chivalry without much of its troubling military substance, omitting any but legendary history and far reducing the characteristic medieval interest in the detail of wars and tournaments. Partly through the huge success of Tennyson's "parabolic" Arthuriad, in the later Victorian period war became the main selling-point of medievalism as symbolic heroism and chivalry, even though, viewed in the cold light of history, medieval war could also be seen as barbarous violence, an indictment of its age. An elderly character in one of Charlotte Yonge's late novels nicely sums up the conflict:

> [Y]ou will laugh, but my enthusiasm was for chivalry, Christian chivalry, half symbolic. History was delightful to me for the search for true knights. I had lists of them, drawings if possible, but I never could indoctrinate anybody with my affection. Either history is only a lesson, or they know a great deal too much, and will prove to you that the Cid was a ruffian, and the Black Prince not much better.[1]

One outcome of such tension, between the Middle Ages as half-symbolic chivalry and medieval violence as barbaric "Other" to the modern, was the increased ideological vulnerability of the symbolism to adverse critiques of medieval history. Medievalist fictions had to find ways to cope with that difficulty, by giving war a more positive and widely applicable narrative treatment. I wish to suggest in this essay that the war discourse of J.R.R. Tolkien's *The Lord of the Rings* can best be understood within this late-nineteenth-century context. As a war story, *The Lord of the Rings*, I argue, is more of a late utterance in a Victorian medievalist poetic, usually thought to have died out after 1916, than either a medieval or a mid-twentieth-century text.

Tolkien's relation to the war of his own century is problematical. Famously, he made others take all responsibility for any connection between *The Lord of the Rings* and World War II. The book was, he said, purely a "feigned" "history," "with...varied applicability to the thought and experience of readers."[2] Yet he hinted that it might have been generally influenced by his dreadful experience in the Great War, more than fifty years before[3]—"By 1918 all but one of my close friends were dead"—and by an even earlier trauma: "The country in which I lived in childhood was being shabbily destroyed before I was ten" (*LR* foreword, xv).

It is not surprising that Tolkien should rate his memories of the Great War as more important than any contemporary reference. The nobility of long memory and the obliviousness of the present time to past sacrifices are major themes in *The Lord of the Rings*, which Tolkien made as deeply nostalgic and past-oriented as he had judged *Beowulf* to be.[4] It abounds in laments for lost landscapes and departed glories, and dwells repeatedly on scenes of decay and desolation. Indeed, given Tolkien's association of the Great War with English rural destruction as his two founding traumas, one might well have expected that a horrific version of modern war would complete *The Lord of the Rings*'s indictment of the twentieth century. This is not the case. Early attempts to read the novel as a political allegory probably arose because much of its discourse of war seemed so distant from most twentieth-century sensibilities. Hugh Brogan has written that for "Tolkien, a man whose life was language,. . .[to] have gone through the Great War, with all its rants and lies, and still come out committed to a 'feudal' literary style. . .looks like an act of deliberate defiance of modern history."[5] Tolkien's references to his own war memories are definitely not "feudal" in style—"the animal horror of the life of active service on the earth—such as trench life as I knew it" (*Letters*, 72).

And yet, despite the author's language here and in the 1968 foreword, *The Lord of the Rings* does not mainly represent war as an "oppression" or "hideous experience" that wastes young lives (*LR* foreword, xiii). Instead, Tolkien principally makes the War of the Ring into a theater of heroic action in which the military prowess of groups and individuals is recognized as necessary, ennobling, and deeply effective. His war may be "grim" and "terrible," but it is often valorous and lofty in style, and of the major friendly characters, only Boromir and Théoden actually die in its fighting. Certainly, the novel also shows evidence of more common modern attitudes. Tom Shippey has commented on the postheroic, "modernistic style of courage" exemplified by the Hobbits.[6] Brian Rosebury,[7] Brogan, and John Garth have all suggested ways in which Tolkien's Great War memories might have influenced horrific and menacing narrative details. Yet Garth's recent book, while fully documenting the evils Tolkien experienced in the trenches and his distaste for war propaganda, still concludes that *The Lord of the Rings* "tackled the themes that Wilfred Owen ruled off-limits: deeds, lands, glory, honour, might, majesty, dominion, power."[8] My focus here is on what cultural factors might have helped to make up such an idealized discourse of war in Tolkien, especially the high style of war narrative he often employs within *The Lord of the Rings*.

It would be natural to suppose that Tolkien, as a learned medievalist, dealt with the memory of "hideous" modern war by transforming it into a superior version directly along medieval lines. In this connection, there have been important studies of his indebtedness to various medieval literatures,[9] and, in obvious ways, Tolkien's war looks "medieval." The heroes in *The Lord of the Rings* fight with favored weapons of the Middle Ages— swords, spears, axes, and bows; they offer and fulfil military service as part of feudal or family obligation; there is a preponderance of medieval combat types, especially siege warfare, sword fights, cavalry charges, and battles in open field; there are numerous single combats within battles that broadly resemble those in medieval historiography and romance; battle description is dominated by features such as distinctive armor and livery, famous swords and horses with special names, banners, heralds, war cries, horns, and so on. There is continued reference to great "tales" of war, in various medieval forms: chronicle, elegy, and heroic lay. And yet, Tolkien's wars are not quite like those in the medieval stories he salutes, in either their overall narrative function or their specific rhetoric.

Of course, medieval literary sources and analogues can often be sighted in Tolkien's war narrative, but they become strangely transmuted in the process. For example, he commonly employs a paratactic sentence structure, which joins up its elements by a chain of "and's" and "then's." In Sir Thomas Malory's *Le Morte Darthur* this is the standard narrative method: matter-of-fact, highly physical, and centered on particular exploits. Malory's paratactic structure is congruent with a whole narrative procedure that takes the reader directly from one deed of arms to the next. Tolkien's major extended battle descriptions, such as the Pelennor Fields episode (*LR* 5.6, 821–22), are quite different in overall effect, although one could easily point to individual features that look "medieval." To begin with, there is a good deal of parataxis, but whereas in *Le Morte Darthur* parataxis is the staple of battle narrative, here it is a high style that embraces both simple actions ("and he spurred to the standard") (*LR* 5.6, 821) and sometimes elaborate figuration: "and the drawing of the scimitars of the Southrons was like a glitter of stars"; "and more skilled was their knighthood with long spears and bitter" (*LR* 5.6, 821). Tolkien's alliance of paratactic structure with highly charged imagery and lyrical cadences will recall the King James Bible or verse derived from it, like Lord Byron's "The Destruction of Sennacherib" or Lord Macaulay's narrative poems, much more than it does Malory or any Old or Middle English prose. The symbolic coloring of the Pelennor scene (white and green, scarlet and black), the complex transferral of literal color to metaphorical use ("red wrath," "white fury. . .burned the hotter"), and the lofty similes ("like a glitter of stars," "like a firebolt in a forest") (*LR* 5.6, 821) indicate their origin in a postmedieval, romantic mindset. Tolkien makes the battle a panoramic, semisymbolic clash of good and evil, quite unlike the basic functionalism of most medieval English war writing with its principal interest in individual "deeds" of arms and the fortunes of the fight and with occasional evocations of the general battlefield atmosphere.

The style and certainly the individual word choices of Tolkien's description of the Pelennor Fields come closer in places to the effect of Old English and Middle English alliterative verse. "Long spears and bitter" recalls collocations like *Beowulf* 2703b–2704a, "wæll-seaxe gebræd, / biter ond beaduscearp" ("drew the deadly knife, keen and battle-sharp"),[10] or *The Battle of Maldon* 110b–111a, "bord ord onfeng, / biter wæs se beadu-ræs" ("Shield received spear-point; savage was the onslaught").[11] In bare meter, at least, "and his spear was shivered as he threw down their chieftain. [/] Out swept his sword, and he spurred to the standard, [/] hewed staff and bearer, and the black serpent foundered" (*LR* 5.6, 821) could almost be lines from the Alliterative *Morte Arthure*.

But in overall effect, Tolkien's writing reads quite differently from any of these medieval poems. This is partly because he has such a mixture of different styles, and they have a fairly consistent style. Another difference occurs because in a twentieth-century prose fiction such abundant parataxis, sentence inversion, and metricality must strike the reader as elements of stylistic individuality, choices to heighten literary "tone," rather than as integral features of a narrative medium that the writer shares as normal with a contemporary audience. Tolkien's war narrative seems to try for elevation by sounding archaic, whereas if Malory or *Maldon* sound lofty to a modern reader (and Malory sometimes does not), they will seem to manage that effect just by being themselves, strikingly different from modern writing, but in modes we imagine to be familiar to the original audience while still sufficiently intelligible to us. They exemplify Virginia Woolf's dictum: "To believe that your impressions hold good for others is to be released from the cramp and confinement of personality."[12]

Tolkien, by contrast, well aware that his impressions did *not* hold good for most literary contemporaries, consciously wielded archaism as an antimodernist cultural weapon. The insistent archaism of battle scenes in *The Lord of the Rings* reveals his cultural campaign to restore a sense of heroic potential to English life, which is symbolically enacted through the novel's revival of earlier English usages. Tolkien attempts to share his heroic mindset with others by employing archaic language as if it were actually contemporary and colloquial. Even small features of Tolkien's high style, such as the elision of the indefinite article in a phrase like "with great press of men" (*LR* 5.6, 821), stand out as effortlessly grand. A reader expects in modern English usage, at a deeper, less negotiable level than individual lexical choices, the form "with *a* great press of men," so what Tolkien offers as a casual, natural parlance cannot be accepted as such. "Great press" is colloquial thirteenth- to sixteenth-century English, but in a modern work its presence creates a complex secondary effect, revealing the writer's impossible desire for archaic forms to pass as both ordinary *and* lofty.

Naturalization of the archaic as a high style was Tolkien's deliberate program, which he once defended in an unfinished letter: "If mod. E. [modern English] has lost the trick of putting a word desired to emphasize (for pictorial, emotional, or logical reasons) into prominent first place, without addition of a lot of little 'empty' words (as the Chinese say), so much the worse for it. And so much the better for it the sooner it learns the trick again. And *some* one must begin the teaching, by example" (*Letters*, 225–26). Although inversion of sentence order and other archaisms might seem appropriate in formal speeches between characters drawn from a past age, archaism has a different effect in a simple narrative utterance like "great press," which, if it *were* natural in form to a modern narrator, as it was to the Wife of Bath,[13] would be quite prosaic. It can only be "high" in Tolkien *because* it is archaic, and so the archaism, implicitly proposed as more impressive than what he called "our slack and frivolous modern idiom" (*Letters*, 225–26), is seen to be valued for its own sake. The frequent archaism, much greater than Tolkien's normal practice, in the battle scenes of *The Lord of the Rings* indicates the special status he gave to military prowess. Battle is consistently made a high subject.[14] Although the love of war for its own sake clearly worried Tolkien, as many critics have noticed, he still very often employs inversion and/or parataxis as a means of ennobling battles and military symbols—"Great was the clash"; "Fewer were they"; "Out swept his sword" (*LR* 5.6, 821); "Very bright was that sword when it was made whole again; the light of the sun shone redly in it, and the light of the moon shone cold, and its edge was hard and keen" (*LR* 2.3, 269).

What helped to form this high style of war? Perhaps one answer lies in the closeness in balance and cadence of the lines on the sword Andúril just quoted to some lines in Tennyson's "The Passing of Arthur": "On one side lay the Ocean, and on one / Lay a great water, and the moon was full."[15] Tennyson was clearly one model for Tolkien's poetry before and around the time he enlisted, as Rosebury notes, and as can be seen in numerous instances quoted by Garth.[16] We need not suppose that the trenches destroyed that influence. Research by historian Jay Winter has suggested that the Great War did not suddenly inaugurate mass modernity by breaking all links with the past, as used to be claimed. Rather, many people, perhaps most, coped with war trauma by performing the work of memory and mourning with their prewar cultural resources. In Winter's words, "The Great War, the most 'modern' of wars, triggered an avalanche of the unmodern."[17] Tolkien's Middle-earth narratives, begun in wartime, might well be understood in this context. It was he who called the Shire "more or less a Warwickshire village of about the period of the Diamond Jubilee" (*Letters*, 230). When he found himself, as a war casualty, faced with the need to invent "a myth for England," it should not be surprising if he was influenced by the very popular "Return of the King" myth presented in Tennyson, Victoria's laureate, who died the year Tolkien was born.[18]

Generally speaking, Tolkien's narrative can be seen as a way of "getting over" the war through its assertion of strong continuities with the nineteenth century. Tolkien does not show nostalgia for the medieval past as a separate period in itself, a lost domain, but he mourns the sudden modern loss of a sense of continuity with that past. In seeking to reconnect the present to the Middle Ages, he therefore binds himself to intervening ages as well, when it was better remembered. So, in *The Lord of the Rings* a privileged discourse of "tree" and "root" connects Norse mythology, English folk-tale, genealogy, and linguistic derivation, and naturalizes their continuing connection with the English landscape. Language, landscape, and identity become intimately close. *Beowulf*, for Tolkien, was a timeless, and therefore a contemporary text for England: "It was made in this land, and moves in our northern world beneath our northern sky, and for those who are native to that tongue and land, it must ever call with a profound appeal—until the dragon comes" ("Beowulf," 33–34).

So much in Tolkien's battle to restore cultural continuity is imaginatively projected in this way from a romantic reading of early heroic narratives that his work might seem to exemplify the nostalgia double bind described by Susan Stewart in *On Longing*:

> Nostalgia, like any form of narrative, is always ideological: the past it seeks has never existed except as narrative, and hence, always absent, that past continually threatens to reproduce itself as a felt lack. Hostile to history and its invisible origins, and yet longing for an impossibly pure context of lived experience at a place of origin, nostalgia wears a distinctly utopian face, a face that turns toward a future-past, a past which has only ideological reality. This point of desire which the nostalgic seeks is in fact the absence that is the very generating mechanism of desire.[19]

In Stewart's terms, one might see a fear of experiential inauthenticity behind Tolkien's grand narrative, fear driving the continuing consolidation of his linguistic and narrative environment against his experience of an environment doubly destroyed. Certainly, within *The Lord of the Rings*, critiques of the heroic view based on empirical history and material culture are branded as loss of faith and associated with demoralized minds like Saruman: "Dotard! What is the House of Eorl but a thatched barn where brigands drink in the reek, and their brats roll on the floor among the dogs?" (*LR* 3.10, 567).

Yet if, for Tolkien, the gap Stewart postulates between history or lived experience, on the one hand, and ideology, on the other, threatens a horror—the debasement of an idealized environment by sordid materialism—it also provides an endless opportunity for fiction. Within the never-sated narrative space, archaism, nostalgia, and the elegiac mode are deployed as active forms of cultural continuity. Tolkien virtually situates himself *within* the tradition of Old English writing, with *The Wanderer* and much of *Beowulf*. In "The Homecoming of Beorhtnoth Beorhthelm's Son," he delights in pointing out that the most famous lines from *The Battle of Maldon* (312–13), spoken in the face of certain defeat—

> Hige sceal þe heardra, heorte þe cenre,
> mod sceal Þe mare þe ure mægen lytlað.
> [Will shall be the sterner, heart the bolder, spirit the greater as our strength lessens.]

—are "not 'original' [to the man who speaks them], but an ancient and honored expression of heroic will."[20] For Tolkien, to assert these lofty battle sentiments yet again is no mere literary quotation but the conscious renewal of a heroic tradition in the face of imminent loss.

Repetition, which for Stewart is a sign of the otherness of experience mediated through narrative and of the inauthenticity of lived experience, for Tolkien acknowledges the loss of the heroic past in a form that consoles it by asserting a community of interest with the vanished heroes and all those who have since believed in them. Consciousness of loss and absence provides prestigious roles for figures who connect present and past: the mage who can interpret ancient vestiges; the survivor who keeps faith with his dead comrades; the exile in whom memory preserves a lost noble world. With these prestigious adversarial roles comes a sense of cultural work as the battle to reimpose on the world an ideal order that is intuited to be lacking. The conception of heroism in *The Lord of the Rings* feeds directly on the difficulties in realizing such an order:

> "Few now remember them," Tom murmured, "yet still some go wandering, sons of forgotten kings, walking in loneliness, guarding from evil folk that are heedless."
>
> The hobbits did not understand his words, but as he spoke they had a vision as it were of a great expanse of years behind them, like a vast shadowy plain over which there strode shapes of Men, tall and grim with bright swords, and last came one with a star on his brow. Then the vision faded and they were back in the sunlit world. (*LR* 1.8, 142–43)

That "few" are aware of these guardians, that they walk "in loneliness," completes an impression of their necessity and rightness, their supreme importance within an imperialist system of meaning. The past is "shadowy" only because the present is "heedless," ignorant, and ungrateful. The import of the vision may seem remote from the material "sunlit world," but it portends a steep learning curve for the Hobbits toward a potential re-ennoblement of the modern life they represent. In that process, the "bright swords" of war become paramount.

Tolkien's conscious reassertion of archaism in the face of modernity is itself a reprise of the young Alfred Tennyson's original framing of "Morte d'Arthur," in "The Epic":

> Why take the style of those heroic times?
> For nature brings not back the mastodon,
> Nor we those times; and why should any man
> Remodel models?[21]

Tennyson's anxiety about reviving a past style was partly disingenuous. Despite the frame of authorial self-doubt, the imagined audience of

"The Epic" act like proto-Inklings: after discussing "the general decay of faith / Right thro' the world," they listen in deep silence to "Morte d'Arthur," and one, at least, dreams that night of a modern Arthur returned, "With all good things, and war shall be no more." Implicitly, as in Tolkien, the problematical archaism of Tennyson's medievalist venture is shown to be its main point, a sign of the struggle to keep faith with a heroic potential against the apparently ineluctable course of the world.

Tolkien resembles Tennyson in numerous more specific ways. First is his lexicon loaded with Tennysonian favorites—"bright," "dark," "fair," "foul," "dim," "pale," "fade(d)," "faint," "clean," "sweet," "weary," "gleam," "flame," "gray," "thin," "shadow," "waste." Second is his habit of displacing psychological and moral analysis onto descriptions of landscape, weather, architecture, and ornament. It could be argued that this is a tendency Tolkien shares with several other writers—the *Beowulf*-poet, *Gawain*-poet and Spenser come to mind—yet, taken in combination with the close similarities in vocabulary, it often creates in his work a distinctly Tennysonian ambience. Direct borrowings are absent, but Tolkien's landscapes generally aspire to what J.S. Mill early identified in Tennyson: "the power of *creating* scenery, in keeping with some state of feeling; so fitted as to be the embodied symbol of it."[22] Examples abound: "to their right a grey river gleamed pale in the thin sunshine" (*LR* 1.12, 195); "The sun grew misty as the day grew old, until it gleamed in a pale sky like a high white pearl. Then it faded into the West, and dusk came early, followed by a grey and starless night" (*LR* 2.8, 370); "Only far away north-west there was a deeper darkness against the dying light: the Mountains of Mist and the forest at their feet" (*LR* 3.2, 419); "Over the last shelf of rotting stone the stream gurgled and fell down into a brown bog and was lost. Dry reeds hissed and rattled though they could feel no wind" (*LR* 4.2, 611). Tolkien's natural world is glossed with psychic and moral suggestions—"thin," "dying," "rotting," and "lost"—to the extent that what John D. Rosenberg writes of *Idylls of the King* applies equally well to *The Lord of the Rings*: it "uses landscape...not as a decorative adjunct to character but as the mythopoeic soil in which character is rooted and takes its being."[23] Further resemblances to Tennyson are seen in Tolkien's striving for aural imitation—"hissed and rattled"—, and in his creation of unease or apprehension by repeatedly giving colorless or imprecise features of description a precise location: a "grey" river viewed "to the right," a "misty" sun fading "into the West," "darkness" to the "north-west." Tolkien's habitual glances to the sun and the horizon simultaneously orient his heroes on a realist map and surround them with an illimitable vista of psychic possibilities.

Tolkien also strongly resembles Tennyson in the broad political reliance he places on the central role of a true king, and particularly in his vision of good rule as environmental and moral cleansing, based on a prior inner cultivation of the self. Arthur praises the reformed Edyrn for "weeding all his heart / As I will weed this land before I go."[24] Arthur's role in "Gereint and Enid" is a political extension of the same theme:

> [A]nd [he] sent a thousand men
> To till the wastes, and moving everywhere
> Cleared the dark places and let in the law,
> And broke the bandit holds and cleansed the land.[25]

Tolkien's version of good kingship is a directly similar scouring and recultivation of the earth. In Aragorn's reign, Gandalf says, "The evil things will be driven out of the waste-lands. Indeed the waste in time will be waste no longer, and there will be people and fields where once there was wilderness" (*LR* 6.7, 971).

If the key to Tolkien's stylistic archaism is his nostalgic desire to reconnect with a heroic past, then the nostalgia is empowered by such links with a recent era of medievalist idealism. In particular, the comparison helps explain how Tolkien, who had, like Tennyson, a well-attested distaste for actual war, could nevertheless make it a "high" subject in the manner I have outlined. Within both writers' works, the description of war often tends more toward ideological symbol than toward direct description of military action: their war is a school of moral order, a preparation for future rule: "That is what you have been trained for," Gandalf tells Merry and Pippin before they "scour" the Shire, removing the "squint-eyed and sallow-faced" Orc-like enemy (*LR* 6.7, 974; 6.8, 981, 992) and restoring ethnic boundaries. As in Tennyson's *Idylls*, the enemy not only causes pollution but *is* moral pollution, "the beast," to be dispelled by force. War is relied on to restore the natural world: "Kill orc-folk!" says Ghân-buri-Ghân. "Drive away bad air and darkness with bright iron!" (*LR* 5.5, 816).

In dealing with war in his novel, Tolkien encountered a problem similar to Tennyson's in the *Idylls*. Like Tennyson he longs for a state beyond war— "the very last end of the War, I hope" (*LR* 6.8, 997)—yet is committed to a story and an ethos in which martial heroism is a major currency. Both writers cope with the issue in a similar way, by moral allegory. Arthur's good wars are made a semisymbolic expression of moral superiority—"a voice / As dreadful as the shout of one who sees / To one who sins"[26]—and his early enemies are inhuman or alien: the "heathen," "beast," and "Roman." Evil war, when his knights have degenerated, in Mordred's civil rebellion, is physically gross:

> Oaths, insult, filth and monstrous blasphemies,
> Sweat, writhings, anguish, labouring of the lungs

In that close mist, and cryings for the light,
Moans of the dying, and voices of the dead.[27]

In *The Lord of the Rings*, battle alignments, as in Tennyson's self-styled "parabolic" wars, are also moral alignments. Tolkien mainly treats the nature of war according to the sides involved, which are identified by the rightness and wrongness of their overall causes. One side, led by Aragorn and advised by Gandalf, fights a "medieval" war of named volunteers and pledged faith, while the bad side is "modern," with its nameless conscripts, machines, slaves, and creatures of Sauron. The desolate Great War landscape of trenches, mud, shell holes, corpses, and total deforestation is associated with Isengard, the Paths of the Dead, or Frodo's and Sam's journey into Mordor, rather than with the book's actual battlefields: "Indeed the whole surface of the plains of Gorgoroth was pocked with great holes, as if, while it was still a waste of soft mud, it had been smitten with a shower of bolts and huge slingstones. The largest of these holes were rimmed with ridges of broken rock, and broad fissures ran out from them in all directions. It was a land in which it would be possible to creep from hiding to hiding, unseen by all but the most watchful eyes" (*LR* 6.3, 913). This wretched Mordor country, unlike the Somme where Tolkien fought in 1916, does not owe its destruction equally to both sides in the war. Rather, while it functions as an expression of Sauron's sterile, dispiriting power, it gives Frodo and Sam the chance to display selfless endurance as they struggle to get rid of the Ring. Where the war landscape does impinge on actual combat in *The Lord of the Rings*, as at Helm's Deep, it is only the Orcs who are associated with the horror of flares, shell bursts, and night raids from the enemy trenches: "For a staring moment, the watchers on the walls saw all the space between them and the dike lit with white light; it was boiling and crawling with black shapes, some squat and broad, some tall and grim, with high helms and sable shields. Hundreds and hundreds more were pouring over the dike and through the breach" (*LR* 3.7, 520). The Orcs must "pour" over a dike, while Aragorn, Legolas, and Gimli watch them from the walls of a medieval stronghold.

The mixture of realism and allegorical significance in such a war discourse is confusing. Tolkien argued that it was a "romance," and hence a nonrealist, quasi-allegorical narrative feature, derived from Christian psychomachia: "In real life they [the Orcs] are on both sides, of course. For 'romance' has grown out of allegory and its wars are still derived from the 'inner war' of allegory in which good is on one side and various modes of badness on the other. In real (exterior) life men are on both sides" (*Letters*, 82). Although the heroic-Germanic coloring may disguise it, in regard to war *The Lord of the Rings* is considerably more romance than epic or novel, because it gives an absolute aesthetic and moral privilege—aesthetics and morality becoming quite indistinguishable—to one side only. Tolkien re-creates, in effect, the "parabolic" war of Tennyson, in which the king's enemies are not merely political or military opponents but thoroughly evil forces who can be understood to represent evil itself. One sign of this is that weapons occasionally become spontaneous agents in battle: "The bow of Legolas was singing" (*LR* 2.4, 291); "Yet my axe is restless in my hand. Give me a row of orc-necks and room to swing. . .!" (*LR* 3.7, 520); "It has been knife-work up here" (*LR* 3.7, 524). Tolkien's use of the motif recalls medieval heroic poetry like *The Battle of Maldon*, but with the thoroughly Tennysonian difference that only the good characters have weapons privileged to act willingly.[28]

Gimli's Norse-like moments of battle-relish are fairly rare in Tolkien's narrative. Through the figure of Aragorn, especially, *The Lord of the Rings* more often displays what has been said about the medieval warriors of Victorian artists, that they are statuesque icons rather than action figures, with "a strong sense of arrested movement."[29] In *Idylls of the King*, Arthur's wars are "rendered mystically"[30] (allegorically) on the gates of Camelot, in a hierarchy rising from bestial savagery to angelic pureness, topped by the statue of Arthur himself.[31] As, over the course of *Lord of the Rings*, Strider turns into Aragorn, he often seems like a new version of the Victorian allegoric statuesque: "The grey figure of the Man, Aragorn son of Arathorn, was tall and stern as stone, his hand upon the hilt of his sword; he looked as if some king out of the mists of the sea had stepped upon the shores of lesser men" (*LR* 3.5, 489). The iconic quality of Aragorn emblematizes the simultaneously desired presence and absence of the past in Tolkien's heroic nostalgia. Is it that a statue has come to life, the heroic past returned, or that Aragorn's new status removes him from the contingent world of time, of "lesser men," into what is already a perfected retrospective understanding? The core of Aragorn's greatness is that it is already archaic. In such moments Tolkien, one might say, equally desires the return of the heroic age and the rememorializing of its loss—a renewal of the Tennysonian covenant with an idealized medievalist violence, but carefully removed from historical scrutiny, as the true idiom of national and personal heroic potential.

It could be argued that *The Lord of the Rings* maintains dialogue with Tennyson's *Idylls* to the very end. For Tolkien leaves us finally not with Frodo or Aragorn but with Sam Gamgee, just as the *Idylls* ends not with Arthur but with Bedivere, also staring westward, as his master's vessel passes beyond sight into a mysterious realm and a new age begins on earth. Both bereft companions grieve, but in comparison to Tennyson, Tolkien distances this world from the one to which his hero has departed. In Tennyson, Bedivere himself sees "the speck that bare the King, / . . .pass on and on. . . / . . .and vanish into light,"[32] and hears, though faintly, Arthur's reception in heaven:

> As from beyond the limit of the world,
> Like the last echo born of a great cry,
> Sounds, as if some fair city were one voice
> Around a king returning from his wars.[33]

In Tolkien, Frodo alone beholds the new day, "white shores and beyond them a far green country under a swift sunrise," and hears "the sound of singing that came over the water" as he nears his final home. With Frodo gone, a dejected Sam sees only "a shadow on the waters that was soon lost in the West," and hears "only the sigh and murmur of the waves on the shores of Middle-earth" (*LR* 6.9, 1007), much as Tennyson's Bedivere (following Malory) has done on his earlier, failed attempts to cast Excalibur away: "I heard the water lapping on the crag, / And the long ripple washing in the reeds."[34] Tennyson's triumphant "Return of the King" motif is absent in Tolkien at Frodo's parting, having been reserved appropriately for Aragorn's elaborate reception in Gondor: "And the shadow departed, and the Sun was unveiled, and light leaped forth; and the waters of Anduin shone like silver, and in all the houses of the City men sang for the joy that welled up in their hearts" (*LR* 6.5, 941–42), followed by "[A]nd amid the music of harp and viol and singing and clear voices the King passed through the flower-laden streets and came to the Citadel" (*LR* 6.5, 947).

It is here, too, that Tolkien most strongly foregrounds another Tennysonian theme—"The old order changeth, yielding place to new"[35]—when Gandalf stresses that the king's triumph means "The Third Age of the world is ended, and the new age is begun" (*LR* 6.5, 949). Aragorn's warfaring and hold on power are, like Tennyson's Arthur's, finally subsumed within the broadest view of historical necessity. Already by the time Frodo and Sam are reunited with him in Ithilien, his sword has become ritual and symbolic, a sign of the right to rule: "On the throne sat a mail-clad man, a great sword was laid across his knees, but he wore no helm" (*LR* 5.4, 932). There can be no suggestion that superior military force alone has won the day in Gondor. This is the image of a "true king."

Tennyson is by no means the only Victorian medievalist who invites relation to Tolkien. Others such as William Morris could perhaps be considered as more direct influences on him. After all, *The Lord of the Rings* is an eclectic text with many possible points of reference. Yet the example of Tennyson best helps us understand the "high" style of war discourse and its symbolic tendencies that puzzle some Tolkien readers so much. It helps us to see how, against his personal experience of war and his political understanding, for reasons of moral allegory, Tolkien displaces the evils of modern war on to the bad side and reserves for the good the "bright swords" of medievalist idealism. The sword—medievalized war's archaic weapon—becomes for Tolkien both the real, which authenticates romantic nostalgia, and the sign of opposition to a debased modernity. As in Tennyson, the idea of war as an ennobling cultural and moral struggle is allowed precedence over the unpleasant history of war itself. Through Tolkien's continuing influence, so prevalent at the present time, we have not yet finished with the agenda of the nineteenth-century British Middle Ages.

Notes

1. Charlotte M. Yonge, *The Long Vacation* (London: Macmillan, 1895), chap. 13.
2. J.R.R. Tolkien, *The Lord of the Rings*, one-volume edn. (London: HarperCollins, 1994), foreword to the 2nd ed., 9 (hereafter cited in text and notes as *LR*).
3. See J.R.R. Tolkien, *The Letters of J. R. R. Tolkien: A Selection*, ed. Humphrey Carpenter with assistance from Christopher Tolkien (London: George Allen and Unwin, 1981), 303 (hereafter cited in text and notes as *Letters*): "Personally, I do not think that either war (and of course not the atomic bomb) had any influence upon either the plot or the manner of its unfolding. Perhaps in landscape. The Dead Marshes and the approaches to the Morannon owe something to Northern France after the Battle of the Somme. They owe more to William Morris and his Huns and Romans, as in *The House of the Wolfings* or *The Roots of the Mountains*."
4. J.R.R. Tolkien, "Beowulf: The Monsters and the Critics," in *"The Monsters and the Critics" and Other Essays*, ed. Christopher Tolkien (London: George Allen and Unwin, 1980), 5–34. See 31: "For *Beowulf* was not designed to tell the tale of Hygelac's fall, or for that matter to give the whole biography of Beowulf, still less to write the history of the Geatish kingdom and its downfall. But it used knowledge of these things for its own purpose—to give that sense of perspective, of antiquity with a greater and yet darker antiquity behind. These things are mainly on the outer edges or in the background because they belong there, if they are to function in this way."
5. Hugh Brogan, "Tolkien's Great War," in *Children and Their Books: A Celebration of the Work of Iona and Peter Opie* (Oxford: Clarendon Press, 1989), 356.
6. T[homas] A. Shippey, *J. R. R. Tolkien, Author of the Century* (London: HarperCollins, 2001), 151.
7. Brian Rosebury, *Tolkien. A Critical Assessment* (New York: St. Martin's Press, 1992), 126.
8. John Garth, *Tolkien and the Great War: The Threshold of Middle-Earth* (London: HarperCollins, 2003), 312.
9. T[homas] A. Shippey, *The Road to Middle-Earth* (London: Allen and Unwin, 1982); Jane Chance, ed., *Tolkien the Medievalist* (London: Routledge, 2003).

10. *Beowulf*, ed. and trans. Michael Swanton (Manchester: Manchester University Press, 1978).
11. *The Battle of Maldon*, in *A Choice of Anglo-Saxon Verse*, ed. and trans. Richard Hamer (London: Faber, 1970).
12. Virginia Woolf, "How It Strikes a Contemporary," in *The Common Reader* (London: Hogarth Press, 1925), 302.
13. Geoffrey Chaucer, "Wife of Bath's Prologue," line 522, in *The Riverside Chaucer*, ed. L. D. Benson (Boston: Houghton Mifflin, 1987), 112.
14. Rosebury, *Tolkien*, 65, points out that "the basic style of narrative and description. . .is. . .largely free from archaic, let alone obsolete, forms."
15. Alfred Tennyson, "The Passing of Arthur," lines 179–80, in *The Poems of Tennyson*, ed. Christopher Ricks (London: Longman, 1969), 1747.
16. Rosebury, *Tolkien*, 82. Garth, *Tolkien and the Great War*, 35, 39–40, 59, 78–79.
17. Jay Winter, *Sites of Memory, Sites of Mourning: The Great War in European Cultural History* (Cambridge, UK: Cambridge University Press, 1995), 2–5, 54.
18. Tennyson's father had even held the living of Bag Enderby, in Lincolnshire, near the poet's birthplace. See Christopher Ricks, *Tennyson*, 2nd edn. (Basingstoke, UK: Macmillan, 1989), 3.
19. Susan Stewart, *On Longing* (Durham, NC: Duke University Press, 1993), 23.
20. J.R.R. Tolkien, "The Homecoming of Beorhtnoth Beorhthelm's Son," in *The Tolkien Reader* (New York: Ballantine, 1966), 124. The translation is Tolkien's own.
21. Alfred Tennyson, "The Epic [Morte d'Arthur]," lines 35–38, in *Poems of Tennyson*, 584.
22. J.S. Mill, review of Tennyson, *Poems, Chiefly Lyrical* [1830] and *Poems* [1833], *London Review July, 1835*, in *Tennyson: The Critical Heritage*, ed. John D. Jump (London: Routledge, 1967), 86.
23. John D. Rosenberg, *The Fall of Camelot: A Study of Tennyson's "Idylls of the King"* (Cambridge, MA: Harvard University Press, 1973), 67–68.
24. Alfred Tennyson, "Gereint and Enid," lines 905–06, in *Poems of Tennyson*, 1575.
25. Tennyson, "Gereint and Enid," lines 940–43.
26. Alfred Tennyson, "The Coming of Arthur," lines 115–17, in *Poems of Tennyson*, 1473.
27. Alfred Tennyson, "The Passing of Arthur," lines 114–17, in *Poems of Tennyson*, 1745.
28. See *The Battle of Maldon*, line 110: "Bogan wæron bysige, bord ord onfeng" ("bows were busy too, / Shield received spear"). See also Alfred Tennyson, " 'Fall battleaxe, and flash brand! Let the King reign," from "The Coming of Arthur," lines 485–86. See also "Coming of Arthur," lines 5–19, 94–120, 475–513.
29. Elizabeth Brewer and Beverly Taylor, *The Return of King Arthur* (Cambridge: D. S. Brewer, 1983), 131.
30. Alfred Tennyson, "The Holy Grail," lines 359, 235–45, in *Poems of Tennyson*, 1672, 1669.

31. Alfred Tennyson, "The Holy Grail," lines 235–45: "And in the lowest beasts are slaying men, / And in the second men are slaying beasts, / And on the third are warriors, perfect men, / And on the fourth are men with growing wings, / And overall one statue in the mould / Of Arthur, made by Merlin with a crown, / And peaked wings pointed to the Northern Star / And eastward fronts the statue and the crown / And both the wings are made of gold, and flame / At sunrise till the people in far fields, / Wasted so often by the heathen hordes, / Behold it, crying, 'We have still a King.' "
32. Alfred Tennyson, "The Passing of Arthur," lines 465–68, in *Poems of Tennyson*, 1754.
33. Tennyson, "The Passing of Arthur," lines 458–61.
34. Tennyson, "The Passing of Arthur," lines 284–85, in *Poems of Tennyson*, 1748.
35. Tennyson, "The Passing of Arthur," line 408, in *Poems of Tennyson*, 1752.

CHAPTER 7

PASTORALIA AND PERFECTABILITY IN WILLIAM MORRIS AND J.R.R. TOLKIEN

Chester N. Scoville

> *Tolkien, while growing up, read the socialist William Morris's Pre-Raphaelite medievalist fantasy. Comparison of works by the two authors shows parallels but also the distinctive ways in which Tolkien responded to the stark nature of twentieth-century life by drawing on his own Christian beliefs, more pessimistic about the prospects of utopia.*

William Morris, the great English polymath of the nineteenth century, made a deep and lasting influence on J.R.R. Tolkien, the most popular author of the twentieth century. So varied was Morris's career—as poet, designer, painter, architect, gardener, socialist, translator from Greek, Latin, Old English, and Old Norse, and, not incidentally, the inventor of the fantasy novel—that getting a grip on his work is difficult. Even more difficult is working out the exact extent and nature of his influence on others. Although such luminaries as Dante Gabriel Rossetti and Edward Burne-Jones were his colleagues in the second wave of Pre-Raphaelitism, and although such major authors as W.B. Yeats and George Bernard Shaw were among his disciples, Morris himself is not often read today, and his reputation is a puzzle. Everyone, it seems, was touched by some aspect of his work, whether they know it or not, but how they were touched is something difficult to measure.

Such is also the case with J.R.R. Tolkien; Morris's influence on him is undeniable but hard to quantify. In *The Annotated Hobbit*, Douglas Anderson states that "William Morris's influence on Tolkien is often underrated."[1] This is so, and the fact is curious. It is well established that Tolkien read and enjoyed Morris, and that his first adult attempts at writing were, by his own admission, inspired by Morris's late-nineteenth-century prose romances with their quasi-medieval setting and diction. The two men temperamentally also have a remarkable amount in common. Morris and Tolkien shared a deep and abiding love for the Middle Ages and saw in them clues to an alternative way of living, different from the shabby, materialist, and industrialized world they saw around them. Both men had at the center of their thinking and writing the image of the tree, especially the contrast between the green tree, symbolic of life and continuation, and the dead or dry tree, symbolic of sterility of thought and action.[2] Morris's self-description as a man "with a deep love of the earth and the life on it, and a passion for the history of the past of mankind"[3] could as easily apply to Tolkien; the two men's love of medieval Icelandic saga is such that Tolkien envied Morris's trips to Iceland and at one point wished to make such a journey himself. Morris was also influential in the way Tolkien saw his social and academic circles; when Tolkien was at King Edward's School, he once suggested that his circle of friends, the Tea Club-Barrovian Society (TCBS), was like the Pre-Raphaelites, the circle to which Morris had belonged—although his classmates disagreed. Again, when Tolkien was at Exeter College, Oxford, in 1914 (which was also Morris's alma mater), Tolkien used the money he won for the Skeat Prize in English to buy some of Morris's books.[4] And when he was teaching at Oxford years later, Tolkien became friends with C.S. Lewis, initially because of a mutual love of, among other things, Morris.[5] Finally, Tolkien's writings and Morris's have had the same unfortunate reception by far too many modernist critics in the twentieth century, a point that needs little belaboring at this point of time.[6]

Anderson traces Morris's specific influence on *The Hobbit* in such things as the naming of Dale and Tolkien's phrase "the wood beyond the Water,"[7] which so closely echoes the titles of Morris's romances *The Wood beyond the World* and *The Water of the Wondrous Isles*—and, I would add, *The Well at the World's End*, of which C.S. Lewis was also fond of, and which features a mysterious figure named "Gandolf."[8] Anderson is not the only one who has made such connections: Tom Shippey cites especially Morris's *The House of the Wolfings*, *The Roots of the Mountain*, and *The Glittering Plain*[9]—the books Tolkien bought with his prize money—while Humphrey Carpenter adds to the list Morris's *The Life and Death of Jason* and Morris's translation of the *Völsungasaga*,[10] and he speculates—very reasonably, I think—that Tolkien's early work *The Book of Lost Tales* owes its structure to Morris's *The Earthly Paradise*.[11] That Tolkien knew this last work is shown by John Garth,[12] and that he knew it well is suggested by Tolkien's letter of November 29, 1943, to his son Christopher, then serving in the RAF in World War II.[13] Morris's famously alienated self-description in *The Earthly Paradise*, "Dreamer of dreams, born out of my due time," reappears in Tolkien's letter in the rueful sentence, "We were born in a dark age out of due time."

Morris's importance to Tolkien, then, was profound. And, as I argue, the two men saw many of the same admirable qualities in the Middle Ages. Yet, their political differences would seem to preclude this. Morris saw the Middle Ages in an essentially Marxian manner; he was, in his time, the best known of English socialists and was deeply committed to the cause. Morris's book *Socialism from the Root Up*, originally published in installments in the *Commonweal* from 1886 to 1888, is to a large extent an exposition of part 7 of *Das Kapital*. In the second part of *Socialism*, Morris declares that medieval society is "based on the fusion of ideas of tribal communism and Roman individualism and bureaucracy"; he only secondarily acknowledges that "this system was mixed up with religious ideas of some sort."[14] In particular, he alleges that the main thrust of the medieval church was not to foster individual devotion to the next life, but rather to bring "the kingdom of heaven to earth by breathing its spirit into the temporal power."[15] In other words, Morris saw in the Middle Ages a constant dialectical struggle between the authentically human yearning for communal property and equality and the artificiality of individual aggrandizement made possible by bureaucratic power. In both forces there is a focus on bringing about some kind of utopia in real life; but one would be a sort of free yeoman republic, while the other would be typical of the various political nightmares that Morris actually saw around him.

Unlike Morris, Tolkien never wrote explicitly political works, and he never seems to have committed himself explicitly to any "ism" other than Catholicism. Tolkien, it is safe to say, had no tolerance for socialism. Yet his politics are more difficult to pin down than might be thought. He himself had difficulty defining them; when he tried, he typically ended up with humorously contradictory assertions such as, "My political opinions lean more and more to Anarchy (philosophically understood, meaning abolition of control not whiskered men with bombs)—or to 'unconstitutional' Monarchy."[16] In one breath, Tolkien expresses his preference for the complete absence of government,[17] and for the complete centralization thereof in one person's whim. One senses him throwing up his hands in frustration at the whole business, both at the business of government and at any attempt to define his thinking about it. It is safe to say, as many have, that he was closer to old Tory conservatism than to anything that modern people would recognize as being on the left (or, I would add, on the modern right), but even there he found problems and oppositions; in the same letter he refers to the Churchill wartime government as "Winston and his gang." Tolkien was a booster for no party.

Yet that, I would suggest, is one reason why Tolkien now appeals to people of differing political opinions themselves, and why he was able to take inspiration from someone like Morris. Ideas and ideals can, of course, migrate all over the political spectrum given the time and the right conditions. In the Victorian England of Morris, the ideal of decentralized, environmentally conscious communities of power and culture—the sort of thinking that many today would call Green and, in the United States and Canada, would associate with the left—was at least as likely—in fact, more likely—to originate from conservatism as from radicalism. Both movements were in positions of resistance and marginalization relative to the liberal, industrial, capitalist mainstream that was in control of the country's history and development. Thus, for example, both Morris and Tolkien would find themselves influenced by John Ruskin, whose ideas about the Gothic were intimately tied to his rejection of liberal economics, which grew directly out of his conservative resistance to Gladstone's industrial policy. We should not now be surprised that people from opposite sides of the political spectrum should share the same ideals when they are both resisting a common opponent.

Yet if Morris and Tolkien shared a set of ideals, and a position of resistance to the mainstream of modern liberal industrialism, the metaphysical underpinnings of their work are entirely different. To view these conclusions at work, let us briefly consider Morris's best-known work, the utopian romance *News from Nowhere* (1890). I cite this book although it is never mentioned in connection with Tolkien. Of course, it is—just—possible that Tolkien did not know this particular work; he never mentions it in his letters, for instance, although that is certainly no positive proof. It is rather more possible that he did know the work and found it not to his taste, for reasons that will become apparent; John Wain states that the Inklings admired Morris but only selectively.[18] Yet it is worth considering what Morris did in this book in contrast to what Tolkien did in his writings. In particular, it is worth comparing Tolkien's portrait of the Shire to Morris's portrait of Nowhere; such a comparison reveals the common uses that the two men made of quasi-medieval Arcadian imagery and traditions, despite coming from such radically different perspectives.

Readers of this volume need no summary of Tolkien's portrait of the Shire; but Morris's *News from Nowhere* perhaps could benefit from a brief introduction. This book, first published, again, in serialized form in the *Commonweal*, takes the form of a dream vision, in which the narrator, one William Guest, finds himself in a London of the twenty-second century, in which the ugliness and illness of industrial society have been replaced by "a well-ordered and well-farmed countryside" (*LR* 1. prologue, 1).[19]

In his wanderings up the Thames, Guest finds that in the inhabitants of this new England are "a merry folk" (*LR* 1. prologue, 2) who, remembering the disasters of industrialism of ages past, are on the whole scornful of most "machines more complicated than a forge-bellows, a water-mill, or a hand-loom," though they are "skilful with tools" (*LR* 1. prologue, 1) and, in fact, love to make many beautiful things. They dress "in bright colours," and in many cases they "wear no shoes" (*LR* 1. prologue, 2) having such "a close friendship with the earth" (*LR* 1. prologue, 1) that, for instance, they feel emotionally the changing of the seasons. They have "hardly any 'government'" and are "generous and not greedy, but contented and moderate" (*LR* 1. prologue, 9). "Nonetheless, ease and peace had left this people still curiously tough" (*LR* 1. prologue, 5). After many conversations with them, and especially with a remarkable woman named Ellen and with her learned grandfather, Guest eventually awakes to the ugliness of nineteenth-century London.

It sounds much like the Shire, a reader might think, and that would be right. I have of course not yet quoted Morris in describing his Nowhere; all the descriptive quotations thus far have been lifted from Tolkien's essay "Concerning Hobbits," at the beginning of *The Lord of the Rings*. Yet they are all—and this is the point—entirely accurate as descriptors of Morris's Nowhere. This is not, I must stress again, an attempt at source study. I am attempting not to demonstrate direct influence but to show that a similarly Arcadian pastoral tradition was strong in both Morris and Tolkien and that both were direct reactions against industrial modernism, despite coming at it from differing political angles.

Although Morris's Nowhere is set in a hypothetical future, it owes its creativity to the past. In describing some of the Nowhereans, for instance, Guest reports, "Their dress was somewhat between that of the ancient classical costume and the simpler forms of the fourteenth century garments, though it was clearly not an imitation of either."[20] The architecture of Nowhere, also, is a curiously eclectic yet thoroughly transformed style of antiquarianism: "It seemed to me to embrace the best qualities of the Gothic of northern Europe with those of the Saracenic and Byzantine, though there was no copying of any one of these styles."[21] In fact, the memory of the Middle Ages and early modern period, and the forgetting of the modern industrial world, is one of the chief characteristics of Nowhere, as Guest notes with pleasure: "I smiled faintly to think how the nineteenth century, of which such big words have been said, counted for nothing in the memory of this man, who read Shakespeare and had not forgotten the Middle Ages."[22]

Nowhere is also an ecologically conscious place; in this, Morris anticipated many of the ideas of today's Green movement. The Nowhereans have rejected the modern (including the socialist) assumption that civilization is essentially built on top of the natural world. Instead, they see their society as a part of the ecosystem: Clara, one of Guest's guides, criticizes previous eras for "always looking upon everything, except mankind, animate and inanimate—'nature,' as people used to call it—as one thing, and mankind as another. It was natural to people thinking in this way, that they should try to make 'nature' their slave, since they thought 'nature' was something outside them."[23] Guest himself compares the Nowhereans' sympathetic attitude toward nature with that of his own people, noting that the Nowhereans have a "passionate love of the earth which was common to but few people at least, in the days I knew; in which the prevailing feeling amongst intellectual persons was a kind of sour distaste for the changing drama of the year, for the life of the earth and its dealings with men."[24]

Morris was at this time the most prominent member of the Socialist League and had, in fact, written *News from Nowhere* in part as a means of encouraging English socialists, who had suffered a series of setbacks. In particular, the events of "Bloody Sunday," November 13, 1887, in which the London police charged a peaceful crowd of socialist demonstrators in Trafalgar Square—including both Morris and George Bernard Shaw[25]— had thrown much of English socialism into dismay. Also, the rise of the ideology of mechanized State Socialism (i.e., the ancestor of Leninism) was a new threat to the vision of libertarian and pastoral socialism that Morris held dear; in particular, Morris was reacting to the American writer Edward Bellamy's book *Looking Backward*, in which a mechanized superstate has created a kind of utopia that both Morris and Tolkien (and, probably, most people nowadays) would find soulless and chilling—"a cockney paradise" was Morris's verdict.[26] *News from Nowhere* is an account of the final defeat of both bourgeois England and mechanized State Socialism. As such, it is a fundamentally optimistic work; Morris was a fundamentally optimistic man. Like many another activists, he believed that the world could be perfected, or nearly so, if only centralized power would get out of the way and let people be free.

In creating this vision, Morris was drawing less on traditional utopian traditions than on pastoral or, more properly, Arcadian traditions.[27] As Tom Middlebro' argues, the values of the Arcadia are typically "spontaneity, creativity, love and freedom," unlike those of the utopia proper, which are "stability, uniformity, efficiency and hierarchy."[28] The Arcadia is typically rural and nostalgic; the utopia is typically urban and philosophic. Above all, the Arcadia is written from the point of view that individual humanity is innately good, and that the overregulation and corruption of urban life is an oppressive burden; the utopia is written from the point of view that individual humanity is essentially weak and corrupt, and that liberty and privacy must be abolished or heavily regulated in order to stave off social chaos.[29] The Arcadia wishes, in Tolkienian terms, not to take the Ring of Power for its own, that is, to place a new central authority in charge of people's lives, but to remove central authority from the picture.

It is also true, however, that, unlike the utopia, the Arcadia need not present itself as absolute but can afford to remain contingent and hypothetical. Such is certainly the case with *News from Nowhere*. As E.P. Thomson has pointed out, for all its Marxist substructure, *News from Nowhere* was never intended to be a literal and programmatic picture of what an ideal communist society would look like. It is, instead, intended as a critique of nineteenth-century capitalism and "a revelation of the powers slumbering within men and women and distorted or denied in class society."[30] As a political Arcadia, it derives at least as much from Rousseau, whose *Social Contract* begins with the famous, ringing assertion, "Man is born free and is everywhere in chains," as it does from Marx. It is worth pointing out also that, despite the various disastrous quasi-Marxist utopian experiments of the twentieth century, Marx himself did not believe in utopias; *The Communist Manifesto* positively sneers at what it calls the "duodecimo editions of the New Jerusalem...castles in the air" of utopian experiments.[31] It is important at this point to realize also that for all its apparently rural characteristics, *News from Nowhere* takes place not in a transformed English countryside but in a transformed London, a "London, small, and white, and clean,"[32] like the fourteenth-century city of Morris's introduction to *The Earthly Paradise*. And it is also true that for all their happiness, the Nowhereans are neither angels nor saints: erotic jealousy, for instance, still exists among them, and during Guest's visit indeed one unfortunate love triangle erupts into sudden violence.[33]

Yet despite these *caveats*, Morris does ultimately believe in the improvement and possible perfection of human society through political action and the freeing of humanity from central authority. Although it is sometimes said that *News from Nowhere* takes the form of a dream vision, that is only half true. After pondering his dream, the narrator asks, "Or indeed *was* it a dream? If so, why was I so conscious all along that I was really seeing all that new life from the outside, still wrapped up in the prejudices, the anxieties, the distrust of this time of doubt and struggle?"[34] In other words, the narrator's own position of alienation from his story leads him to believe that what he experienced was not merely internal and psychological, not merely private wish fulfilment, but something historical and therefore objectively possible. The book ends not with nostalgia but with an exhortation: " 'Go on living while you may, striving, with whatsoever pain and labour needs must be, to build up little by little the new day of fellowship, and rest, and happiness.' Yes, surely! and if others can see it as I have seen it, then it may be called a vision rather than a dream."[35] For all the contingencies and complexities, Morris finally believed in the Earthly Paradise and in the fundamental goodness of humanity.

For Tolkien, no such earthly paradise could exist, at least not after the Fall of Man. The Shire, which bears so much superficial resemblance to Morris's Nowhere, is not a utopia and never could be one; nor is it an Arcadia, despite its rural setting. If one were to describe its chief virtues in Middlebro's terms, they might be "much stability, some spontaneity, some uniformity, some hierarchy, some freedom, some efficiency, and some love"; it is, in other words, a mixture of contradictory elements rather than a perfected ideal. Its people are neither perfect nor perfectible but, for all their love of peace and harmony, live in a sublunar, fallen world. As Shirriff Robin Smallburrow observes ruefully in the midst of Saruman's temporary rule, "Even in the Shire there are some as like minding other folk's business and talking big" (*LR* 6.8, 979). Whereas in Nowhere this sort of egotism is shrugged off as a relic of an artificial and dead economic system,[36] in the Shire it is simply part of human (or Hobbit) nature. There is no indication that Saruman had to *do* anything to those Hobbits, like Ted Sandyman, who become quislings; he simply found the concupiscence that was naturally already there and used it.

When Frodo and his companions encounter Ted Sandyman lounging outside the new mill in "The Scouring of the Shire," Frodo remarks, "I hope there are not many more Hobbits that have become like this." Yet really, there is no evidence that Ted Sandyman has "become" ontologically different. He is, as Merry states, "dirty and insolent" (*LR* 6.8, 994), but the former condition is literally skin-deep, and the latter was already much in evidence as far back as the beginning of *The Fellowship of the Ring*, when he dismisses the ancient lore of Middle-earth as "moonshine" and shows himself more interested in scoring cheap debating points than he is in arriving at the truth (*LR* 1.2, 44). Under Sharkey's regime, Ted has merely found a system that suits him, and he has taken on the mannerisms of those in power, such as saying "Garn" like an Orc (*LR* 6.8, 993). But he has not, in fact, been changed in any way by the system, merely given more opportunities to exercise his more unsavory qualities.

Of course, Ted is unusual in his eagerness to go along with the new regime. As Farmer Cotton notes, "Only that fool Ted was pleased" by the industrialization of Hobbiton, including the rebuilding of his mill (*LR* 6.8, 990); most of the Hobbits are going along merely to avoid trouble. Yet the very fecklessness of the Hobbits, their inability to defend themselves without being rallied by Merry and his magical Rohirric horn, suggests another flaw in the Shire and its pastoral system of life. Even though the defeat of the ruffians proves to be, in Farmer Cotton's words, "almost too easy after all" (*LR* 6.8, 988), the Hobbits are entirely unfit for the task of resistance to injustice, having lost all of their traditions of self-defence. As Gandalf remarks in *The Hobbit*, "In this neighbourhood heroes are scarce, or simply not to be found. Swords in these parts are mostly blunt, and axes are used for trees, and shields as cradles or dish-covers."[37] Although the Shire may seem permanent, although its roots may seem deep, it is actually quite fragile, having forgotten or discounted most of its history, and lost its sense of context.

The Shire, then, is far from a perfect place at the best of times. As Tolkien remarked in a letter to *New Statesman* book reviewer Naomi Mitchison in 1954, "*Hobbits* are not a Utopian vision, or recommended as an ideal in their own or any age. They, as all peoples and their situations, are an historical accident...and an impermanent one in the long view. I am not a reformer nor an 'embalmer'! I am not a 'reformer'...since it seems doomed to Sarumanism. But 'embalming' has its own punishments" (*Letters*, 196–97). Here, again, we see Tolkien's reluctance to subscribe to any political program, or to declare himself for any party or ideology.

Yet of course, as mentioned before, Tolkien always declared himself, boldly and openly, for Christianity. Tolkien could never have said, with Morris, merely that in the Middle Ages, or in any age, life "was mixed up with religious ideas of some sort."[38] For him, religion was central even when it was not explicit: to him, for instance, the *Beowulf*-poet was, like himself, a Christian writing about pre-Christians, who saw "the supreme quality of the old heroes...[as] their special endowment by God."[39] Likewise, his perception of the truth and importance of original sin and the fallen state of the world precluded him from imagining that perfection could ever be achieved in this life. "Always after a defeat and a respite," says Gandalf, "the Shadow takes another shape and grows again" (*LR* 1.2, 50). But, of course, it is perfectly possible for a hell to exist on earth, as the example of Mordor shows. The duty of those of us who dwell in Middle-earth is not to hope for a final defeat of the shadow—not to bring about an illusory perfection in this life, but to stand fast and fend off the darkness for as long as we can. Man—or Hobbit—is *not* born free in Tolkien's universe, or not wholly free. The chains of sin and imperfection are with him from the moment of his birth, and remain until his death.

For Morris, the Middle Ages provided clues that could lead humanity to heaven on earth or something very close to it; for Tolkien, they provided clues that could—just—hold off hell on earth, so that humanity could still have inklings of, and desire for, the real heaven. Both viewpoints run contrary to the prevailing ideas of modernism, in which nothing *before* the modern is of any use whatever. Thus, it is easy to mistake them for each other; and, in embattled situations, even natural opponents may end up in unlikely alliances. But when placed next to each other, it is hard to imagine two more different conclusions from the same starting point. Although both Morris and Tolkien used traditions and images of the pastoral, for Morris they represented an ideal in which human society could achieve perfection; for Tolkien, no such perfection was possible or necessary, for even the best human society was not an end in itself.

Notes

1. J.R.R. Tolkien, *The Annotated Hobbit*, ed. Douglas A. Anderson, rev. edn. (London: HarperCollins, 2003), 243n4.
2. W.B. Yeats, "The Happiest of the Poets," in *Essays and Introductions* (New York: Macmillan, 1961), 53–64.
3. William Morris, "How I Became a Socialist" (1894), repr. in *Political Writings of William Morris*, ed. A.L. Morton (New York: International Publishers, 1973), 243.
4. Humphrey Carpenter, *J.R.R. Tolkien: A Biography* (London: George Allen and Unwin, 1977), 69.
5. Humphrey Carpenter, *The Inklings: C. S. Lewis, J. R. R. Tolkien, Charles Williams, and Their Friends* (London: George Allen and Unwin, 1978), 29.
6. Joseph Pearce, *Tolkien: Man and Myth* (San Francisco: Ignatius Press, 1998), 1–6; and Norman Talbot, introduction to William Morris, *The Water of the Wondrous Isles*, ed. May Morris (1913; repr., London: Thoemmes Press, 1994), viii.
7. Tolkien, *Annotated Hobbit*, 243–45, n4.
8. William Morris, *The Well at the World's End* (1896), ed. Lin Carter, 2 vols. (New York: Ballantine, 1970), 1:261.
9. T.A. Shippey, *The Road to Middle-Earth*, 2nd edn. (London: HarperCollins, Grafton, 1992), 301.
10. Carpenter, *Biography*, 69–70.
11. Carpenter, *Biography*, 90.
12. John Garth, *Tolkien and the Great War: The Threshold of Middle-Earth* (London: HarperCollins, 2003), 185.
13. *The Letters of J. R. R. Tolkien*, ed. Humphrey Carpenter (Boston: Houghton Mifflin, 1981), 64.
14. William Morris, "Socialism from the Root Up," reprinted in *William Morris on History*, ed. Nicholas Salmon (Sheffield, UK: Sheffield Academic Press, 1996), 148, 149.
15. Morris, "Socialism from the Root Up," 149.
16. Tolkien, *Letters*, 63.
17. If Tolkien had no tolerance for socialism, Morris had none for anarchism. In William Morris, *News from Nowhere, or, An Epoch of Rest: Being Some Chapters From a Utopian Romance* (1890), ed. David Leopold (Oxford: Oxford University Press, 2003), two characters "burst out laughing very

heartily" (77) at the suggestion that pure anarchism would lead to anything like happiness.
18. Quoted in Colin Duriez, *Tolkien and C. S. Lewis: The Gift of Friendship* (Mahwah, NJ: Hidden Spring, 2003), 129.
19. J.R.R. Tolkien, *The Lord of the Rings*, reset one-volume edn. (London: HarperCollins, 1994).
20. W. Morris, *News from Nowhere and Other Writings* (New York: Penguin, 1993), 13.
21. Morris, *News from Nowhere*, 21.
22. Morris, *News from Nowhere*, 43.
23. Morris, *News from Nowhere*, 154.
24. Morris, *News from Nowhere*, 178.
25. May Morris, *William Morris: Artist, Writer, Socialist*, 2 vols. (1936; repr., New York: Russell and Russell, 1966), 2:260–75; E.P. Thompson, *William Morris: Romantic to Revolutionary* (London: Lawrence and Wishart, 1955), 574–78; Michael Fellman, "Bloody Sunday and *News from Nowhere*," *Journal of the William Morris Society* 8, no. 4 (1990): 9–18; Fiona MacCarthy, *William Morris: A Life for Our Time* (London: Faber and Faber, 1994), 567–73.
26. William Morris, letter 1613 to John Bruce Glasier, May 13, 1889, in *The Collected Letters of William Morris*, ed. Norman Kelvin (Princeton, NJ: Princeton University Press, 1996), 3:59.
27. For a fascinating contrast between the two, see Roger C. Lewis, "*News from Nowhere*: Arcadia or Utopia?" *Journal of the William Morris Society* 7, no. 2 (1987): 15–25.
28. Tom Middlebro', "Brief Thoughts on *News from Nowhere*," *Journal of the William Morris Society* 2, no. 4 (1970): 8–13, here, 11.
29. Middlebro', "Brief Thoughts," 12. See also Martin Delveaux, "From Pastoral Arcadia to Stable-State Mini-Cities: Morris's *News from Nowhere* and Callenbach's *Ecotopia*," *Journal of the William Morris Society* 14, no. 1 (2000): 76–81.
30. Thompson, *William Morris*, 806.
31. Karl Marx and Friedrich Engels, *Manifesto of the Communist Party* (English edn. 1888, ed. Engels), in *The Marx-Engels Reader*, ed. Robert C. Tucker (New York: Norton, 1972), 361.
32. William Morris, *The Earthly Paradise* (1868–70), ed. Florence S. Boos, 2 vols. (New York: Routledge, 2002), 1:69, line 5.
33. Morris, *News from Nowhere*, 142–43.
34. Morris, *News from Nowhere*, 181.
35. Morris, *News from Nowhere*, 182.
36. Morris, *News from Nowhere*, 77.
37. Tolkien, *Annotated Hobbit*, 53–54.
38. William Morris, "Socialism from the Root Up," in *William Morris on History*, 149.
39. J.R.R. Tolkien, "Beowulf: The Monsters and the Critics," in *The Monsters and the Critics and Other Essays*, ed. Christopher Tolkien (Boston: Houghton Mifflin, 1984), 42.

CHAPTER 8

ENGLISH, WELSH, AND ELVISH: LANGUAGE, LOSS, AND CULTURAL RECOVERY IN J.R.R. TOLKIEN'S *THE LORD OF THE RINGS*

Deidre Dawson

> *Language is central to the development of Tolkien's fantasy and that of James Macpherson. Macpherson wrote modern versions of purportedly ancient Celtic legends composed in old Gaelic; Tolkien wrote a mythology to correspond to Elvish languages based on his knowledge of early Celtic and Finnish languages.*

Celtic languages and oral traditions occupy an important part of the multilingual and multicultural universe of Middle-earth. This seems paradoxical, since Tolkien, by his own admission, approached Celtic culture with a certain reserve. Indeed, Tolkien admitted to finding "both Gaelic and the air of Ireland wholly alien" (*Letters*, 219).[1] In response to the statement of Edward Cranshaw that "Quenta Silmarillion" and "The Gest of Beren and Lúthien" had "something of that mad bright-eyed beauty that perplexes all Anglo-Saxons in face of Celtic art," Tolkien wrote to his publisher Stanley Unwin, "I do know Celtic things (many in their original languages Irish and Welsh), and I feel for them a certain distaste: largely for their fundamental unreason. They have bright colour, but are like a broken stained glass window reassembled without design. They are in fact 'mad' as your reader says—but I don't believe I am" (*Letters*, 25–26).

Tolkien certainly was not "mad" in understanding that the Celtic languages of Britain had played an important role in forging the island's history and identity. Thus, the reconstruction of an ancient British language as much akin as possible to the one(s) that existed in England before foreign invasions altered the linguistic landscape would play as important a role in Tolkien's effort to compose a mythology for England as his use of Anglo-Saxon as an inspiration for the language and names of the Riders of Rohan. Anglo-Saxon was, after all, a Germanic import. And while Éowyn and Éomer's names are constructed from the Anglo-Saxon word "eo," meaning "horse," are not the Riders of Rohan themselves, by virtue of the fact that they are such excellent horsemen (and women), reminiscent of the Celtic tribes of Briton and Gaul that dazzled and terrified the Roman infantry with their extraordinary equestrian skills in battle? While Rohan itself may have been closely modeled after Anglo-Saxon society, as Tom Shippey and others have noted, it was a Celtic tribe that produced the courageous woman warrior Boudicca, who led the Britons in a revolt against the Romans in AD 61. Éowyn's name may be Anglo-Saxon, but the inspiration of her character—her fearlessness in the face of death, her determination to avenge her slain kinsmen and her refusal to be dominated by a foreign power—are very Celtic.

The destiny of the Celtic languages once spoken in Tolkien's England was closely linked to the history of its people, who had spent hundreds of years resisting foreign invaders by the time of the Norman Invasion of 1066. Despite the presence of the Romans in southern Britain for over 400 years (55 BC to AD 410), the language of the colonizers left few linguistic traces on the colonized peoples (though some significant clusters of church-related words in Welsh and Irish); it was only in the wake of the Norman Conquest that vast numbers of words of Latin origin made a permanent incursion into the vernacular linguistic territory of Britain as it was conquered by England. This is in stark contrast to the situation in Gaul, Iberia, and other parts of the Mediterranean basin, where the local Celtic languages disappeared more rapidly, as the vulgar Latin required for commercial and political dealings began to evolve into archaic forms of the Romance languages at a very early stage, shortly after the fall of the Roman empire. Celtic philologists generally agree that "P Celtic, Brythonic, Old Brythonic or Common Brythonic was spoken in Britain south of the rivers Forth and Clyde down to the middle of the sixth century AD. Before the rise of the neo-Brythonic languages, from the middle to the end of the century, we observe the formation of dialects."[2] According to Kenneth Jackson, these dialects included "a western and northern dialect (in Wales, the West Midlands, northern England and southern Scotland) from which later Welsh and the 'Cumbric' spoken in the northwest in the Dark Ages were descended...and a south-western dialect...which on the one hand evolved into the now extinct Cornish, and on the other...became established in Brittany as the Breton that still flourishes there today."[3] In Tolkien's beloved Warwickshire, located in the West Midlands, the western dialect descending from Old Brythonic (or Brittonic) eventually gave way to the language of the Anglo-Saxons, although recent archaeological evidence indicates that "Brittonic speakers remained in very large numbers within the Anglo-Saxon kingdoms for several centuries."[4] While Tolkien considered himself a Saxon, he acknowledged the fact that his Saxon ancestors were relative newcomers to the British Isles. He described himself thus in his lecture entitled "English and Welsh," given in Cardiff in 1963: "Indeed, a Saxon in Welsh terms, or in our own one of the English of Mercia. And yet one who has always felt the attraction of the ancient history and pre-history of these islands, and most particularly the attraction of the Welsh language itself."[5]

Linguistic authenticity was an essential component of Tolkien's attempt to recover England's ancient past. Tolkien therefore based one of his Elvish languages, Sindarin, on a reconstruction of a "lost" early Brittonic language, as he explains in a letter to the publisher Houghton Mifflin: "The 'Sindarin,' a Grey-elven language, is in fact constructed deliberately to resemble Welsh phonologically and to have a relation to High-elven to that existing between British (properly so-called, sc., the Celtic languages spoken in this island at the time of the Roman invasion) and Latin" (*Letters*, 219); in another letter Tolkien describes Sindarin as "very like (though not identical to) British-Welsh" (*Letters*, 176). The research of philologist Kenneth Jackson, cited above, indicates that Old Cumbric was very similar to Welsh. Tolkien's creation of Sindarin, with its close resemblance to Welsh, was therefore a close approximation of one of the early Brittonic languages that had disappeared in the wake of the Anglo-Saxon invasions. Aside from this intriguing philological aspect, Sindarin served an aesthetic purpose: just as Tolkien reveled in the pure beauty of the Welsh language—"Welsh is of this soil, this island, the senior language of the men of Britain; and Welsh is beautiful" ("English and Welsh," 11)—so his own readers could delight in the historical and linguistic richness that Sindarin brought to Tolkien's own mythological universe: "If I may once again return to my own work, *The Lord of the Rings*, in evidence: the names of persons and places in this story were mainly composed on patterns deliberately modeled on those of Welsh (closely similar but not identical). This element in the tale has given perhaps more pleasure to more readers than anything else in it" ("English and Welsh," 41).

Another important aspect of the linguistic authenticity that Tolkien considered essential to his project of cultural recovery is his use of different registers of language—a range of styles, vocabulary, and tone—which he deemed appropriate to specific characters and situations. Not all of his readers fully understood or appreciated what Tolkien was trying to achieve, however. In a letter written in December 1954, Hugh Brogan told J.R.R. Tolkien that he found the style of several passages from the *Two Towers*, in particular the chapter "The King of the Golden Hall," "Ossianic" (*Letters*, 225–26). This was not intended as a compliment; the third edition of the *Oxford Universal Dictionary* defines "Ossianic" as "of or pertaining to Ossian or to the poems ascribed to him; of the style or character of Macpherson's rhythmic prose rendering of these poems; hence, magniloquent, bombastic."[6] Tolkien did not answer the letter, and when Brogan wrote several months later to apologize, Tolkien wrote a response that he never sent. In his draft response, dated September 1955, Tolkien explained that "a real archaic English is far more *terse* than modern; also many of the things said could not be said in our slack and often frivolous idiom." Tolkien understood "Ossianic" to mean the deliberate use of a vocabulary, syntax, and tone in keeping with the historical setting of a narrative.

The language used by King Théoden in "The King of the Golden Hall," then, is deliberately "Ossianic." To have a king speak in modern style would result in "an insincerity of thought, a disunion of word and meaning," in Tolkien's view. "I can see no more reason for not using the much *terser* and more vivid ancient *style*, than for changing the obsolete weapons, helms, shields, hauberks into modern uniforms," he remarks later in the letter. To illustrate his point, Tolkien "translates" the words of King Théoden into modern English: " 'Nay Gandalf!' said the King. 'You do not know your own skill in healing. It shall not be so. I myself will go to war, to fall in the front of the battle, if it must be. Thus shall I sleep better,' " becomes "Not at all my dear G. You don't know your own skill as a doctor. Things aren't going to be like that. I shall go to the war in person, even if I have to be one of the first casualties. . . .I should sleep sounder in my grave like that rather than if I stayed at home" (*Letters*, 225–26). Even to a contemporary ear, the archaic language of King Théoden rings truer. Perhaps, had Tolkien been asked to revise the entry for "Ossianic" in the third edition of the *Oxford Universal Dictionary* when it was corrected and revised in 1955, he would have rewritten it thus: "of the style or character of Macpherson's rhythmic prose rendering of these poems; hence, *sincerity* of thought, a *unity* of word and meaning" (italics mine).

Tolkien makes no further references to Ossian or things "Ossianic" in his correspondence, but he shared similar linguistic and historical preoccupations with James Macpherson, who claimed to have translated the *Poems of Ossian* from the ancient Gaelic. A concern for "authenticity" and "sincerity" of language underlies both Tolkien's and Macpherson's work, and while this emphasis takes different forms in the works of each author, in each case language is seen as the key to reviving, recovering, or reconstructing an ancient culture and mythology. In his *Critical Dissertation on the Poems of Ossian*, Hugh Blair, a leading figure of the Scottish Enlightenment, drew attention to the authentic tone of the poems' language as proof of the authenticity of the poems themselves: "The manner of composition bears all the marks of the greatest antiquity. No artful transitions; nor full and extended connection of parts; such as we find among the poets of later times, when order and regularity of composition were more studied and known; but a style always rapid and vehement, in narration concise even to abruptness."[7] Blair's comments on the "rapid and vehement" and even "abrupt" style of the *Poems of Ossian* as proof of their antiquity can be compared with Tolkien's defense of King Théoden's speech as closer to the "a real archaic English" by virtue of its "terse" nature. Philological concerns are at the core of both *The Poems of Ossian* and *The Lord of the Rings*. Tolkien insisted on the primacy of philology in the genesis of his work: "The invention of languages is the foundation. The stories were made rather to provide a world for the languages than the reverse" (*Letters*, 219).

As we have seen, Tolkien's creation of the Sindarin language was a deliberate attempt at linguistic reconstruction of a lost Celtic language of Britain that had been spoken until the middle of the sixth century. For his part, Macpherson translated into English original Gaelic ballads that he had heard in his youth or that he collected on his travel to northwest Inverness-shire, the Isle of Skye, the Outer Hebrides, the Argyllshire coast, and the islands of Skye and Mull. His project was more one of recovery than of reconstruction, since many medieval ballads were still in circulation at the time of the publication of *The Poems of Ossian*. On the subject of the original Gaelic ballads on which Macpherson based his translations, Donald Meek notes, "The ballads which circulated in oral transmission in the Highlands after 1600 were composed, for the most part, in the classical period of Gaelic culture, between 1200 and 1600. They were composed in Classical Common Gaelic, the shared literary language of Ireland and Gaelic Scotland, and they employed a loose form of syllabic metre."[8]

Although the Ossianic ballads that Macpherson may have heard were composed, according to Meek, no earlier than the thirteenth century, their subject matter was much more ancient, relating events that would have occurred during the heroic period of the history of the Celtic peoples of Scotland and Ireland, between the first and third centuries AD. In his "A Dissertation concerning the Antiquity &c. of the Poems of Ossian the Son of Fingal," Macpherson explained to his readers that he made these journeys "in order to recover what remained of the works of Ossian the son of Fingal, the best, as well as the most ancient of those who are celebrated in tradition for their poetical genius."[9] Macpherson's mission to collect and transcribe the Ossianic ballads still in circulation in the Scottish Highlands of his day was not futile. According to Paul J. deGategno, "Evidence exists to validate his success in finding Gaelic fragments of ballads and of other tattered manuscripts; he transcribed as well some oral recitations of Ossianic legend that he gathered from various residents. In just a few weeks Macpherson had collected nearly forty-five hundred words of authentic Gaelic poetry and had received promises from a number of his collaborators for further deliveries of material."[10]

The most striking parallel between Tolkien and Macpherson is that they both understood the relevance of preserving the epic language used to record the ancient deeds of a nation to preserve the cultural integrity of a nation itself. Macpherson's attempt to reconstruct a prehistoric history for Scotland through his Ossianic poems can be compared in some respects with Tolkien's project to create a mythology for England through the creation of languages and proper names that reflected England's past cultural diversity. Both authors sought to write missing chapters in the history of their respective cultures. As translator of the ancient Gaelic ballads, Macpherson sought to restore to urbanized Lowland Scots who knew no Gaelic a national epic that had remained buried in obscurity in the most remote parts of the Highlands and the isles for more than a millennium. In response to readers of *Fragments of Ancient Poetry* who wondered why "poems admired for many centuries in one part of the kingdom should be hitherto unknown in the other," Macpherson offered the following explanation: "This is to be imputed to those who understood both languages and never attempted a translation. They. . .despaired of making the compositions of their bards agreeable to an English reader. The manner of these compositions is so different from other poems, and the ideas so confined to the most early state of society, that it was thought they had not enough of variety to please a polished age."[11] Like Tolkien, Macpherson understood that language is at the root of national identity. His translation and reconstruction of the Gaelic ballads attributed to the bard Ossian was as much an attempt to reclaim for Scotland heroes such as Cú Chulainn and Fingal as it was an effort to preserve the ancient Gaelic tongue. Macpherson devotes a good portion of the dissertation that serves as an introduction to *Temora, an Ancient Epic Poem*, at the beginning of the second volume of *The Works of Ossian, the Son of Fingal*, to proving that Scottish Gaelic was more ancient (and thus more authentic) than the Irish Gaelic from which it was thought to descend:

> The first circumstance that induced me to disregard the vulgarly-received opinion of the Hibernian extraction of the Scottish nation, was my observations

on their antient [*sic*] language. That dialect of the Celtic tongue, spoken in the north of Scotland, is much more pure, more agreeable to its mother language, and more abounding with primitives, than that now spoken, or even that which has been writ for some centuries back, amongst the most unmixed part of the Irish nation. . . . This affords a proof, that the Scotch Galic [*sic*] is the most original, and consequently, a language of a more antient [*sic*] and unmixed people.

Significantly, Macpherson's claim that the Scots are a more ancient people than the Irish is based on purely linguistic considerations: "From internal proofs it sufficiently appears, that the poems published under the name of Ossian, are not of Irish composition. The favourite chimaera, that Ireland is the mother-country of the Scots, is totally subverted."[12]

As Fiona Stafford notes in *The Sublime Savage*, Macpherson's effort to translate or reconstruct Gaelic poetry would have not met with as much controversy had he omitted his "Dissertation" from the volume containing *Temora*. Macpherson's claims about the greater antiquity and purity of Scottish Gaelic provoked a host of rebuttals from scholars of Irish Gaelic and Welsh as well as skepticism from early supporters of Macpherson, such as his fellow-Scot David Hume and the English poet Thomas Gray. Accusations of historical inaccuracy were followed by accusations of forgery, particularly from Samuel Johnson, who had never believed in the authenticity of any of the poems. However, Stafford makes another point that is more pertinent to the reception of the poems than questions about their historical authenticity: scholars and literati aside, the vast majority of readers *did not care* whether the poems were a translation of originals, a reconstruction of fragments, or a product entirely of Macpherson's own poetic imagination: "Despite the critical attention that Macpherson received from scholars and antiquarians, most of the enthusiasm for Ossian came from readers who were quite unconcerned about the sources of the work. They sought ancient literature not for historical or philological reasons, but as an escape from the advancing civilisation of eighteenth-century Europe."[13]

In the "Note on the Shire Records" that is found at the end of the prologue to the *Lord of the Rings*, Tolkien writes as a scribe/narrator who is retelling for his own audience a story that has already been told and retold by many other scribes: it is a story so ancient that it can be traced to an age when histories, poems, and tales existed only in oral form, as in the Celtic heroic age celebrated by Macpherson: "At the end of the Third Age the parts played by the Hobbits in the great events that led to the inclusion of the Shire in the Reunited Kingdom awakened among them a more wide-spread interest in their own history; and many of their traditions, up to that time still mainly oral, were collected and written down" (*LR*, prologue, 13). Unlike Macpherson, Tolkien never claimed that *The Hobbit*, *The Lord of the Rings*, or *The Silmarillion* were anything other than his own creations. However, Tolkien explained to Milton Waldman, an editor at Allen and Unwin, that "always I had the sense of recording what was already 'there', somewhere: not of 'inventing' " (*Letters*, 145). Tolkien's own project, therefore, was not unlike the project of the Hobbits as described by the narrator of the prologue; he wished to reconstruct in writing a history that "was already 'there', somewhere." Whether they were working from texts that actually existed (as is the case with some of Macpherson's Ossianic poems) or reconstructing a history that might have existed, "somewhere," the literary genius of Macpherson and Tolkien lay in their ability to create myths for their own time in a style that was accessible to their contemporary audiences without losing a sense of historical and linguistic authenticity.

But the very act of reconstructing or recovering implies that something has been lost or is about to disappear. For Macpherson, this was the elimination of the traditional way of life and the language—Scottish Gaelic—of the Scottish Highlands through conquest and assimilation. As Fiona Stafford notes in her introduction to *The Poems of Ossian*, "It is in the context of systematic cultural destruction that Macpherson's efforts to collect old heroic poetry can be seen; they were, at least in part, an effort to repair some of the damage to the Highlands sustained in the wake of the Jacobite uprisings."[14] James Macpherson was only nine years old when the last attempt of the Stuarts to reclaim the thrones of Scotland and England came to a bloody end on the battlefield of Culloden. The crushing of the Jacobite forces led by Charles Edward Stuart, "Bonnie Prince Charlie," was more than a military defeat. In the wake of their victory, English forces led by the Duke of Cumberland pillaged, plundered, and burned their way through the last Jacobite strongholds in the Highlands, including the Macpherson stronghold in Ruthven. The young James Macpherson thus witnessed a heroic "last stand" of the Highlanders, and this would have an enormous impact on his reconstruction of the figure of the ancient Gaelic warrior in his Ossianic poetry: "The picture of these beaten men contradicted the young boy's vision of his countrymen as heroes—men whose humanity blended with courage in all their actions. Though his sentiments were shaken by the reality of the scene, Macpherson would never abandon his belief in the valor and nobility of the Highland warrior."[15]

During the years after Culloden, Macpherson saw the beginnings of the notorious Highland Clearances. "Crofters," or small landholders, were forced off their land, so that landlords could exploit the pastures for commercial purposes. As historian T.M. Devine notes, this was part of a trend that was destroying traditional ways of life in much of Europe: "The eighteenth and nineteenth centuries were an epoch of persistent rise in population, urban growth and industrial expansion and in virtually every European country the rural economy had to produce more food and raw materials at acceptable prices to feed and support the growing urban masses. . . .land was now principally to be seen as an asset and a productive resource to be managed according to its capacity for earning profit rather than as a basic source of support for the rural population."[16] The crofters received little economic compensation for their loss, and many succumbed to starvation when unable to support themselves by other means. John Prebble's preface to his history of the Highland Clearances, written in 1963, is in fact a moving elegy of the Highlander and a bitter reminder that "progress" does not come without a price: "It has been said that the Clearances are now far enough away from us to be decently forgotten. But the hills are still empty. In all of Britain only among them can one find real solitude, and if their history is known there is no satisfaction to be got from the experience. . . .The chiefs remain, in Edinburgh and London, but the people are gone. Finally we have become so civilized in our behaviour, or more concerned with profit than men, that this story holds no lesson for us."[17]

The overwhelming sense of loss that Prebble felt when he gazed upon the hills of the Highlands was mitigated for the eighteenth-century visitor by the spirit of Ossian. Stafford cites Tobias Smollett's novel *Humphrey Clinker* as one of many artistic and literary works from the latter part of the eighteenth century that bears witness to the healing effect that Macpherson's poems, real or invented, had on many of his compatriots: "These are the lonely hills of Morven, where Fingal and his heroes enjoyed the same pastime: I feel an enthusiastic pleasure when I survey the brown heath that Ossian wont to tread; and hear the wind whistle through the bending grass—When I enter our landlord's hall, I look for the suspended harp of that divine bard, and listen in hopes of hearing the aerial sound of his respected spirit."[18]

The childhood and early manhood of both Tolkien and Macpherson were marked by war and ensuing destruction and loss. The defining moment for the young James Macpherson was his witnessing of the defeat of the Highland warriors, and the ancient traditions they represented, at the hands of a more organized, imperial army, followed by the gradual disappearance of indigenous Highland culture. As a combatant in World War I, the young J.R.R. Tolkien was also a witness to scenes of death and destruction that would leave their impact on his work. While Tolkien did not believe that either World War I or World War II had any influence on the development of the actual plot of *The Lord of the Rings*, he did acknowledge that "The Dead Marshes and the approaches to the Morannen owe something to Northern France after the Battle of the Somme" (*Letters*, 303). In *Tolkien and the Great War*, John Garth evokes the gruesome landscape of the Western Front through which Tolkien and his comrades stumbled after a "victory" over German forces: "This was land newly taken from the Germans, and at high cost. So it was on the approach to Ovilliers that Tolkien first encountered the lost of the Somme: heralded by their stench, darkly hunched or prone, or hanging on the wire until a stab of brightness revealed them, the bloated and putrescent dead."[19] These horrific memories of the Somme are echoed in "The Passage of the Marshes," in which Frodo and Sam, led by Gollum, come face to face with the dead of an ancient battle. Frodo says: "They lie in the pools, pale faces, deep deep under the dark water. I saw them: grim faces and evil, and noble faces and sad. Many faces proud and fair, and weeds in their silver hair. But all foul, all rotting, all dead" (*LR* IV. 11, 614). Tolkien's loss was also deeply personal, as all but one of his closest friends were killed in the war.

For Tolkien, the sense of loss was not linked to one defining moment but was rather an accumulated sense of loss of which he had always been aware. "I was from early days grieved by the poverty of my own beloved country—it had no stories of its own (bound up with its tongue and soil), not of the quality that I sought, and found (as an ingredient) in legends of other lands" (*Letters*, 144). In England, the loss of a native language and lore had begun with the Roman invasion of Britain and had continued throughout the subsequent Saxon and Norman invasions. This has long posed a challenge not only to philologists like Tolkien but also to archaeologists, anthropologists, and historians: "For, unlike such peoples as the Goths and the Anglo-Saxons, the Britons were disrupted in the process of forming Iron Age identities by the Romans, who introduced (or imposed) other identities: Roman (cultural Romanization), *civis* (political citizenship), and eventually (for some) Christian. Then, with the Roman political and military apparatus withdrawn ca. 410, the Britons were forced once more into reexamining their identity, this time in the face of Germanic invaders/settlers."[20]

Tolkien was also deeply concerned with the loss of a traditional lifestyle and landscape in his native Warwickshire: "Nobody cares for the woods as I care for them" could have been spoken just as well by Tolkien himself as by Treebeard, the Ent, head shepherd of the trees, who rouses the other Ents and the very forest itself to destroy Saruman's munitions factory at Isengard (*LR* 3.4, 461). In a letter to the Houghton Mifflin Company, Tolkien felt it important to mention his love for all living things, especially trees: "I am (obviously) much in love with plants and above all trees, and always have been; and I find human mistreatment of them as hard to bear as some find ill-treatment of animals" (*Letters*, 220). In another letter, Tolkien remarked that while there was no specific post–World War II reference in *The Lord of the Rings*, "the spirit of 'Isengard' if not of Mordor, is always cropping up. The present design of destroying Oxford in order to accommodate motor-cars is a case" (*Letters*, 235).

For Tolkien, loss was a continuous process. In this light, it is understandable that Tolkien would be somewhat irritated by allegations that *The Lord of the Rings* was an allegory of World War II: to link his work to that particular war, as horrible as it was, would be to overlook much of what Tolkien was elegizing in his work. Aragorn's response to Frodo when asked about the "Tale of Tinúviel" could serve as a poetic response to Tolkien's readers who asked about the "meaning" of the *Lord of the Rings*: "It is a long tale of which the end is not known. . . . It is a fair tale, though it is sad, as are all the tales of Middle-earth, and yet it may lift up you heart" (*LR* 1.XI,187).

As Aragorn's comment suggests, the telling of a tale—even a sad tale—provides solace for the poet or performer and the listener alike. Tolkien's characters, each in their own turn, fulfill the role of the bard in ancient Celtic society "Pleasant are the words of the song, said Cuchullin, and lovely are the tales of other times."[21] Through the poetic process, things and persons who have long disappeared are remembered and recovered in language, and thus become part of the eternal present, the present of the very act of telling a tale or listening to a song. *The Lord of the Rings* abounds with songs, tales, and poems in elegiac form, evoking beings who have long departed Middle-earth, but who continue to live on in collective or individual memory. Thus the fallen of the Battle of Pelennor Fields are eulogized many years later by a poet who was not even an eyewitness to the event:

So long afterward a maker in Rohan said in his song of the Mounds of Mundburg:
We heard of the horns on the hills ringing,
The swords shining in the South-kingdom.
Steeds went striding to the Stoningland
As wind in the morning. War was kindled. . . ,
Death in the morning and at days's ending
Lords took and lowly. Long now they sleep,
under grass in Gondor by the Great River.
Grey now as tears, gleaming silver,
Red then it rolled, roaring water. (*LR* 5.6, 831)

The fallen of the battle, Théoden, Thengly, Hirluin the Fair, Horn and Fastred, and others, are called to mind by their names and are preserved not only in the maker's song, but in the very landscape itself. The use of the present tense to describe what has become of the warriors, "Long now they sleep under grass in Gondor. . .," has a soothing effect, as it suggests that Théoden and his companions in arms are still present in the land on which they fought. One notes a similar use of the elegiac form, with a pre-romantic emphasis on nature as reflective of human emotions, in the ossianic poems of the James Macpherson:

> Autumn is dark on the mountains;
> grey mists rest on the hills. The whirlwind
> is heard on the heath. Dark rolls the river thro'
> the narrow plain. A tree stands alone on a hill,
> and marks the grave of Connal.[22]

In Tolkien's work, however, the natural world does not exist merely to enhance or reflect the thoughts and feelings of humans; beings in Middle-earth, whether they be humans, Elves, Dwarves, hobbits or Ents, as part of an organic whole; all feel sadness and distress as they witness the loss and destruction of any part of their universe. Thus Treebeard the Ent laments the lands upon which he once strode, and which now lie under the waves (*LR* 3.4, 458), Merry and Pippin are lulled to sleep by the song of Bregalad, "that seemed to lament in many tongues the fall of trees that he had loved" (*LR* 3.4, 472), Legolas laments the loss of Nimrodel and her lover Amroth (*LR* 2.6, 332), Gimli recalls the golden age of the Dwarrowdelf, realm of Durin, when "The world was young, the mountains green, No stain yet on the moon was seen" (*LR* 2.4, 308), and so on. There is a pervasive sense of loss throughout *The Lord of The Rings*, of a world which is slipping away before the characters' (and the readers') eyes, and which will never return, except in songs and stories. Treebeard, whose memory is among the longest in Middle-earth, understands fully well that while language may memorialize the past, it can never fully revive it. " 'Now the last march of the Ents may be worth a song. Aye,' he sighed, 'we may help the other peoples before we pass away. Still, I should have liked to see the songs come true about the Entwives. I should dearly have liked to see Fimbrethil again. But there, my friends, songs like trees bear fruit only in their own time and their own way; and sometimes they are withered untimely' " (*LR* 3.4, 475).

Treebeard's words, spoken as he leads the other Ents in their last march toward Isengard, where they will take a stand against the evil perpetrated there before disappearing from Middle-earth, could be read as a commentary on the limitations of the recuperative power of language. If language only helps one remember what has been lost, but is incapable of bringing it back, then one might conclude that Tolkien's effort to construct a national identity for England through reconstructing past languages, history, and mythology was merely a linguistic and literary tour de force, which commands our admiration, and even "lifts up our hearts," to paraphrase Aragorn, but will likely bear no fruit for future generations. Treebeard, in his wisdom, understands that when language ceases to create meaning, when it is used only to recall a dead past, civilization itself is threatened: "Elves began it, of course, waking trees up and teaching them to speak and learning their tree-talk. . . .But then the Great Darkness came, and they passed away over the Sea, or fled into far valleys, and hid themselves, and made songs about days that would never come again" (*LR* 3.4, 457).

Language can be used, in appropriate circumstances, to memorialize, but its primary function is to communicate, to express meaning in ways that others around us can understand. Language is also a reflection of culture, in that the language or languages that spring from a particular culture reflect the way in which that culture experiences and understands the world. Middle-earth is a multilingual and multicultural universe in which linguistic changes reflect the history of its peoples. Thus Quenya and Sindarin develop into separate languages after the sundering of the Elves, and the Hobbits abandon their original language for the Common Tongue, or Westron, once they settle in the westlands of Eriador. During the time frame of the story, the Third Age, the Elves, the Dwarves, the Ents, the Rohirrim, the Wild Men and the Dunlendings still speak their own languages, although most can communicate with other groups in the Common Tongue, the *lingua franca* of the free peoples of Middle-earth. The ability and willingness to communicate with other ethnic and linguistic groups is an important trait of most of the inhabitants of Middle-earth, and a key factor in the ultimate defeat of Sauron by the free peoples. The members of the Fellowship can all communicate in the Common Tongue; in addition to this, Aragorn and Frodo have varying degrees of competence in Elvish.

The Orcs, by contrast, have trouble communicating even among themselves. After he is abducted by a group of Uruk-Hai and bound hand and foot, Pippin lies listening to the sounds of orc voices: "There were many voices round about, and though orc-speech sounded at all times full of hate and anger, it seemed plain that something like a quarrel had begun, and was getting hotter. To Pippin's surprise he found that much of the talk was intelligible; many of the Orcs were using ordinary language. Apparently the members of two or three quite different tribes were present, and they could not understand one another's orc-speech" (*LR* 3.3, 435). The orcs' inability to communicate with each other reflects their selfish, unempathetic nature and the fact that they are not united in a common cause, but are out for individual gain. Perhaps the most poignant illustration of the healing and empathetic language can be found in a passage in "The Mirror of Galadriel." After Celeborn castigates Gimli for provoking Gandalf's death through passing through the mines of Moria, ancient dwelling of the Dwarves, Galadriel comes to Gimli's defense by describing the "many-pillared halls of Khazad-dûm" as fair in Elder Days: "And the dwarf, hearing the names given in his own ancient tongue, looked up and met her eyes; and it seemed to him that he looked suddenly into the heart of an enemy and saw there love and understanding" (*LR* 2.7, 347) Galadriel's willingness to use language of the demonized "Other" smooths over the enmity that exists between Elf and Dwarf; prejudice and mistrust melt away, as Celeborn apologizes for his words, and Legolas, to the astonishment of all of the company, becomes Gimli's closest friend.

Tolkien's claim that his stories were written primarily to provide a world for his languages provides an important insight into the function of language not only within these stories, but also within society. If the invention of languages is the foundation of *The Lord of the Rings*, then it is clear that Tolkien's project of historical and linguistic reconstruction has, first of all, significant implications for understanding the importance of language in the shaping of nations and cultures. When Legolas sings a song in Sindarin, for example, it is because that language is the best expression of the collective memory of his people. His willingness—when able—to translate such a song into the Common Tongue is a sign of his desire to understand and be understood by others. Tolkien and Macpherson both understood that when a language disappears from the earth, a culture will likely follow it into oblivion, and this is why they insisted so much—in their own ways—on linguistic authenticity in their works. Secondly, if language is the foundation for Middle-earth, Tolkien's recreation of an English past that could have been, then the England that Tolkien is presenting as a foundation of today's English society is a multiethnic, multicultural and multilingual one, in which the coexistence of various linguistic idioms within the same borders enhances, rather than threatens, harmony between the various ethnic groups represented by these idioms.

The key to ultimate victory of the free peoples of Middle-earth over the standardization and mechanization represented by Isengard is a respect for the Other, exemplified in a willingness to understand and communicate in the language of the Other. The ramifications of Tolkien's multilingual universe for the linguistic and political map as it is currently evolving in the developed world is profound. The existence of one or several global "common tongues" should not—must not—lead to the disappearance of other languages. As beautiful as it is, Sindarin is not the same as the lost Britonnic language on which it is based. Had the Celtic languages, poetry, and ancient epics of Tolkien's England survived, *The Lord of The Rings* may never have been written; but then, this would have been another great cultural loss.

Notes

1. J.R.R. Tolkien, *The Letters of J.R.R. Tolkien: A Selection*, ed. Humphrey Carpenter, with the assistance of Christopher Tolkien (London; Boston: G. Allen and Unwin, 2000), 219 (hereafter cited in text and notes as *Letters*).
2. Karl Horst Schmidt, "Insular Celtic: P and Q Celtic," in *The Celtic Languages*, ed. Martin J. Ball (London: Routledge, 1993), 75.
3. Kenneth Jackson, "The British Languages and Their Evolution," in *The Mediaeval World*, ed. D. Daiches and A. Thorlby (London: Aldus Books, 1973), 113, quoted in Schmidt, "Insular Celtic: P and Q Celtic," 75.
4. Christopher A. Snyder, *The Britons* (Oxford: Blackwell Publishing, 2003), 255.
5. J.R.R. Tolkien, "English and Welsh," in *Angles and Britons: O'Donnell Lectures*, ed. J.R.R. Tolkien et al. (Cardiff: University of Wales Press, 1963), 1, 11 (hereafter cited in text and notes as "English and Welsh").
6. *The Oxford Universal Dictionary on Historical Principles*, 3rd edn. (1964; repr. London: Oxford University Press, 1933), s.v. "Ossianic."
7. Hugh Blair, "A Critical Dissertation on the Poems of Ossian, the Son of Fingal" (1763), in *The Poems of Ossian and Related Works/James Macpherson*, ed. Howard Gaskill (Edinburgh: University Press, 1966), 354.
8. Donald Meek, "The Gaelic Ballads of Scotland: Creativity and Adaptation," in *Ossian Revisited*, ed. Howard Gaskill (Edinburgh: Edinburgh University Press, 1991), 20.
9. James Macpherson, "A Dissertation concerning the Antiquity &c. of the Poems of Ossian the Son of Fingal," in *The Works of Ossian the Son of Fingal, in Two Volumes, Translated from the Galic [sic] Language, vol. I containing Fingal, an Ancient Epic Poem in Six Books and Several Other Poems* (London, 1765), in Gaskill, *The Poems of Ossian and Related Works*, 51.
10. See Paul J. deGategno, *James Macpherson* (Boston: Twayne Publishers, 1989), 31. See Meek, "The Gaelic Ballads of Scotland," 20.
11. Macpherson, "Dissertation," 50.
12. James Macpherson, "A Dissertation," in *The Works of Ossian the Son of Fingal, in Two Volumes, Translated from the Galic [sic] Language, vol. II containing Temora, an Ancient Epic Poem in Eight Books and Several Other Poems, the Third Edition to which is subjoined "A Critical Dissertation on the Poems of Ossian," by Hugh Blair* (London, 1765), in Gaskill, *The Poems of Ossian and Related Works*, 216–17.
13. Fiona Stafford, *The Sublime Savage: A Study of James Macpherson and the Poems of Ossian* (Edinburgh: Edinburgh University Press, 1988), 171.
14. Fiona Stafford, "The Ossianic Poems of James Macpherson," introduction to Gaskill, *The Poems of Ossian and Related Works*, x.
15. deGategno, *James Macpherson*, 11.
16. T.M. Devine, *The Scottish Nation: A History, 1700–2000* (New York: Viking, 1999), 178.
17. John Prebble, foreword to *The Highland Clearances* (Harmondsworth: Penguin Books, 1969).

18. Tobias Smollett, *Humphrey Clinker* (1771), ed. L.M. Knapp (London, New York: Oxford University Press, 1966), 240, quoted in Stafford, *Sublime Savage*, 167.
19. John Garth, *Tolkien and the Great War: The Threshold of Middle-Earth* (Boston and New York: Houghton Mifflin, 2003), 164.
20. Snyder, *Britons*, 4.
21. James Macpherson, *Fingal, an Ancient Epic Poem in Six Books*, in *The Works of Ossian the Son of Fingal, in Two Volumes, Translated from the Galic [sic] Language, vol. I containing Fingal, an Ancient Epic Poem in Six Books and Several Other Poems*, the Third Edition (London, 1765), in Gaskill, *The Poems of Ossian and Related Works*, 73.
22. James Macpherson, *Fragments of Ancient Poetry, Collected in the Highlands of Scotland, and translated from the Galic [sic] or Erse language*, The Second Edition, 1760, in Gaskill, *The Poems of Ossian and Related Works*, 354.

PART THREE

CONFRONTING MODERN IDEOLOGIES IN MIDDLE-EARTH: WAR, ECOLOGY, RACE, AND GENDER

CHAPTER 9

FANTASTIC MEDIEVALISM AND THE GREAT WAR IN J.R.R. TOLKIEN'S *THE LORD OF THE RINGS*

Rebekah Long

This essay examines Tolkien's project in tandem with David Jones's In Parenthesis, *with special attention to the ways in which each post–World War I text echoes Chaucer's* Knight's Tale *to speak to the horror of the Great War.*

Never since the Middle Ages, when the church taught its lessons by means of pictures to people who could not read the written word, has art been called upon to serve in so many ways.

—Anonymous Critic

You feel exposed and apprehensive in this new world.

—David Jones

In 1918, the last year of his life, Wilfred Owen wrote "Strange Meeting."[1] An artifact of Owen's war experiences, this dense poem breaks through the borders of war-language by articulating a supernatural postmortem exchange between the dreaming speaker of the poem and the enemy he killed in battle. Owen's poem renders a jagged portrait of the merciless effects of modern warfare and violence. As Allen Frantzen has noted, "Strange Meeting" is a "visionary work," rejecting an earlier "realism," and imagining instead a new language of violence that burns out from the inside, ravaging bodies, ruining the integrity of its participants.[2] Words are corroded as poetic phrases double back on themselves, while the clanging consonant slant rhymes establish a mood of tense, dissonant familiarity:

> Courage was mine, and I had mystery,
> Wisdom was mine, and I had mastery:
> To miss the march of this retreating world
> Into vain citadels that are not walled.
> Then, when much blood had clogged their chariot-wheels,
> I would go up and wash them from sweet wells,
> Even with truths that lie too deep for taint.
> I would have poured my spirit without stint
> But not through wounds; not on the cess of war.
> Foreheads of men have bled where no wounds were.
>
> I am the enemy you killed, my friend.
> I knew you in this dark: for so you frowned
> Yesterday through me as you jabbed and killed.
> I parried; but my hands were loath and cold.
> Let us sleep now. . . .[3]

Through Owen's use of assonance, the enemy's sense of "mystery" becomes something that is missed, the numinous victim to the cold, bleak hardness of war; "mastery" fades into the march of war's caustic energy, its brutal, inflexible syntax. The poem switches voice from the speaker to the enemy, who indicates his status as the one "you jabbed and killed, my friend," with a recognition of mutual complicity in an act that has left both the speaker and his victim in a blank hell laced with despair, ultimately robbed of language as the poem's contracted last line falls off into silence.

In the epigraph from A.E. Gallatin's 1919 discussion of art's political role during the Great War, the quotation from David Jones's 1937 epic Great War poem *In Parenthesis*, and in my reading of Owen's "Strange Meeting," we discover several themes that find expression in the fantastic medievalism of World War I veteran J.R.R. Tolkien.[4] Literature of the fantastic and the experience of war share a fundamental bond. In each maps are redrawn, new worlds are created, and the given is dismantled. An unlearning takes place: "Wisdom *was* mine, and I *had* mastery." As Brian Attebery has delineated in his analysis of the fantastic as mode, "The fantastic strain of storytelling is particularly dependent upon the open-endedness of language: the fact that there are always more sentences available to the native speaker than there are situations to call for them."[5] Unlike the mode of literary realism, which relies upon an "economy of significance," fantastic literature relentlessly reconceives existing systems of meaning-making; the limits of language are tested.[6]

The reader of fantasy and the soldier find themselves inhabiting an in-between twilight space, a No-Man's Land of linguistic disintegration. "Violence destroys fiction," James Dawes contends in *The Language of War*, "shattering the cherished fictions that structure our routines of life." "In landscapes of blasted homes and bloated corpses," Dawes explains, "words of explanation fall to the ground like brittle and frail autumn leaves."[7] In Tolkien's 1954 novel *The Lord of the Rings* the Great War's violence defies the prescriptions of realism, accosting us with an "arresting strangeness."[8] Tom Shippey, in *J.R.R. Tolkien: Author of the Century*, observes that the turn to the fantastic in twentieth-century literature is linked to the experience of modern warfare, not as avoidance, "the flight of the deserter," but as testimony to the newness of this horror,[9] an opinion shared by Tolkien biographer John Garth.[10] War informs the fantastic landscape of Tolkien's narrative; in *The Lord of the Rings* verbal topography is unearthed, widened, and resown.

In a letter dated September 25, 1954, Tolkien writes to Naomi Mitchinson about *The Lord of the Rings*: "But in any case this is a tale about war, and if war is allowed (at least as a topic and a setting) it is not much good complaining that all the people on one side are against those on the other. Not that I have made even this issue quite so simple: there are Saruman, and Denethor, and Boromir; and there are treacheries and strife even among the Orcs."[11] Tolkien responds in this letter to criticisms of the portrayal of the fight between good and evil in *The Lord of the Rings* as "simple-minded"—as Tolkien phrases it, "just a plain fight between Good and Evil." Tolkien remarks that this reductive tendency is "pardonable, perhaps (though at least Boromir has been overlooked) in people in a hurry, and with only a fragment to read" (*Letters*, 197). To reduce *The Lord of the Rings* to a "plain fight between Good and Evil" relies upon a fragment of its narrative, a superficial shard, obscuring its depths, its intricately resolved forms of medievalism. It is a book about war; it is also an important fiction about remembering.

Tolkien once stated, "One war is enough for any man."[12] If this is the case, that to suffer war, with its waste, is *enough*, then why spend over a decade returning to the psychological situation of war by writing a book seared by its violence? And a book about war that speaks from the past to the present? *The Lord of the Rings* was written during World War II, but is shadowed by the world-ending violence of World War I. In the foreword to the second edition of *The Lord of the Rings*, Tolkien famously denies that his massive, ambitious novel is an allegory of World War II, telling his audience, who may have "forgotten," "that to be caught in youth" by the Great War was "hideous." This call to remember is followed by the well-known statement: "By 1918 all but one of my close friends were dead."[13] The proximity of Tolkien's rejection of a particular, limited mode of interpretation to his rhetorically graceful pairing of communal forgetting *and* personal loss suggests a way of receiving *The Lord of the Rings* as a commemorative fiction. We can view *The Lord of the Rings* not as an allegory of the Great War, enacting a crude correlation between historical event and artistic representation, but as a recollection of it—a literary work, like Owen's "Strange Meeting" and David Jones's *In Parenthesis*, which investigates the creative work of memory in reply to the trauma of war. Fantasy, conceived in Tolkien's novel as a dialogic process of invention and remembrance, allows for a return to the war that is not documentary or allegorical in approach but *memorial*.

"To write about World War I, or any war," Allen Frantzen writes in *Bloody Good: Chivalry, Sacrifice, and the Great War*, "is to ask how the living can learn from the dead."[14] During the Great War, as Frantzen shows, the "dead" medieval past was being revived; medieval iconography and chivalric narratives were being revisited and called up in a rich conversation concerning chivalric motifs of "sacrifice" and "antisacrifice" in this new martial context. "The Middle Ages and World War I were inextricably linked by the enduring power of chivalry to symbolize both prowess and principle in warfare," Frantzen argues.[15] Tolkien, a postwar writer, poses questions about our recollections of the Middle Ages by remembering the dead in a manner that responds to reclamations of the medieval past during the Great War. Tolkien's look backward is not nostalgic or a reveling in "betrayed idealism."[16] It is a conscious and sophisticated meditation on the stakes of medievalism, a revelation that our view of the medieval past is tinted by modern appropriations of it.

The concerns that drive Tolkien's fiction can also be seen in the poetry of his contemporary David Jones. By using a form of fantastic medievalism, *In Parenthesis* treats the intersection of the Middle Ages with modern warfare in a manner comparable to that of *The Lord of the Rings*. Jones's poem invites the medieval past into the reader's present by focusing the panorama of the war through the eyes of the poem's central figure John Ball, the enigmatic preacher of the 1381 Peasants' Revolt, here resurrected in the trenches. In his preface to *In Parenthesis*, Jones indicates that at every moment during his World War I military service he was reminded of past poetic portrayals of war, "complexities of sight and sound" making present past literary–martial episodes, while every man's speech was a "perpetual showing" of John Ball, of the commons-in-arms.[17] *In Parenthesis* is a protean linguistic entity, exploring dialects and tones, Welsh, and cockney. Jones's difficult poem explores and elaborates on this verbal significance—the way words register war. Language in the poem undergoes a revision; representation acquires a startling expansiveness as evidenced in the moment John Ball endures a shell-fire attack:

> John Ball stood patiently, waiting for the
> eloquence to spend itself. The tedious flow continued, then
> broke off very suddenly. He looked straight at Sergeant Snell
> enquiringly—whose eyes changed queerly, who ducked in
> under the low entry. John Ball would have followed, but
> stood fixed and alone in the little yard—his senses highly
> alert, his body incapable of movement or response. The
> exact disposition of small things—the precise shapes of
> trees, the tilt of a bucket, the movement of a straw, the
> disappearing right foot of Sergeant Snell—all minute
> noises, separate and distinct, in a stillness charged through
> with some approaching violence. . .—registered not by the ear
> nor any single faculty—an on-rushing pervasion, saturating
> all existence; with exactitude, logarithmic, dial-timed,
> millesimal—of calculated velocity, some mean chemist's
> contrivance, a stinking physicist's destroying toy.[18]

Jones's poetic language is furious, splitting the bounds of the poetic form itself as phrases, strung together with commas and dashes, rush forward. In this stanzaic sepulcher, Jones's backward glance is shown to be polemical and provocative, not tinged with a Victorian golden twilight. This is not the John Ball of William Morris's *A Dream of John Ball*, who speaks to the Victorian time-traveling narrator about life after death and self-sacrifice in the name of a cause, who trusts in Morris's narrator's socialist vision; nor is this the wandering heretic, armed with "pleasing words," of Thomas Walsingham's or other fourteenth-century chroniclers' reports.[19] The John Ball of *In Parenthesis* has been asked to stand in and see on behalf of the twentieth-century reader, as a fantastically out-of-time observer of the Great War's violence.

In his introduction to *In Parenthesis*, T.S. Eliot gives a description of Jones's poem that shares similarities with Tolkien's own accounts of *The Lord of the Rings*: "It is a book about War, and about many other things as also, such as Roman Britain, the Arthurian Legend, and diverse matters which are given association by the mind of the writer."[20] Jones's poem, displaying, as Eliot puts it, "the Celtic ear for the music of words,"[21] marries the fantastic to the medieval to rework the legacy of the Great War, to unravel its war-language. John Ball's gaze is sharp and his reactions raw, not narrowed by martial ideals, by fantasies about what war means, but achingly aware, silently watching the deadening aftermath, "ashen."

By reading Jones's poem alongside *The Lord of the Rings*, we can appreciate both the writers' exquisite sensitivity to the aesthetic and linguistic representation of violence (with what words we speak about war) and their attentiveness to the problems of associating it with the Middle Ages. In *The Lord of the Rings* violence resists displacement into an idealized, flattened chivalric history—an empty simulacrum of martial idealism—to erupt instead into the present, into the reader's awareness, with a resounding forcefulness. Critical accounts of *The Lord of the Rings* that read its interest in the medieval as sentimental fail to recognize the complex treatment of war in both Tolkien's novel and its medieval influences and the conversation, vibrant, powerful, and political, that takes place between them. Tolkien interrogates the chivalric code in *The Lord of the Rings*, responding critically to strains of medieval-themed propaganda circulating in England during the Great War, including notions of chivalry displayed in the iconography of well-known recruitment posters featuring England's patron saint, St. George, slaying the dragon. Allen Frantzen comments on the weird tranquility of this popular, seductive image: "A massive bloody war is represented and glorified in single combat."[22]

Like Jones and Owen, Tolkien was marked indelibly by the Great War; he witnessed the Battle of the Somme. The Somme remained a lingering memory for Tolkien, a memory brought to life in *The Lord of the Rings* in a chapter entitled "The Passage of the Marshes." In this chapter, Frodo the Ringbearer, his friend Sam Gamgee, and Gollum make their way across the Dead Marshes, the site of a long-past battle, on the way to Mordor. In the Dead Marshes the wartime dead refuse to be frozen into patriotic memories; instead, vacant faces linger in dark pools of water. Tolkien states that Frodo's description of the marshes owed something to the battle of the Somme, its landscape of endless disruption, bodies reemerging perpetually from the earth: "They lie in all the pools, pale faces, deep deep under the dark water. I saw them: grim faces and evil, and noble faces and sad. Many faces proud and fair and weeds in their silver hair. But all foul, all rotting, all dead. A fell light is in them" (*LR* 4.2, 614).[23]

The Dead Marshes act as a sort of war memorial, as a textual actualization of the processes of memory, in which the dead refuse to be resolved into statuelike icons, idealized narratives of victory or defeat traced across their frozen surfaces. Instead, the dead *accuse*. Here we might think of Jay Winter's and Susan Sontag's discussions of the French film *J'accuse*, in which the Great War's dead confront the living. Sontag describes the film's final images, which share uncanny similarities to the Dead Marshes, as "a sea of impassive ghosts overrunning the cowering future combatants and victims of *la guerre de demain*."[24] Tolkien scholars have known that the landscape of the marshes was influenced by the torn earth, mud, and blood of the

Somme, but I would like to extend our reading of it past this analogy to consider how, and what, this textual moment asks us to recall.

In the Dead Marshes, the dead demand recognition, not for what was accomplished, but because they suffered. The dead have been forgotten, their suffering discounted, and they have been reduced to unnamed participants in a battle of the Second Age that has fallen out of memory. There is a sameness in suffering and death, "Elves and Men and Orcs" as Gollum says, distinctions eroded by the conjunctions. In Middle-earth, acts of remembrance are always foregrounded; here the dead demand the release of commemoration, but not the static tribute of a standard memorial. Black and gray, like the collodion plate images that depicted scenes from the Crimean War,[25] the marshes with their undead show us that death's brutal physicality defies attempts to shape war's ruptures into confined single-thread narratives. As witnesses to the marshes, we ask: who sees? Who will speak of this?

Here and elsewhere in *The Lord of the Rings*, Tolkien refuses to treat war as something-to-be-viewed, as a play of spectral knights assembled from assorted pieces of ghostly longings. It is, instead, a volcanic conversation in which myriad voices take part, uttering memories, mercy, rage, and, above all, grief. In this attention to the verbal–visual presentation of war inheres an interesting correspondence between *The Lord of the Rings* and one of its possible influences, Chaucer's "Knight's Tale."[26] David Aers has argued that, in the "Knight's Tale," Chaucer refuses to avoid the violence of chivalry, differing from Boccaccio by inserting a protracted section with "a sharply particularized focus on the body," concentrating on the "clinical detail" of bodily decay in the account of the death of Arcite.[27] War in the "Knight's Tale" is self-consciously treated and exposed as spectatorial—Theseus builds an elaborate, literal, "noble theater" of war in which to showcase the rivalry between Palamon and Arcite, an architecture of sheer artifice the knight lavishly describes:

> The circuit a myle was aboute,
> Walled of stoon, and dyched al withoute.
> Round was the shap, in manere of compas,
> Ful of degrees, the heighte of sixty pas.[28]

Throughout the knight's material-minded description of the theater, and the violent battle that takes place within it, the verb "to see" is emphatically repeated: the statue of Venus is "glorious for to se";[29] the night before the contest, "every wight" gets proper rest "for to seen the grete fight" in the morning.[30] Yet the dazzle of the initial parade into the theater, the bright shields and bridles, buckle into the battlefield; bodies are convulsed as the glittering facade of war gives way. We learn to read war not as a series of superficial visual cues but as a set of terms that will be bitterly redefined. What we see, and *how* we read these surfaces—flashing veneers as opposed to (literally) spoiled insides—is radically altered. Our eye acts as a vehicle of recognition and compassionate attachment—the martial play is no longer distant and in impersonal perspective so that every man can see but close, pungent, and pressing in its uncomfortable proximity. Our field of vision constricts to an image of Arcite's ruined body, as delight in engorged spectacle focuses into an acute sympathetic engagement that transforms the chivalric exercises in the noble theater of war into personal, physical devastation, "And every lacerte in his brest adoun / Is shent with venym and corrupcioun."[31] In *The Language of War*, James Dawes proposes that "sympathy is capable of becoming, as act, a point of shared psychic experience that allows for entry into the position of the other."[32] In the "Knight's Tale," and in *The Lord of the Rings*, our eyes see war's waste through moments of empathetic reciprocity. Frodo hides his eyes in his hands, turning away from the pale, pleading faces of the ghosts in the marshes, as the secrets these shifting phantasms reveal—sad stories of war that remain strangely unpunctuated, incapable of ending—nearly overwhelm. Meeting the gaze of the marshes' undead entails recognition, and this moment of recognition, this flash of sympathy, shatters, and converts.

Frodo covers his eyes; however, his view gradually changes, voiced finally in his urgent wish for "no killing" in the book's bitter second-to-last chapter, "The Scouring of the Shire": "All the same," said Frodo to all those who stood near, "I wish for no killing; not even of the ruffians, unless it must be done, to prevent them from hurting hobbits" (*LR* 6.8, 986–87). With its images of a spoiled Shire and murdered Hobbits, "The Scouring of the Shire" has a lasting sadness and a narrative resignation that makes its petty injustices seem excessively cruel. As readers, we long for respite after the War of the Ring with its desperate denouement, yet here we discover not rest but the novel's starkest explorations of violence, which approach us unexpectedly and without the clink of medieval warfare. Tolkien tells us that Hobbits have never been warlike; therefore, pictures of Hobbits killing and being killed, pictures made vivid through the wordplay of aggressive verbs ("hew," for example) that ring out oddly in the verbal topography of the Shire, seem incongruous and jarring, rough tears in the novel's aesthetic integration.

Tom Shippey raises the point that "one might wonder again about the 'applicability' of 'the Scouring of the Shire,' " noting Tolkien's denial that the chapter is an allegory of postwar industrialization. Tolkien claimed that the chapter had been "foreseen from the outset," Shippey recounts, rooted in Tolkien's early personal history.[33] Even so, it underwent a series of revisions, as Christopher Tolkien details, most conspicuously marked in Frodo's change from a figure "warlike and resolute in action" to a figure whose relationship to "weapons was personal."[34] It is in this chapter that war wrenches free from medieval history—the linguistic parameters of war's violence broaden again to spill into this last enclave, into the reader's presence.

Tolkien fundamentally rethinks the representation of violence in *The Lord of the Rings*, transforming it out of frameworks that seal bloodshed into a phantasmic and unreal chivalric history, through an innovative medievalism rooted in the novel's syntax and semantics, in the songs of the Rohirrim and the echoes of medieval elegy that haunt Lórien's verbal landscape.[35] The Shire, our territory as readers,[36] has been, at last, crippled by a language of violence that floats eerily into our consciousness, waking us, like a dimly tolling bell, from our dream. While the chapter laments industrialization, its aggression is not only directed internally at the fictional landscape; it lashes out, prompting us to look within. In the *Middle English Dictionary*, we find that the verb *scouren* ranges in semantic usage from the purely practical, "to cleanse or scrub;" to the martial, "to get rid of (an enemy)"; to the spiritual, "to spiritually scour."[37] This spiritual purgation, seen in the *MED*'s citation of the verb's usage in the fifteenth-century *Jacob's Well*, is enabled through unflinching self-reflection; the search for external threats becomes inwardly directed. If we think that once cleansed of Sharkey and his ruffians the Shire will wash its hands of the spot of war, we learn instead that war has become uncomfortably, insistently *personal* on both the level of narrative and in the chapter's aesthetics—we feel exposed and apprehensive as its violence shadows us in our return. "At last all was over," but we are haunted.

The Lord of the Rings understands the violence of war as a confrontation in words, one that asks us to acknowledge its diverse repercussions by rejecting the distorting lenses of ideologies, which used simplified narratives decorated with medieval iconography as persuasive propaganda during the Great War. In *The Great War and Modern Memory*, Paul Fussell writes that Tolkien and his contemporaries were raised on "Victorian pseudo-medieval romance" and brought these dreams of war into the trenches, while the language of euphemism obscured the actualities of the war.[38] In reaction to this euphemism, Tolkien in his fiction, like Jones in his poetry, searches for a new language of violence, and this language is set in the terms of an involved recovery (not evacuation) of the medieval past. John Garth, in his recent biography of Tolkien's World War I experiences, hopes we may someday see Tolkien as the epic poet of the Great War. He elaborates, "Middle-earth...looks so familiar to us and speaks to us so eloquently because it was born with the modern world and marked by the same terrible birth pangs."[39] Concerned with imbuing forgotten poetic forms and languages with new life, Tolkien wrought his romance out of the past and turned its words into an account of the misery of war.

"I think that 'victors' can never enjoy 'victory'—not in the terms that they envisaged," Tolkien wrote in a letter dated 1956.[40] The experience of war calls for a fundamental transformation of literary representation. That effect results in a consciousness of the limited depth and reach of terms not interrogated before the disruption of the battlefield. It nurtures a desire to stretch language out of stasis into awareness, away from framed reflection to the fantastic: "as to this hour / when unicorns break cover / and come down."[41]

Notes

I would like to thank Douglas A. Anderson and Fiona Somerset for reading earlier drafts of this essay and for offering thoughtful suggestions for revision. I would also like to thank audiences at the 25th annual International Conference on the Fantastic in the Arts, March 2004, and the 39th annual International Congress on Medieval Studies, May 2004, for suggestions and comments on earlier drafts of this essay. A special thanks goes to Brian Attebery and the members of the ICFA awards committee who selected my essay as the 2004 recipient of the Outstanding Graduate Student Paper award.

1. The first epigraph is taken from a quotation credited to an unnamed critic in A.E. Gallatin, *Art and the Great War* (New York: E. P. Dutton, 1919), 33. Gallatin comments that artists served an important function as propagandists during the Great War: "This was the first war artists, as such, were used by their governments, and art became a powerful weapon" (21). The second epigraph comes from David Jones, *In Parenthesis* (New York: New York Review Books, 2003), 9. Wilfred Owen, "Strange Meeting," in *The Poems*, vol. 1 of *Wilfred Owen: The Complete Poems and Fragments*, ed. Jon Stallworthy (New York: Norton, 1984), 148–49. Stallworthy states the poem was likely composed "between January and March 1918" (149). Stallworthy provides a helpful, detailed biographical outline of Owen's life and military service at the beginning of his book.
2. Allen Frantzen, *Bloody Good: Chivalry, Sacrifice, and the Great War* (Chicago: University of Chicago Press, 2004), 258–63, 258. I am indebted to Frantzen's suggestive discussion of the poem. Also helpful on Owen is Douglas Kerr, *Wilfred Owen's Voices: Language and Community* (Oxford: Clarendon, 1993). Informing Frantzen's study of violence (and my own thinking of the language of violence) is René Girard's *Violence and the Sacred*, trans. Patrick Gregory (Baltimore: Johns Hopkins University Press, 1977).
3. Owen, "Strange Meeting," in *Complete Poems*, ed. Stallyworthy, 148–49.
4. In his foreword to *In Parenthesis* W.S. Merwin comments that Jones drew on his memories of his service in the Somme: "The six months in the forward trenches, and then the attack on Mametz Wood, were the period that became

the subject for *In Parenthesis*" (iv). My analysis in this essay focuses on Jones's strategies as a medievalist and does not attempt to situate Jones within a particular vein of literary modernism. I have found the following studies to be useful for my reading of Jones's poem: the excellent study by Thomas Dilworth, *The Shape of Meaning in the Poetry of David Jones* (Toronto: University of Toronto Press, 1988); together with David Blamires, *David Jones: Artist and Writer* (Toronto: University of Toronto Press, 1972); and Janet Gemmill, "*In Parenthesis*: A Study of Narrative Technique," *Journal of Modern Literature* 1 (1971): 311–30. I was first inspired to write an article comparing Jones and Tolkien after reading Paul Fussell's rather unsympathetic remarks on Jones, which do not recognize the innovations of Jones's strategies as a medievalist. Fussell describes Jones's "rescue" of "pre-industrial religious and ethical connotations" as "Quixotic" (145): "The trouble is that the meddling intellect, taking the form this time of a sentimental Victorian literary Arthurianism after Tennyson and Morris, has romanticized the war" (147). See Paul Fussell, *The Great War and Modern Memory* (London: Oxford University Press, 1975), 144–54. Lamentably, only one earlier article, written by Barton Friedman, "Tolkien and David Jones: The Great War and the War of the Ring," *Clio* 11, no.2 (1982): 115–36, brings these two writers together in conversation. I admire and am indebted to Friedman's attempt; however, I find his reading of *The Lord of the Rings* unsatisfying, and I do not consider the resulting discussion particularly illuminating for the case of either writer in terms of thinking about how they query the representation of violence in relationship to the medieval. Friedman tends to oversimplify: "For Tolkien, like the Jones of 'Art in Relation to War,' is celebrating the delight of war rather than deprecating its slaughter" (118). For a general history of the Great War I have consulted John Keegan, *The First World War* (New York: Alfred A. Knopf, 1999).

5. Brian Attebery, *Strategies of Fantasy* (Bloomington, IN: Indiana University Press, 1992), 6. Throughout this paper I will be thinking of the deployment of "fantasy" following Attebery's analysis of fantasy as mode (1–17). While I recognize that "fantasy" is a broad term, I apply the descriptor "fantastic medievalism" to both Jones's poem and Tolkien's novel to enable a conversation between these two works. Brian Attebery's chapter "Is Fantasy Literature? Tolkien and the Theorists" (18–35) is enormously useful for thinking about the prickly critical reception history of *The Lord of the Rings*.

6. Susan Stewart, *On Longing* (Durham, NC: Duke University Press, 1993), 26: "What does it mean to describe something? Descriptions must rely upon an economy of significance which is present in all of culture's representational forms, an economy which is shaped be generic conventions and not by aspects of the material world itself."

7. James Dawes, *The Language of War* (Cambridge, MA: Harvard University Press, 2002), 131. Dawes's remarkable book, which focuses on war and language in American literature, has helped me refine some of my thinking about war's effects on language. He explains, "War thus initiates a semantic crisis, a crisis of meaning premised upon disbelief in language's ability

effectively to intervene in the material world" (131). I would like to thank Monique Allewaert for bringing this book to my attention after hearing an earlier version of this essay.
8. J.R.R. Tolkien, "On Fairy Stories," in *The Monsters and the Critics and Other Essays*, ed. Christopher Tolkien (Boston, MA: Houghton Mifflin, 1984), 109–61, 139: "Fantasy, of course, starts out with an advantage: arresting strangeness."
9. Tom Shippey, *J. R. R. Tolkien: Author of the Century* (Boston, MA: Houghton Mifflin, 2001). See especially 112–60. See also Shippey's invaluable study: *The Road to Middle-earth*, rev. edn. (Boston, MA: Houghton Mifflin, 2003). Arthur Machen, a contemporary of Jones and Tolkien, also explored the fantastic in his war-related fiction: see the World War I-era "The Coming of the Terror," in *Tales before Tolkien*, ed. Douglas A. Anderson (New York: Ballantine, 2003), 264–301.
10. John Garth, *Tolkien and the Great War* (Boston, MA: Houghton Mifflin, 2003), 285–311 in particular. Garth extends Shippey's comments on the ways in which Tolkien's book confused its critics and asks valuable questions about how we might interpret and contextualize Tolkien's writing about war. Garth's biography of Tolkien's war experiences is an important and groundbreaking new study and has enriched my sense of the war's effects on Tolkien's literary activities. Also helpful for thinking about the place of Tolkien's fiction: Brian Rosebury, *Tolkien: A Cultural Phenomenon* (New York: Palgrave, 2003), 147–157.
11. *The Letters of J. R. R. Tolkien*, ed. Humphrey Carpenter (Boston, MA: Houghton Mifflin, 1981), 196–99, 197 (hereafter cited in text and notes as *Letters*).
12. Tolkien, *Letters*, 54. The quote is taken from a 1945 letter to Michael Tolkien.
13. J.R.R. Tolkien, *The Lord of the Rings*, 3 vols. (Boston, MA: Houghton Mifflin, 1999) (hereafter cited in text and notes as *LR* followed by book, chapter, and page), Foreword to the 2nd ed., xv. Of course the novel is not an allegory of any war, but Tolkien's experiences in the Great War transform the "setting" (I argue the verbal landscape) of *The Lord of the Rings*.
14. Frantzen, *Bloody Good*, 258. Frantzen is referring to Owen's "Strange Meeting" specifically, although I think that this remark can also be taken more broadly as a way of thinking about receptions of the Middle Ages during the Great War.
15. Frantzen, *Bloody Good*, 13
16. Frantzen, *Bloody Good*, 2. "Chivalry was born in the court of King Arthur and laid to rest in the trenches of World War I," Frantzen states, reciting conventional views about the medieval versus the modern, noting that this "scenario is an emblem of various themes—betrayed idealism, bitterness, the futility of pitting men against machine. . ." (1–2) As Frantzen elaborates, his interest is in "points of continuity" between chivalric themes and the Great War, not in the idea of the Middle Ages as idealized contrast to "the weapons of a new age" (2).

17. Jones, *In Parenthesis*, xi.
18. Jones, *In Parenthesis*, 24.
19. *A Dream of John Ball* is excerpted in William Morris, *News from Nowhere and Other Writings* (New York: Penguin, 1993), 25–39. For accounts of "John Ball" during the 1381 rebellion see R.B. Dobson, ed., *The Peasants' Revolt of 1381* (London: Macmillan, 1983), especially 372–78. The phrase "pleasing words" is taken from Thomas Walsingham (see 373–75). Fussell suggests that John Ball's "name may have reached Jones through the agency of Morris's romance of 1888, *The Dream of John Ball*" and that "Jones's John Ball is no leader of revolts" (147). Fussell's statements mask Jones's extraordinary gesture of locating Ball in the trenches, a gesture which does not support a "romanticized" medievalism, blurred by the "sentimental," but a complexly radical and political aesthetic impulse.
20. T.S. Eliot, introduction to Jones, *In Parenthesis*, vii.
21. Eliot, introduction to Jones, viii.
22. Frantzen, *Bloody Good*, 14: "Myth, art, and propaganda conspire to suppress blood and struggle—to say nothing of war—and present the surface of heroic masculinity as a free-floating fantasy while leaving the substance of the virtue unexamined."
23. Tolkien, *Letters*, 303: "The Dead Marshes and the approaches to the Morannon owe something to Northern France after the Battle of the Somme. They owe more to William Morris and his Huns and Romans, as in *The House of the Wolfings* or *The Roots of the Mountains*." Hugh Brogan, Hugh Cecil, Barton Friedman, and John Garth all discuss the Great War imagery of the marshes: Brogan, "*Tolkien's Great War*" in *Children and Their Books: A Celebration of the Work of Iona and Peter Opie*, ed. Gillian Avery and Julia Briggs, 362 (Oxford, UK: Clarendon Press, 1989); Hugh Cecil, *The Flower of Battle* (Vermont: Steerforth Press, 1996), 6: " 'Here nothing lived, not even the leprous growths that feed on rottenness,' wrote J.R.R. Tolkien forty years later, drawing on his memories of war to describe a scene of desolation in his epic, *The Lord of the Rings*"; Friedman, "*Tolkien and David Jones*," 115–16 (Friedman cites similar references made by several of Tolkien's contemporaries, including Siegfried Sassoon); Garth, *Tolkien and the Great War*, 308–09. Another crucial moment of sympathetic reciprocity in *The Lord of the Rings* occurs when Sam considers the body of a Southron soldier, an incident that takes place later in the novel than the passage through the marshes: "He wondered what the man's name was and where he came from; and if he was really evil of heart, or what lies or threats had led him on the long march from his home; and if he would not really rather have stayed there in peace—all in a flash of thought which was driven quickly from his mind" (*LR* 4.4, 646). A moment quite similar to this is brilliantly realized in Lewis Milestone's 1930 film version of Erich Remarque's *All Quiet on the Western Front*, when Paul kills a French soldier and then repents his actions.
24. Jay Winter, *Sites of Memory, Sites of Mourning: The Great War in European Cultural History* (Cambridge, UK: Cambridge University Press, 1995),

15–18; and Susan Sontag, *Regarding the Pain of Others* (New York: Farrar, Straus, and Giroux, 2003), 16–17. Sontag is referring to the 1938 version of Abel Gance's *J'accuse*. Her book features a compelling exploration of the role of photography in war and the viewer's relationship to "the pain of others." I am driven in this essay by questions Sontag raises throughout her book about what it means to behold another person's pain.

25. For an analysis of nineteenth-century war photography, including the Crimean War, see Sontag, *Regarding the Pain of Others,* 47–58. Sontag discusses the work of Crimean war photographer Robert Fenton and American Civil War photographer Mathew Brady in particular.
26. J.R.R. Tolkien, "Chaucer as a Philologist: 'The Reeve's Tale,'" *Transactions of the Philological Society* (1934): 1–70. The essay is a groundbreaking study of Chaucer's use of northern Middle English dialect in the "Reeve's Tale." Tolkien's relationship to Chaucer remains underexplored; yet Tolkien would have known the "Knight's Tale" very well and would have been remarkably sensitive to the linguistic and aesthetics shifts in its realization of the tournament that takes place in the theater of war.
27. David Aers, *Chaucer, Langland, and the Creative Imagination* (London: Routledge, 1980), 184. Aers notes that the phrase "clinical detail" is borrowed from Elizabeth Salter. Other studies have been assistive for my analysis here: Lawrence Clopper, "The Engaged Spectator: Langland and Chaucer on Civic Spectacle and the *Theatrum,*" *Studies in the Age of Chaucer* 22 (2000): 115–39; V.A. Kolve, *Chaucer and the Imagery of Narrative* (Stanford, CA: Stanford University Press, 1984); Lee Patterson, "The Knight's Tale and the Crisis of Chivalric Identity," in *Chaucer and the Subject of History* (Madison, WI: University of Wisconsin Press, 1991), 165–230; and, especially, Elizabeth Salter, *Chaucer: the "Knight's Tale" and the "Clerk's Tale"* (London: E. Arnold; New York: Barrons, 1962).
28. Geoffrey Chaucer, "The Knight's Tale," in *The Canterbury Tales,* ed. Larry Benson (Boston: Houghton Mifflin, 2000), lines 1887–92.
29. Chaucer, "The Knight's Tale," line 1955.
30. Chaucer, "The Knight's Tale," line 2489.
31. Chaucer, "The Knight's Tale," lines 2753–54.
32. Dawes, *The Language of War,* 47.
33. Shippey, *J.R.R. Tolkien,* 166. See pages 166–68 for the entire discussion.
34. See Christopher Tolkien, ed., *Sauron Defeated: The End of the Third Age* [part 4 of *The History of "The Lord of the Rings"*], vol. 9 of *The History of Middle-Earth* (Boston: Houghton Mifflin, 1992), 93; together with *Letters,* 195.
35. Tom Shippey explores the medieval-linguistic resonances of Tolkien's fiction at length in *The Road to Middle-Earth*; for his analysis of the Anglo-Saxon aspects of the Rohirrim, see pp.122–31. Elsewhere I argue (extending Shippey's observations on this same point in *Author of the Century,* 196–200) that Tolkien invokes the fourteenth-century dream-vision *Pearl* in his description of Frodo's first look at Lórien in *The Fellowship of the Ring.* Tolkien published a poem based on *Pearl* in 1927 titled "The Nameless

Land"; for Shippey's mentions of "The Nameless Land" see Shippey, *The Road to Middle-Earth*, 286 and *J.R.R. Tolkein: Author of the Century*, 197, 278–79.

36. For a discussion of the Shire as a "polder" that leads the reader into the fantastic world, see the entry on Tolkien in *The Encyclopedia of Fantasy*, ed. John Clute and John Grant (New York: St. Martin's Griffin, 1997), 950–55, and for "polder," 772–73; also, Shippey, *J. R. R. Tolkien: Author of the Century*, 1–49.
37. The entry for *scouren* can be found on pages 233–34 of *The Middle English Dictionary*, ed. Hans Kurath et al. (Ann Arbor: University of Michigan Press, 1952–2001).
38. Paul Fussell, *The Great War and Modern Memory*; see the chapters "Myth, Ritual, and Romance" and "Oh What a Literary War" for Fussell's discussion of these points (the phrase "Victorian pseudo-medieval romance" can be found on page 135). Garth, in *Tolkien and the Great War*, notes that Tolkien's "imaginary war" "packed with high diction" appeared to be out of the tradition Fussell describes (287). Friedman and Brogan also discuss Fussell's writing on "feudal language" and the implications for Tolkien's fiction, see Friedman, *The Great War and the War of the Ring*, 122, and Brogan, "Tolkien's Great War," 356, respectively.
39. Garth, *Tolkien and the Great War*, 307.
40. *Letters*, 235. Carpenter notes that the letter was part of a series of drafts that were intended for Michael Straight but never sent.
41. Jones, *In Parenthesis*, 168.

CHAPTER 10

TOLKIEN'S COSMIC-CHRISTIAN ECOLOGY: THE MEDIEVAL UNDERPINNINGS

Alfred K. Siewers

Tolkien's fascination with Celtic otherworldly narrative traditions helps to illumine the ecologically centered aspects of his fantasy. Views of nature that emerged in early-medieval literature from incarnational, cosmic emphases of Christianity (in tandem with earlier mythology) provided a narrative base for Tolkien's critique of modern objectifying views of nature.

At the start of the third millennium, readers still immersed in the end of the Third Age in J.R.R. Tolkien's *The Lord of the Rings* included tree-house-living eco-pagan activists blocking motorway construction in England and evangelical Christians at conservative Wheaton College (Illinois) dedicating a new library in honor of Tolkien and his literary friends the Inklings. "The beauty of the road-protests was that they enabled us as young adults to fully indulge those escapist fantasies," said activist eco-pagan Andy Letcher, "whilst engaging in a meaningful ecological struggle. . . . Tolkien grounded us, and made us relevant."[1] In the heartland of an American consumer culture that Tolkien abhorred,[2] Wheaton College faculty member Jerry Root noted that texts like *The Lord of the Rings* remain an oasis of sorts for conservative traditionalists as well. "People today are underdeveloped spiritually, they're famished," said Root, who teaches courses on the Inklings on a campus where students pledge not to drink as a form of religious practice, even as contemporaries in Letcher's Tolkien-inspired "tribe" turn to hallucinogenic mushrooms in theirs. "These authors. . .say to us: How can anybody look with an imaginative eye and not see a world that is infused with the divine?"[3]

In an era of ever-sharpening cultural divides between self-described traditionalists and progressives, Tolkien's major work stands out for its ability to engage people of all political and religious stripes with its anti-modernist and essentially "Green" environmental perspective. Indeed *The Lord of the Rings* has become more than fantasy in impacting a mass audience with an ecological message of valuing life above global consumerism.[4] Yet this contemporary edge of Tolkien's retro-medieval modern fantasy strangely mirrors its medieval inspiration, and in those roots lies the source of its real-life power to create broadly based communities of readers today. Tolkien's fantasy replicates a pattern of ecologically centered narrative design from the early Middle Ages, explained below as "overlay landscape," that helped originally inspire his project. His sources, which he at times termed "Celtic," emerged in a patristic Christian milieu (the period of mainly Greek texts of the Christian "church fathers," from the apostolic era to roughly the ninth century in the West), and served in their own day to bridge pagan, classical intellectual, and Christian traditions in connecting physical and spiritual realms through narrative.[5] They, in some ways, serve a similar function in Tolkien's reconstruction.

Early Celtic (really Welsh and Irish) Otherworld texts helped provide Tolkien with a pattern for an ecocentric Middle-earth—that is, for portraying the natural world as a central character beyond human control or even human concerns, integrated rather than separated from the divine, representing a kind of premodern version of Aldo Leopold's twentieth-century "land ethic."[6] The elves and their realms, the Ents and Tom Bombadil's domain, all have precedents in indigenous narratives of northern Europe shaped by an earlier, more cosmically oriented Christianity with which Tolkien was familiar through his scholarship. The relation of these narratives to early Christian cosmological traditions (explicit for example in the works of the Irish philosopher John Scottus Eriugena) helps to explain how Tolkien's fantasy could stretch beyond his own Augustinian Catholicism to embrace the imaginations of a wide range of religious and secular beliefs. The mingling of his Catholic faith with an interest in Celtic languages was responsible.

Tolkien in constructing an ecocentric Middle-earth from early models was drawing upon views of nature that emerged before the formative "Twelfth Century Renaissance" of Western Europe. Andrew Louth explained the transition from early-medieval views of the physical body to later-medieval Catholic views as "moving from seeing the body as microcosm reflecting in itself a cosmic story, to seeing the body as interpreter of human inwardness."[7] That same transition inevitably involved changes in the way Creation or physical nature (identified with the human body) was viewed, as medieval Western cosmology formed. In fact, the body can be extrapolated to nature in Louth's statement, in describing a transition "from seeing nature as microcosm reflecting in itself a cosmic story, to seeing nature as interpreter of human inwardness," from integrating the Other to objectifying it. In the earlier view, Kallistos Ware notes, "The body is directly involved in the vision of God,"[8] and again in extending attitudes toward the physical to the cosmos as a whole, one could as truly say that in that era "nature was directly involved in experience of the divine," as illustrated by active engagement of a worshipper with the divine through meditative asceticism in the desert tradition.

It was in this earlier Christian literary milieu of a nature integrated with the divine that the Celtic story pattern of the Otherworld was formed, in texts featuring an overlay landscape of the spiritual realm integrated with the physical, drawing on pagan mythology but reflecting a cosmic Christian theology. The Otherworld, in texts such as the so-called Ulster and Mythological Cycles of early Irish literature, was an ancestral realm of the old gods that also reflected Christian notions of Paradise, all interwoven with "real world" natural topography in a way analogous to the Australian aboriginal Dreamtime. Rather than an allegorical backdrop or structure of vertically separated physical and spiritual landscapes (such as in Dante's *Divine Comedy*), this integrative cultural landscape was more a horizontal experiential engagement of the two, as are Tolkien's fantasy landscapes: a polycentered reality, not merely an objectification of earthly reality as human desire. This overlay-landscape pattern of early otherworldly story forms the deep structure of Tolkien's ecocentric view of nature.

The Lord of the Rings As Ecocentric Narrative

"Green"/antimodernist popular readings of Tolkien across disparate cultural communities are stronger than ever in the wake of recent film portrayals of Saruman's Isengard as a forest-consuming industrial hellhole engaged in genetic engineering. The wasteland of Isengard, as portrayed by director Peter S. Jackson, and the even more desolate volcanic wasteland of militarism and black magic that is Mordor, stand out in bold relief for a new generation of Tolkien fans against the greenways of the Shire, elven realms, and tree-shepherd Ents.[9] Indeed, an ecocentric theme is even more pronounced in the book's accounts of Tom Bombadil and Goldberry, the Old Forest, Radagast the Brown, and a large miscellany of scenes and details down to the point of view of a fox in the Shire observing Hobbits traveling[10]—features left out of the movies. One of the most-noted connections between films and text was Jackson's use of New Zealand's stunning landscape to match Tolkien's scenery. Framing both projects is the Western sea.

Ecocritic Lawrence Buell concluded that one of the goals of literary studies in an era of massive environmental degradation should be to seek to counter such trends from within the structure of culture, "to take stock of the resources within our traditions of thought" for developing more ecologically centered narratives of the world.[11] Tolkien's fantasy is in fact a textbook case of adapting ecocentric literary traditions from the past as a basis for cultural restoration in the present. The effort parallels another (primarily nonenvironmental) modern literary project of cultural recovery: William Butler Yeats's effort to draw on early Irish mythology for texts that he hoped would be the basis for fashioning a new national culture for Ireland, bridging social divisions. Though Tolkien's effort by his own account was not so intentional, his foreword to the second edition of *The Lord of the Rings* suggests that the industrialization and development of the English countryside were on his mind while writing what could be read in part as a deliberately "retro" literary intervention in that process (as in "The Scouring of the Shire").[12]

Indeed, the fantasy realm of Middle-earth to Tolkien was the real earth of England. His term relates to the Old Icelandic or Old Norse term *miðgarðr*, part of a belief system involving a sense of multiple worlds with our Earth in the center, terminology from an Old Norse culture whose worldview Tolkien felt was analogous in important ways to that of the Anglo-Saxons. The name could be read in both pagan and Christian terms ("middle" Earth being also between chaos and the realm of the gods, or Hades and heaven in later medieval Christian cosmology), like Tolkien's favorite Old English poem, *Beowulf*. The view of Middle-earth as a place that through its very position is integrative of mythical or spiritual and physical realms (as in Christian belief is Christ's body) is implied in a passage from *The Lord of the Rings* that illumines the text's ecocentricity:

> "Do we walk in legends or on the green earth in the daylight?"
> "A man may do both," Aragorn said. "For not we but those who come after will make the legends of our time. The green earth, say you? That is a mighty matter of legend, though you tread it under the light of day!"[13]

Tolkien's sense of the integral interrelationship of our Middle-earth (in a pre-Ice Age European past) and spiritual or mythical realms is glimpsed in the reconstruction of a famous "real-world" conversation between C.S. Lewis and himself:

> Myths are "lies and therefore worthless, even though breathed through silver." *No*, said Tolkien. *They are not lies*. . . . You look at trees, he said, and call

them "trees," and probably you do not think twice about the word. . . . To you, a tree is simply a vegetable organism, and a star simply a ball of inanimate matter moving along a mathematical course. But the first men to talk of "trees" and "stars" saw things very differently. To them, the world was alive with mythological beings. . . . Christianity (he said) is exactly the same thing—with the enormous difference that the poet who invented it was God Himself, and the images He used were real men and actual history.[14]

There is an implied relationship (and potential engagement) here between the realm of imagination/language and the physical world, and thus between the spiritual and the physical, in Tolkien's cosmic philology, exemplified in the Incarnation but present in various indigenous religions and mythologies. (In addition to Celtic material, for example, Tolkien drew on nature-related mythology from a nineteenth-century reimagination of Finnish folklore, *The Kalevala*, whose traditions emerged in a borderland Russian Orthodox milieu similar in syncretic cosmology to early Christian Ireland.)

Tolkien's Ecocentricity and Celtic Narrative Patterns

The overlay landscape of the Elven realms in Tolkien's fantasy is its most distinctive Celtic element, echoing the Otherworld common to both early Welsh and Irish literatures. In Tolkien's fantasy we see immortal realms interlaced with the everyday world of physical experience and natural topography, as in the early medieval Welsh *Mabinogi* and the Irish *Táin Bó Cuailnge*.[15] The effect is a deeper dimensionality to landscape and ultimately nature that undergirds the ecocentricity of Tolkien's work. A similar overlay of spiritual and physical landscapes is seen in the layering of natural and spiritual forces, and history and in descriptions of other landscapes in Tolkien as well such as Weathertop, and the Old and Fangorn Forests. It is reflected in characters such as Tom Bombadil, Radagast the Brown (who communicates with animals) and Gandalf in his relation to elements of nature, all of whom are reminiscent of the shamanistic "wild man of the woods" motif in early Irish and British Celtic literature.[16] The woods of Middle-earth themselves provide an example of a specific analogue with early Celtic traditions. The relationship between oaks and druids is well known, and a medieval Welsh poem suggests an importance and agency given to trees: "Cad Goddeu," attributed to Taliesin (whose poetic voice and persona are echoed in the figures and chanting of both Tom Bombadil and Treebeard) seems to tell of a rallying of trees to war in Entish style.[17] There are other analogues as well. Giving animals a "life of their own" so to speak, as with the giant eagles, echoes the untamable bulls at the center of the *Táin* and the salmon in the Welsh tale *Culhwch ac Olwen*.[18] The rising up of the waters at the boundary of Rivendell upon the approach of the Black Riders parallels the rivers defending Ulster in the *Táin*, and the music and otherworldly light of the Elves echo Celtic otherworldly tales, and are reminiscent of "uncreated light" associated with Byzantine saints.[19]

Tolkien's readaptation of the early-medieval technique of overlay landscape enables an heteroglossic nature in a Bakhtinian sense, in which forests, rivers, mountains, and animals become characters, not really anthropomorphized, but representing powers larger than or beyond the human, a cosmic poly-centered focus for the narrative. To offer a more specific example of how this use of overlay landscape reflects Celtic otherworldly narrative patterns, consider the Four Branches of the *Mabinogi*, a probably early-twelfth-century Welsh text of anonymous authorship that reflects earlier traditions. In it the mound of Arberth in South Wales is a real topographical place that is also a focus of interaction between the Otherworld, a spiritual realm associated with ancestral tradition and forces of nature, and the everyday human world with which it is integrally interlaced. There Pwyll, the prince of Dyfed, an actual medieval Welsh kingdom (following an earlier encounter with an otherworldly hunter in the woods that results in Pwyll becoming prince of the Otherworld as well as of Dyfed), sees Rhiannon, a figure drawn from Celtic horse-goddess lore, riding through the natural landscape. She has chosen him to be her husband, as he learns at their encounter. Later, the mound becomes the center of resistance to an enchantment placed on the kingdom of their son.

This normalized presence of the Otherworld in the land lends to the landscape itself a dynamic, and as it were a voice of its own, which is larger than human control and concerns, a mystery that is experiential but beyond objectification. In this context, human characters such as Pwyll are actualized by their coming into relationship with this larger cosmic reality, as opposed to a more modern notion of identity as formed through a differentiation that occurs in the context of external social relations, and a distancing from the Other. This has implications for the perception of the relation of human beings to their physical environment, which in both Tolkien and many early Celtic texts tends to reflect the early-medieval view outlined by Louth and Ware above. The resulting living landscape of such a polyphonic text of nature can be seen in an early Irish passage in which St. Columba converses with an otherworldly youth, asking (among other questions about the origins of things) what the lake before them used to be:

> The youth answered: "I know that. It was yellow, it was flowery, it was green, it was hilly; it was rich in liquor, and strewn rushes, and silver, and chariots. I have grazed it when I was a stag; I have swum it when I was a salmon, when

I was a seal; I have run upon it when I was a human. I have landed there under three sails: the yellow sail which bears, the green sail which drowns, the red sail under which flesh was conceived. Women have cried out because of me, although father and mother do not know what they bear."[20]

John Carey identifies this text as a probable source for the early-eighth-century text *Immram Brain*, with its famous description of the sea-god Manannán Mac Lír leading Bran through an Otherworld inlaid in the sea.[21] The seemingly pagan motif of moving through water as if on earth, combining both spiritual and physical dimensions, and experience of both the past and the present, relates to Tolkien's use of overlay landscape in *The Lord of the Rings*. The motif also echoes patristic exegeses of the description in Genesis 1 of waters above the firmament, envisioned as a kind of watery-greenhouse "cloud cover" for Paradise, imbibed with the logoi or divine energies of the original Creation.[22] The image of the sea, associated in early Irish literature with the Otherworld as a teemingly fertile oeuvre and oeuf of life, including lost underwater realms, serves a similar role in Tolkien's mythology of Middle-Earth, and probably for similar reasons related to the engagement of Christian and pagan traditions just cited. In his analysis of the early Irish poem "Lament of the Old Woman of Beare," Carey notes that "the expectation of a future realm of blessed ever-living ones [is] contrasted with the lost antediluvian kingdoms and hidden Otherworld which seem to have played so important a part in the world-view of the pagan Irish.... Christian spirituality defines itself by contrast with beliefs of which it retains a sophisticated understanding—a fascinating dialectic which seems characteristic of the intellectual culture of early medieval Ireland."[23] More than a contrasting dialectic, however, the impression of moving through a cosmic sea while on earth is a trope of cosmological pagan–Christian engagement that Tolkien draws upon for textual atmospheric oxygen in his fantasy, as did the early Irish. As Kay Muhr has noted, "The positive water and sea imagery in Christian Irish literature may be partly derived from familiarity with the sea, and from the connection between water and revelation in pagan belief, but it also seems to have been closely associated with the two most important Christian sacraments, for, as St. Paul said, the Israelites were all baptized in the cloud and the sea, so they all drank the same spiritual drink, the water 'from the rock which was Christ.' "[24]

The blessed lands beyond the sea, the Elven realms of Rivendell and Lothlórien, the Old Forest and Fangorn, and many descriptions of place throughout *The Lord of the Rings*, all reflect a similarly dynamic and relatively non-objectified sense of place. Tolkien's otherworldly places are often defined by water in various ways, and explicitly identified with longing for the sea in the Elven realms. In them, too, being on the Earth seems to involve walking in an atmosphere of Paradise or original creation, which in the opening chapters of Genesis (so closely read in early-medieval Ireland) was associated with a juncture of the spiritual and material in waters that the Spirit moves or broods over, which are separated above and below the firmament, and which are expressed atmospherically as a mist rising from the earth. Layers of history and of spiritual presence intermingle with the physical scenery and subject in Tolkien's textual "spots of time." The Earth as a whole is by them imbibed with the same numinosity by which manmade mounds in the "real" Irish and Welsh lands become portals for the Otherworld in early stories. Earth becomes, more powerfully alive than metaphor, a metonymy (as Eriugena defined place in his *Periphyseon*, using the analogy of a fish in water)[25] for the multidimensional life of an integrated spirit and body.

Northrop Frye developed a model for the integrative function of overlay landscape in two early-modern authors drawing on Celtic themes, Shakespeare and Spenser, especially their *A Midsummer Night's Dream* and *The Faerie Queene* respectively. (A similar text familiar to Tolkien is the Celtic-influenced Middle English poem *Sir Gawain and the Green Knight*.) Frye describes the "rhythmic movement from normal world to green world and back again" that "makes each world seem unreal when seen by the light of the other."[26] In Middle-Earth, this back-and-forth lends a sense of permanent instability to human constructions and objectifications of nature.

Tolkien himself specifically fingered the Celtic influence on his work. His early fascination with Welsh inspired one of his Elven languages.[27] He said that *The Lord of the Rings* "contains, in the way of presentation that I find most natural, much of what I personally have received from the study of things Celtic." In "*The Lord of the Rings*. . .the names of persons and places in this story were mainly composed on patterns deliberately modeled on those of Welsh. . . . This element in the tale has given perhaps more pleasure to more readers than anything else in it."[28] He would also fondly refer in his famous essay on *Beowulf* to "less severe Celtic learning," in contrast with his main field of study in early English literature.[29] And he mentioned that he meant the term *elf* to be understood "in its ancient meanings, which continued as late as Spenser," who drew on Irish fairy and Welsh Arthurian lore. Tolkien said too he wanted to create in his epic a mythology for England that would possess "(if I could achieve it) the fair elusive beauty that some call Celtic (though it is rarely found in genuine ancient Celtic things)."[30] That last qualification recognizes the inevitable refashioning of early traditions in "retro" modes; in Tolkien's case his epic was also "a fundamentally religious and Catholic work; unconsciously so at first, but consciously in the revision."[31] He also wrote that he knew many "Celtic things" in their original languages but had a "certain distaste" for them due to their "fundamental unreason," seeing them as "a bright color" but "like a broken stained glass window reassembled without design" and "mad."[32] Tolkien's confidence in recovering an underlying philological and religious order from the material enabled him to feel comfortable about reassembling in narrative the shiny pieces that had long fascinated him. Yet the cosmic order reflected in that early material was profoundly Christian, if exotically jarring even to a conservative modern Catholic such as himself.

Tolkien's Christian Ecology: The Early Medieval Underpinnings

The story of the fall from grace in the biblical account of the Garden of Eden has in the West long served as an illustration of the separation of the human from the natural, and been regarded as a narrative forming the basis for ecological cultural disjunction, especially in the emphasis on that narrative of the Fall in the central Western theological works of Augustine.[33] Augustine's four distinctive cosmological emphases—on the Fall; on Original Sin; on effective identification of the Son with the Father in explaining the Trinity (thus to an extent marginalizing Creation further in tandem with the Holy Spirit); and on the distance between reality, sign, and signifier in both theophany and semiotics—were all crucial in the formation of medieval Western views of nature. But in the early medieval period in which Celtic narratives were fashioned, Augustine's complex of emphases represented only one strand in patristic exegeses shaping Insular monastic literary cosmologies. Harold Weatherby summed up the broader, non-Augustinian, patristic take on nature thus: "The Greek Fathers consistently interpret the Transfiguration as both manifesting and effecting the deification of nature."[34] Nature was a book in the sense of a mystery with which to be engaged, like an Irish illuminated manuscript as icon, rather than a text needing to be decoded and possessed by a reader.

It is this Christian approach to cosmology that lies behind the story traditions partly revived in the Elven landscapes of Tolkien's Middle-earth. The Incarnation for Athanasius and other "non-Augustinian" early patristic writers opened up the potential for deifying human beings, and with them nature, in a kind of restoration of Paradise, through a process of becoming one with uncreated divine energies experienced in Creation.[35] The exploration of this cosmic energy or activity in nature proved to be a prime interest of early Christian writers, including the Irish John Scottus Eriugena and his mentor, the earlier Greek writer Maximus the Confessor. That exploration was also a focus of early-medieval Irish hexaemeronic exegeses, especially *De Mirabilibus Sacrae Scripturae*.

In the early Irish otherworldly narrative involving St. Columba, cited above, we see exemplified the way in which early Christian literary culture in Wales and Ireland sought to integrate ancestral pagan and Christian, both physical and spiritual, perspectives on the land. Carey notes the pagan resonance of the text's description of cyclical living or rebirth, although it also echoes the early Irish Christian color scheme for describing types of martyrdom, and thus a return to God, paralleled in colors assigned to the winds.[36] More than that, the motif of moving through water as if on earth in the narrative (already discussed), combining both spiritual and physical dimensions and using water as medium for the overlay landscape, echoes Antony's famous comment in Athanasius's fourth-century *Vita* of the saint (a text that helped inspire John Cassian and early Celtic monasticism), that, for a monk, to be in the desert was to be a fish in the sea, whereas to be in the city was to be a fish out of water.[37] In the early-medieval British Isles there were plenty of watery monastic "deserts" in the form of islands and coastal hermitages, adding their own overlay of a spiritual sea of landscape, evocative again of Genesis.[38]

The overlay landscape pattern was thus a way of incorporating Christianity in ancestral beliefs and legends about places in the natural landscape. In one early Irish text cited by Carey, the Tuatha Dé Danann of the fairy mounds are referred to as "exiles who came from heaven," reminiscent of the status of Galadriel and other elves in Tolkien's writings as exiles (but not evil fallen beings) come to Middle Earth from the Blessed Realm.[39] Two other early Irish texts are noted by Carey in which such otherworldly beings voice similar statements about their nature, one noting that: "The Fall has not touched us. . ."[40] These otherworldly beings or fairies (their human-or-greater stature borrowed by Tolkien for his Elves) could also be read in their early medieval context as figures of what human beings would be like as unfallen immortals in Paradise—as examples of deified human beings or "natural" saints, if not always saintly-seeming. Carey concludes that, "the radical idea that the old gods are unfallen humans survived in Ireland throughout the Middle Ages."[41] Such figures were part of the deifying of nature referred to by Weatherby, related also to traditional localized cults of saints in Celtic lands. Tolkien echoes this personal sense of the divine in nature in *The Silmarillion* when the messengers of Manwe tell the Numenoreans, "it is not the land of Manwe that makes its people deathless, but the Deathless that dwell therein have hallowed the land."[42] True nature is not a "what" but a "who" in early Christian cosmology, as on Middle-earth.

It was Maximus in the seventh century in Greek, and Eriugena in the ninth century in Latin, who fully articulated the cosmology of the overlay-landscape pattern's approach to nature, with its adapted echo in *The Lord of the Rings*. Maximus's writings undergirded what became the dogma of

Christ's two natures at the Sixth Ecumenical Council, on the significance of Creation. As he put it, "The one Logos is many logoi, and the many logoi are one."[43] Preexistent principles, these logoi (both "words" and "reasons" in Greek) are more than archetypes or linguistic signs, but callings to participate in God, similar to Eriugena's theophanies or unfoldments of the divine in nature. The logoi, as personal expressions of God related to the incarnate Logos, were not objects to be enslaved. In the early Middle Ages they were seen as dynamic divine energies, with the effect of instilling a plurality and sense of difference in a monotheistic Creation, and operating in a kind of middle ground between God and physical Creation—in effect, the realm of the Otherworld, in which the physical, imaginary and divine images can be integrated.[44] As Maximus put it, the one Logos is unspeakable but "this same Logos is manifested and multiplied in a way suitable to the good in all the beings who came from Him. . . .and He recapitulates all things in Himself. . . .For all things participate in God by analogy, insofar as they came from God."[45]

Athanasius, writing of the relation of words (logoi) to reality in the Psalms, said: "The one who hears, in addition to learning these things [scriptural tradition], also comprehends and is taught in it the emotions of the soul, and, consequently, on the basis of that which affects him and by which he is constrained, he also is enabled by this book to possess the image deriving from the words."[46] In a similar way, the singing words of Tom Bombadil echo the original singing of creation described in *The Silmarillion*, as do the chants of the Ents. There is likewise a link between word and reality, including the physical environment, in Maximus's logoi, which re-sacralizes nature. This reflects what Carey sees in the early Irish cosmological treatise known as *The Ever-new Tongue*, a "perennially immanent" cosmic language, outside of time.[47] Julia Kristeva, describing psychological aspects of this cosmic language of early-medieval Christianity, writes that in it "the Spirit loses its immanence and identifies with the kingdom of God as defined through germinal, floral, nutritional, and erotic metamorphoses that imply, beyond the cosmic energy theory often viewed as specific to the East, the openly sexual fusion with the Thing at the limits of the nameable."[48] This also could describe the philologically motivated engagement with nature in Tolkien's overlay landscapes.

In Tolkien's worldview, as an Edwardian Roman Catholic, the Augustinian Fall was always present, as seen in the ending of the Third Age and the departing of the Elves and (implicitly) of beings such as Hobbits and Ents from the realms of human beings. But the most significant contribution of his writing to a modern ecocentric literature in the West is his imaginative recovery, for a mass global audience, of a non-Augustinian Western cosmological narrative, one based in Christian patristics that still resonate with indigenous religious traditions. The overlay landscapes of *The Lord of the Rings* defy human objectification or control. Yet they invite human engagement and actualization in participation with a larger mystery of the cosmos. In the process they embody a textual re-sacralization of both his and our Middle-earth, bespeaking the power of recovering alternative Western narrative traditions in shaping new coalitions for ecological healing.

Notes

This paper was originally given at the symposium on "Tolkien's Modern Middle Ages" at Bucknell University, Lewisburg, Pennsylvania, April 7, 2003; subsequent versions were given as talks at St.Mary's College, MD, March 26, 2004, and at Pennsylvania State University at Altoona, January 26, 2005. Thanks to Charles D. Wright for guidance on an earlier project from which this grew, and also to Kevin Murray for helpful bibliographic suggestions.

1. Andy Letcher, "The Scouring of the Shire: Fairies, Trolls and Pixies in Eco-Protest Culture," *Folklore* 112 (2001): 147–61. Comments are from an e-mail, January 26, 2004. On Tolkien's Green connections, see Patrick Curry, *Defending Middle-Earth: Tolkien, Myth and Modernity* (New York, St. Martin's, 1997), rebutted by Verlyn Flieger in "J.R.R. Tolkien and the Matter of Britain," *Mythlore* 87, 23, no. 1 (2000): 47–59.
2. J.R.R. Tolkien to Christopher Tolkien, letters 53 and 100, in *The Letters of J.R.R. Tolkien: A Selection*, ed. Humphrey Carpenter with assistance from Christopher Tolkien (London: HarperCollins, 1995), 65, 115.
3. See "The Marion E.Wade Center," http://www.wheaton.edu/learnres/wade/. Root's comments are from David Crumm, *Detroit Free Press on-line* (May 14, 2001), http://www.freep.com/features/books/rings14_20010514.htm.
4. A newspaper recently opined, "People familiar with either the books or the movies can easily pick up on ecological issues and Tolkien's love and concern for nature." Jennifer Switala, "*Return of the King*: Professor Offers Insight on Tolkien and *Lord of the Rings*," Sunbury (PA) *Daily Item* December 17, 2003: D8. And an eco-Tolkien park is proposed: http://www.tolkiensociety.org/t_park/proposal_tolkienpark_2000.html.
5. The term Celtic can be problematic because of romanticized and stereotyped overtones: see Patrick Sims-Williams, "The Visionary Celt: The Construction of an Ethnic Preconception," *Cambridge Medieval Celtic Studies* 2 (1986): 71–96, but is still a useful term for early Welsh and Irish texts that share linguistic and cultural connections.
6. But see Sims-Williams's cautions regarding stereotyping early Celtic views in "The Invention of Celtic Nature Poetry," in *Celticism*, ed. Terence Brown (Amsterdam: Rodopi, 1996), 97–124. For a qualified view of ecocentric emphases of early Irish and Welsh texts, see Alfred K. Siewers, "Landscapes of Conversion: Guthlac's Mound and Grendel's Mere as Expressions of Anglo-Saxon Nation-Building," in *Viator* 34 (2003): 1–39.

7. Andrew Louth, "The Body in Western Catholic Christianity," in *Religion and the Body*, ed. Sarah Coakley (Cambridge, UK: Cambridge University Press, 1997), 129.
8. Kallistos Ware, "The Body in Greek Christianity," in *Religion and the Body*, ed. Sarah Coakley (Cambridge, UK: Cambridge University Press, 1997), 108.
9. See, for example, Tolkien, *The Lord of the Rings*, 2nd edn., revised (one-volume edn.) (Boston, MA: Houghton Mifflin, 1994), 3.4, 462 (hereafter *LR*) when Treebeard says Saruman, "has a mind of metal and wheels; and he does not care for growing things." The Shire is featured especially in the opening chapters of the epic and then in nostalgic memories throughout, and finally as a kind of fallen ecotopia in need of restoration in the anticlimactic but essential chapter, 6.8, "The Scouring of the Shire," left out, however, by the films. On Elven realms, see *LR* 1.3, 78–83, about otherworldly Elves in a natural setting; 1.12, 209, regarding the powers of the waters of Rivendell, and on that valley's natural/magical fertility, 2.1, 219–20 and 2.2, 233; and 2.6, 328, to 2.8, 369, on Lothlórien's natural-magical realm.
10. See *LR* 1.3, 71, about this now-famous fox; regarding Bombadil, Goldberry, and the Old Forest, see especially 1.6–1.8, inclusive, but also 2.2, 258–59; on Radagast's natural powers 2.2, 250–51, and on Saruman's disdain for those powers and how they yet won the day against Saruman, 2.2, 252 and 254–55.
11. Lawrence Buell, *The Environmental Imagination* (Cambridge, MA: Belknap Press, 1995), 21.
12. Tolkien, *LR*, "Foreword to the Second Edition," xvii.
13. Tolkien, *LR* 3.2, 424.
14. Humphrey Carpenter, *The Inklings: C. S. Lewis, J. R. R. Tolkien, Charles Williams, and Their Friends* (Boston, MA: Houghton Mifflin, 1979), 43–44.
15. John Carey has defended the modern scholarly concept of the Celtic Otherworld in "The Irish 'Otherworld': Hiberno-Latin Perspectives," *Éigse* 25 (1991): 154–59.
16. Pádraig Ó Riain, "A Study of the Irish Legend of the Wild Man", *Éigse* 14 (1971–72): 179–206.
17. Patrick Ford, *The Mabinogi* (Berkeley, CA: University of California Press, 1977), 183–87; also see Marged Haycock, "The Significance of the 'Cad Goddeu' Tree-List in the Book of Taliesin," *Current Issues in Linguistic Theory* 68 (1990): 297–331.
18. The motif of an eagle carrying a shaman figure is found in the *Kalevala*, but birds as beings interacting with humans (or as shape-shifted humans) are a Celtic motif as well, as in the Fourth Branch of the Welsh *Mabinogi*, the Hiberno-Latin *Voyage of St. Brendan*, and stories of the birth and wasting-sickness of Cúchulainn in the Irish Ulster Cycle.
19. See John Carey, "The Encounter at the Ford: Warriors, Water and Women," *Éigse* 34 (2004): 10–24.
20. John Carey, *A Single Ray of the Sun: Religious Speculation in Early Ireland* (Andover, MA, and Aberystwyth, Wales: Celtic Studies Publications, 1999),

4–5, and his "The Lough Foyle Colloquy Texts: *Immacaldam Choluim Chille ₇ ind Óclaig oc Carraic Eolairg* and *Immacaldam in Druad Brain ₇ inna Banfátho Febuil ós Loch Febuil*," *Ériu* 52 (2002): 53–87. See also Carey, "The Location of the Otherworld in Irish Tradition," in *The Otherworld Voyage in Early Irish Literature*, ed. Jonathan Wooding (Dublin: Four Courts Press, 2000).
21. Carey, *Single Ray of the Sun*, 7.
22. See, especially, the fourth-century St. Basil of Caesarea's *Hexaemeron*, trans. Blomfield Jackson, *Basil: Letters and Select Works*, Nicene and Post-Nicene Fathers, second series, vol. 8 (1895; repr. Peabody, MA: Hendrickson, 1999), 52–107. For the relation of notions of divine energy, found in writings of Basil but developed across following centuries, to Maximus the Confessor's seventh-century cosmology of logoi, expressed by John Scottus Eriugena, see also Joseph P. Farrell, *Free Choice in St. Maximus the Confessor* (South Canaan, PA: St. Tikhon's Seminary Press, 1989), especially pp. 181 and 191.
23. John Carey, "Lament of the Old Woman of Beare," in *Celtica* 23 (1999): 30–37.
24. Kay Muhr, "Water Imagery in Early Irish," in *Celtica* 23 (1999): 193–210.
25. John Scottus Eriugena, *The Periphyseon*, trans. Myra L. Uhlfelder (Indianapolis: Bobbs-Merrill, 1976), 42–54.
26. Northrop Frye, "The Argument of Comedy," in *Shakespeare, Modern Essays in Criticism*, ed. Leonard F. Dean (London: Oxford University Press, 1967), 86, 88.
27. See Deborah Webster Rogers and Ivor A. Rogers, *J.R.R. Tolkien* (Boston, MA: Twayne Publishers, 1980), 42; and John Garth, *Tolkien and the Great War: The Threshold of Middle-Earth* (Boston, MA: Houghton Mifflin, 2003), 14, 32, 35, 82, 213, 236.
28. Tolkien, "English and Welsh," in *The Monsters and the Critics and Other Essays*, ed. Christopher Tolkien (London: HarperCollins, 1997).
29. Tolkien, *Letters*, letter 131, p. 143.
30. Tolkien, *Letters*, letter 131, p. 144.
31. Tolkien, *Letters*, letter 142, p. 172.
32. Tolkien, *Letters*, letter 19, p. 26; see also his reference to Irish in *Letters*, letter 165, p. 219. A similar mosaic image is used by Ireneaus in his polemic against Gnostic exegeses; see Irenaeus, *Against Heresies*, in *Ante-Nicene Fathers* 1 (1885), trans. Alexander Roberts and James Donaldson (repr. Peabody, MA: Hendrickson, 1999) 1.8.1, p. 326.
33. See the discussion in Siewers, "Landscapes of Conversion," 8.
34. Harold Weatherby, "Greek Fathers," in *The Spenser Encyclopedia*, ed. A.C. Hamilton et al. (Toronto: University of Toronto Press, 1990), 303.
35. Kallistos Ware, *The Orthodox Way* (Crestwood, NY: St. Vladimir's Seminary Press, 1999), 22.
36. Discussed in Alfred K. Siewers, "How Green was my Martyrdom? Ec(o)centricity in early Irish texts," at the International Medieval Congress, Kalamazoo, MI, May 6, 2004, a later version of which was presented to the Early Irish Department seminar, University College Cork, Ireland, November 10, 2004.

37. Athanasius, *The Life of Antony*, par. 85, in *The Life of St. Antony and the Letter to Marcellinus/Athanasius*, trans. Robert Gregg (New York: Paulist Press, 1980), 93.
38. Máire Herbert, "The Legend of St. Cothíne: Perspectives from Early Christian Ireland," *Studia Hibernica* 31 (2000): 27–35.
39. Carey, *Single Ray of the Sun*, 19–20.
40. Carey, *Single Ray of the Sun*, 30.
41. Carey, *Single Ray of the Sun*, 36.
42. Tolkien, *The Silmarillion* (London: HarperCollins, 1994), 317.
43. Maximus the Confessor, *Ambigua* 22, PG 91:1257AB, in *Free Choice in St. Maximus the Confessor*, trans. Joseph P. Farrell (South Canaan, PA: St. Tikhon's Press, 1989), 181.
44. See Farrell, *Free Choice*, 137, 179.
45. *Ambigua* 7, PG 91:1080AB, quoted in *Christ in Eastern Thought*, trans. John Meyendorff (St. Vladimir's Seminary Press, 1969), 102.
46. Athanasius, "A Letter to Marcellinus," in *The Life of Antony and the Letter to Marcellinus/Athanasius*, trans. and ed. Robert Gregg (New York: Paulist Press, 1980), 108.
47. John Carey, "Etymology and Time," *Temenos Academy Review* 5 (2002): 98.
48. Julia Kristeva, "Dostoevsky, the Writing of Suffering, and Forgiveness," in *Black's Sun*, trans. Leon Roudiez (New York: Columbia University Press, 1987), 209.

CHAPTER 11

FEAR OF DIFFERENCE, FEAR OF DEATH:
THE *SIGELWARA*, TOLKIEN'S SWERTINGS,
AND RACIAL DIFFERENCE

Brian McFadden

> *Tolkien has been criticized either for ignoring persons of color or for depicting them in a manner consistent with negative stereotypes, typical of Edwardian England's popular prejudices. However, Tolkien's depiction of dark-skinned Swertings or Southrons was shaped by his reading of Latin and Old English descriptions of the Sigelwara, or Ethiopians.*

In an article on fantasy in *Time* magazine, Lev Grossman notes of the film version of *The Lord of the Rings* that "on the political correctness meter *The Lord of the Rings* is radioactive. . . .The Fellowship is still as much a boy's club as Augusta National. And whiter, too. Don't let all the heartwarming Elf–Dwarf bonding between Legolas and Gimli fool you. The only people with dark skin in Middle-earth are the Orcs." However, Grossman also puts this statement into the context of a discussion on the role of fantasy literature and asks, "[A]re we escaping reality just to find it again and wrestle with it in disguise?"[1] I believe that J.R.R. Tolkien's literary work is neither simplistic nor particularly exclusionary with respect to race;[2] it reflects many elements of the literature and Roman Catholic faith that its author professed, and while many of those views tend to be expressed in terms of binary oppositions, Tolkien's matter of Middle-earth is more open and subtle than has often been realized until recently. Paul Ricoeur notes that science fiction, and fantasy for the purposes of this essay, presents "puzzling cases" that allow people to confront difficult ideas about selfhood and otherness[3] in a way that realistic fiction cannot, as T.A. Shippey has also pointed out.[4]

This essay examines Tolkien's treatment of the Swertings (probably derived by Tolkien from Old English *sweart*, "dark, black")[5] or Haradrim, the dark men of the South. I argue that Tolkien's encounters with the Haradrim draw on the depictions of the *sigelwara*, or Ethiopians, in Anglo-Latin and Old English literature; they are potentially threatening at first glance but vulnerable, human, and less fearsome on closer contact. To Tolkien, discord and enmity result from manipulation of the perception of difference and are not inherent in difference. The Swertings are feared because they are unfamiliar, and they are enemies because they serve Sauron, but once his influence is removed, the Swertings negotiate and interact with the men of the West as an equal people. I go on to argue that the difference with the most salient effect on perceptions of otherness in Tolkien's works is mortality and immortality;[6] the fear of death and the envy of immortality are the prime weapons that Morgoth and Sauron use to divide humans against both the Elves and each other. However, embracing this key difference yields greater self-knowledge to both Elves and, potentially, humans of all races; it also reveals the artificiality of racial difference, since Númenoreans and Haradrim alike are subject to death and can be manipulated by fear of it.

Tolkien knew something of being excluded as an Other. When Tolkien's mother converted to Catholicism, she was ostracized by her family;[7] also, most of Tolkien's colleagues at Oxford would not have been Catholic, and some would certainly have been hostile to Catholicism.[8] Given the divisions within Christianity, it is perhaps ironic that two key biblical stories can be interpreted to show that one effect of human sinfulness is to fear the Other. In the creation story in Genesis, the first effect of the Fall is to reveal sexual difference to Adam and Eve, and they react with fear and shame: "Then the eyes of both of them were opened and they realized that they were naked" (Genesis 3:7).[9] In this reading, the consequences of their disobedience—physical toil, labor in childbirth, sexual hierarchy, enmity between human and animal, and the fear of death—arise from awareness of evil and its assignment to the Other; Adam immediately passes the blame to Eve, and Eve in turn to the serpent. Where there was once peaceful coexistence of man, woman, and animal without the consciousness of difference, there is now dissension and conflict based on it, and the passages often read as God's punishments may simply be a statement of the results of the human tendency to call "evil" what differs from one's conception of the self. In this reading, fear of difference is a result of the Fall. In the story that supposedly made Tolkien's career of philology necessary, the builders of the Tower of Babel attempt to reconstruct lost human unity and to regain Paradise. Humanity has chosen to know difference, however, and God lets them know it: " 'So they are all a single people with a single language!' said Yahweh. 'This is but the start of their undertakings! There will be nothing too hard for them to do. Come, let us go down and confuse their language on the spot so that they can no longer understand each other.' Yahweh scattered them thence over the whole face of the earth, and they stopped building the town" (Genesis 11:6–9). Pride is punished again by distancing people from each other, in this case linguistically and geographically; the tendency to misunderstand, fear, and resent the Other that first appeared as a result of the Fall is now expanded to the scale of peoples rather than individuals.

The *Silmarillion* contains several parallels to these Scriptural stories. The Elves who do not heed the summons of the Valar to return to Aman become separated from the Noldor, resulting in the sundered languages of Quenya and Sindarin. Likewise, the bloody consequences of the Oath of Fëanor and the exile of the Noldor from Aman arise from both Fëanor's desire to keep the light of the Two Trees for himself and his preference of his own good and his family's to that of the Valar and the world in general; his mistrust of others is a result of the lies of Morgoth. When the Noldor return to Middle-earth, the divisions between Noldor and Sindar are exacerbated by awareness of the Kinslaying and the rebellion against the Valar, to the point where Thingol forbids the use of Quenya in his realm.[10] In addition, the first encounter between the Elf-lord Finrod Felagund and the human Bëor reveals that the humans have fled west because "a darkness lay upon the hearts of Men" (*Silm*, 141) in the east, where Tolkien implies the Fall of Man had taken place at Morgoth's instigation.[11] Difference is present but innocuous at the beginning of both Christian and Tolkienian narrative; the result of the choice to break with unity is mistrust of the Other and fear of difference.

The most visible difference in Tolkien's work at first glance appears to be that of light and darkness, which had several implications in the Middle Ages for race issues. In many medieval texts, dark humans are associated with demons. The main encounter with dark men in Old English literature is with the *sigelwara*, or Ethiopians.[12] In the Old English lives of St. Margaret, for instance, demons appear as dark men; in the London, British Library, Cotton Tiberius A.iii, version of the legend, the saint is confronted with a devil in the shape of a "dark man" (*sweartne man*), and in the Cambridge, Corpus Christi College 303, version, the demon appears "black and ugly" (*sweart ond unfæger*).[13] Tolkien notes four places where the *sigelwara* are equated with demons in Anglo-Saxon homilies and sermons.[14] However, a common trait of medieval monster texts is to make unusual beings distant and inaccessible; the monsters' perceived threat often comes from a lack of certain knowledge about the beings, not necessarily from any overtly hostile acts, and this is the case for most of the occurrences of the *sigelwara*.[15] In the eighth-century *Liber monstrorum*, for instance, in Africa "there are Ethiopians black all over their body, whom the sun burning with very great heat is always searing because they live below the third, most hot and parched circle of the earth's zones, and from the vapor of the most burning stars are protected by the hideaways of the world."[16] The Ethiopians are not described as particularly harmful or dangerous, unlike many other beings in the text; they are merely distant and subject to the extremes of the sun, and the earth seems to be willing to protect them from it, suggesting human vulnerability rather than monstrous difference. In addition, their distance from the safe zones of the world may be read as protection from the threat posed by the reader and the society that treats the Ethiopians as Other. As Tolkien notes with apparent regret, "Ethiopia was hot and its people black. That Hell was similar would occur to many."[17] In *Wonders of the East* in the *Beowulf* MS (London, British Library, Cotton Vitellius A.xv), the presence of the *sigelwara* in the distant world is likewise noted but not evaluated: "There is a race of men who are dark of color [*sweartes hiwes*] to the sight, whom men call the *silhearwan*."[18] Again, where exactly "there" is unspecified; the Ethiopians are not described as threatening, nor do they appear to be threatened by the reader's society. The Israelites pass north of the land of the Ethiopians in the poem *Exodus* without any mention of hostility;[19] likewise, in Ælfric's *De temporibus anni*, we find that they dwell on the island Meroe,[20] and in the Paris Psalter version of Psalm 86, the *folc sigelwara naman* (people by the name of Ethiopians) are mentioned, but no hostile interaction with them is noted.[21] In *Fates of the Apostles*, Matthew is put to death by King Irtacus, but "the truth arose among the Ethiopians," suggesting a willingness to hear him among the people, if not by the king.[22] *Sigelwara* are not mentioned in the *Letter of Alexander to Aristotle*; however, races of human, humanoid, and semihuman Others appear (including an Indian high priest who is ten feet tall with black skin,[23] the dog-headed Cynocephali, and the nine-foot Ictifafonas), and as I have recently argued, the monsters (monstrous from Alexander's viewpoint) seem only to want to be left alone. Their attacks on Alexander's army respond to his invasion of their territory; his culture (and, by implication, the reader's) is the threat.[24] When Alexander can establish communication with a race, he seems to be able to win them over by persuasion; when he cannot communicate, he fights,[25] suggesting a willingness to treat others as humans but to treat as monstrous those beings who cannot or will not reason with him as humans do.[26] In most of their appearances in Old English literature, the *sigelwara* are initially feared, mistrusted, and contained due to lack of communication; in all but a few instances, however, when encountered directly, they appear harmless, vulnerable, and very human.

In Tolkien's narrative, this idea of communication as a humanizing and equalizing trait demonstrates the equality of the Swertings to the Western humans. When Sauron is finally defeated, Aragorn as King Elessar negotiates with his former enemies: "And embassies came from many lands and peoples, from the East and the South. . . . And the King pardoned the Easterlings that had given themselves up, and sent them away free, and he made peace with the peoples of Harad."[27] The Wild Men of the woods likewise negotiate with Aragorn: " 'The Forest of Drúadan he gives to Ghân-buri-ghân and to his folk, to be their own for ever; and hereafter let no man enter it without their leave!' Then the drums rolled loudly, and were silent" (*LR* 6.6, 954). In both cases, Aragorn is an authority figure and grants favors from a position of superiority; however, he treats other peoples as his own people and their leaders as equals to himself. As with Alexander, Aragorn rules peaceably through language and negotiation.

The ultimate barrier to communication is death; dead men tell no tales and cannot defend themselves because their thoughts are lost forever.[28] However, Tolkien allows death to be a site for humanization when a Swerting warrior falls in front of Samwise: "He was glad that he could not see the dead face. He wondered what the man's name was and where he came from; and if he was really evil of heart, or what lies and threats had led him on the long march from his home; and if he would not really rather have stayed there in peace—all in a flash of thought which was quickly driven from his mind" (*LR* 4.4, 646). Sam's distraction is the onslaught of the Mûmak or Oliphaunt, and even in its otherness, Sam finds wonder and pity:

> To his astonishment and terror, and lasting delight, Sam saw a vast shape crash out of the trees. . . . Fear and wonder, maybe, enlarged him in the hobbit's eyes, but the Mûmak of Harad was indeed a beast of vast bulk, and the like of him does not walk now in Middle-earth. . . . His upturned hornlike tusks were bound with bands of gold and dripped with blood. His trappings of scarlet and gold flapped about him in wild tatters. The ruins of what seemed a very war-tower lay upon his heaving back,. . . and high upon his neck still desperately clung a tiny figure—the body of a mighty warrior, a giant among the Swertings. (*LR* 4.4, 646–47)

One of the tactics of "othering" a race is to see it as subhuman or to demonize it,[29] and Tolkien does neither in these passages; he makes Sam's first impulse to try to see the man's humanity and to imagine what he would be like if there had been no war. Sam attempts to explain to himself why the man would be serving evil; while allowing the possibility that the man is evil himself, Sam gives him two possible mitigating factors, fear or deception, neither of which are lacking in Sauron's domain. He brings out the possibility that, like the monstrous races in *Alexander to Aristotle*, the person had no real desire to be fighting and may well have wanted to be left alone. Elephants occur in the *Liber monstrorum*, *Alexander to Aristotle*, and *Wonders* as fearsome creatures sometimes used for military purposes, although Alexander is attacked by wild elephants.[30] The monster is a source of delight and fear to Sam, just as the Anglo-Saxon texts noted above report the creatures and their wondrous traits but also contain them textually by emphasizing their distance from the reader. In addition, in comparison to the Oliphaunt, even the body of the giant warrior is seen as small and desperate, again paralleling the vulnerability of the others in *Liber monstrorum* and *Wonders*. By allowing the Swerting to have a will, although one that may have been overpowered by fear or force, Tolkien attempts to demonstrate that the Swertings, although on the wrong side, are human, vulnerable, and not inherently evil. Racial difference does not imply evil to Tolkien; the dead human and wondrous beast in this passage produce ambivalent emotions, and only as Sauron's servants are they considered "Other."

The image of the dead Haradrim suggests an issue that Tolkien raises in his letters, that death is a equalizing factor for all humans; its omnipresence suggests common ground between west and south in Middle-earth. Although many scholars have argued that the key issue in *The Lord of the Rings* is power,[31] Tolkien himself felt that it was only a means of telling the main story: the opposition of life and death. In a letter to Herbert Schiro, Tolkien states: "But I should say, if asked, the tale is not really about Power and Dominion: that only sets the wheels going; it is about Death and the desire for deathlessness" (*Letters*, 262).[32] Sam's immediate assumption of threat or deception implies that a fear of death may be the motivation for the Haradrim to serve Sauron; terror is the major weapon of the Nazgûl in *The Lord of the Rings*, and in the *Silmarillion*, fear of death is the wedge driven by Sauron between the Valar and the Númenoreans. Freedom from the fear of death is the goal of the Ring quest; responding to W.H. Auden's review of *Return of the King* in 1956, Tolkien states that "the quest had as its object not the preserving of this or that polity,. . .but the liberation from an evil tyranny of all the 'humane'—including those, such as 'easterlings' and Haradrim, that were still servants of the tyranny" (*Letters*, 241).[33] This statement suggests that racial difference does not diminish the Haradrim's humanity in Tolkien's eyes.

In fact, one might argue that the greatest instance of othering in Tolkien's work is the separation of immortal Elf and mortal human; the vulnerability that unites humanity also separates it from its closest friends and allies, making the qualitative difference between immortality and mortality and not the artificial difference of race paramount in the mythology. A key example of the Elven and human boundary is the history of Eärendil and his descendants, mentioned in *The Lord of the Rings* but most fully developed in the *Silmarillion*. Eärendil is the son of Tuor and Idril, a human and an Elf, and has two sons, Elrond and Elros. When it appears that Morgoth is about to overrun Middle-earth, he constructs the ship *Vingilot* and sails into the west to enlist the aid of the Valar on behalf of both Elves and humans. His wife Elwing holds a Silmaril that is being sought by the surviving sons of Fëanor, and when they attempt to take it, she plunges into the sea with it. However, she is turned into a seabird[34] and flies away, catching up with Eärendil and going into the west with him. When he arrives, he is greeted warmly but questioned about his presence, since humans are not allowed to come to Valinor. However, Ulmo defends him: "Say unto me: whether is he Eärendil Tuor's son of the line of Hador; or the son of Idril, Turgon's daughter; of the Elven-house of Finwë?" (*Silm*, 249). The matter is turned over to Manwë, who decides that Eärendil and Elwing, having experienced the Blessed Realm, cannot return to Middle-earth, and that they and their sons must choose to live either as Elves or as humans. Eärendil is stellified with *Vingilot* and the Silmaril, Elwing is allowed to change into bird-form to meet him when she will, and both choose to be counted as Elves. Elrond chooses to be treated as an Elf and eventually founds the stronghold of Rivendell, but Elros decides to be treated as a human, becoming the first king of the Númenoreans. What is important to note about these characters is that the Valar (and Tolkien as author) will not allow them to be in any in-between category; they must be either Elven or human. Eärendil and Elwing are placed in the sky, distant from the human world; like the hybrid monsters of *Liber monstrorum*, *Alexander to Aristotle*, and *Wonders*, they are separated from humanity, having transgressed the human and nonhuman boundary in several ways (half-Elven and half-human for Eärendil, and animal and human for Elwing). Elrond and Elros are forced to pick a category so that they may remain in Middle-earth and Númenor respectively; while their ancestry is undeniably mixed, they cannot have the best of both worlds, perpetual life and the ability to leave the world (which Tolkien would probably have seen as self-contradictory in any event), and must contain themselves within a category so that Valar, Elves, and humans may know how to deal with them. Tolkien does not seem to think that any particular kind of human is better than any other, but he does note qualitative differences between humans and Elves, and while Elves and humans may interact, the boundary of mortality and immortality cannot be abolished.

As David Williams has argued, medieval monsters often cross boundaries in some way, which makes them both fearsome and awesome; without a clear-cut way of containing wondrous beings in an intellectual category, humans are forced to reconsider their categories and may perceive, although darkly, a divinity that in itself transcends human understanding.[35] This kind of thought appears to be similar to Tolkien's view of the relation between immortal Elves and mortal humans; Elves have a long and more comprehensive view of Middle-earth and must remain in it until its end, while humans, who must eventually leave Middle-earth through death, can only perceive immortality as a continuation of their life in Middle-earth and do not understand that their fate is essentially different from that of Elves. While the differences between humans of the North and the Haradrim are negated by death, death only serves to highlight the true difference between human and Elf. As the messengers of Manwë tell the Númenoreans, "[If] you came indeed to Aman, the Blessed Realm, little would it profit you. For it is not the land of Manwë that makes its people deathless, but the Deathless that dwell therein have hallowed the land" (*Silm*, 264). While humans may know what immortality is, they do not fully understand its implications; likewise, the Elves know that humans die, but all they know is that the home of Men is not in the world. The separation of the Elven and human races seems to be divinely ordained; when Ar-Pharazôn attempts to cross the ocean boundary to conquer Aman, the world is changed to prevent both his return and any further attempts to come to Valinor. By separating the human and Elven races, Tolkien suggests that only Ilúvatar has a complete knowledge of the workings of Middle-earth, and to make a good life with incomplete information,[36] to encounter and to attempt to understand the Other without fear, is a task for both mortals and immortals. Humans and Elves both have to reexamine their categories to perceive even a glimpse of Ilúvatar's mind; despite their friendship and interaction, they will always remain Others to each other, and they will not know the mind of Ilúvatar until the end of time. They may, however, learn something of themselves in the process.

Part of this opposition may be a reflection of Tolkien's Catholicism on his view of mortality and immortality; however, this view also reveals a nuance in Tolkien's use of binary oppositions. In the development of Christian theology, Christ's nature was eventually defined as being fully human and fully divine; as intercessor between the Father and humanity, the Son must have the power and wisdom of God but must also be able to suffer and die to redeem humanity. By returning from death and interacting with others, Christ shows to Christians the immortal part of their being;

their souls must leave the world and cannot return, but they believe that there is a place for them after death. Christ also challenges difference: "There are no more distinctions between Jew and Greek, slave and free, male and female, but all of you are one in Christ Jesus" (Galatians 3:28). As David Williams has argued, medieval monsters who cross categories may be read as signs of the divine transcendence of human categories,[37] including life and death. In Middle-earth, however, Ilúvatar allows uncertainty in humans; they cannot know their ultimate home as the Elves do. In the *Silmarillion*, although Beren and Lúthien choose mortality after Lúthien's pleading before Mandos and their return to Middle-earth, they do not interact with anyone after their return (*Silm*, 188); Eärendil and Elwing choose immortality, but having been to Valinor they are prohibited from interacting with humans or Elves ever again in Middle-earth. Elrond and Elros, never having seen Valinor, may remain in Middle-earth after their choice. The Númenoreans, however, fear and resent death because they do not know for sure what comes after; in response to Manwë's messengers, they ask, "Why should we not envy the Valar, or even the least of the Deathless? For of us is required a blind trust, and a hope without assurance, knowing not what lies before us in a little while" (*Silm*, 265).[38] This lack of certainty breeds the mistrust that Sauron will exploit; the Númenoreans see Valinor only as a *locus amoenus*, not as a pretty prison for beings who may eventually desire to escape deathlessness.[39]

Although divinity was seen as immanent in the medieval world[40]—an immanence that in the *Silmarillion* is certainly echoed in the influence of the Valar, especially Ulmo, in Middle-earth, and in the presence of Elves who have been to Valinor—modern Christianity tends to emphasize the separation between the natural and the supernatural worlds, and Tolkien's separation between mortals and immortals may be seen as an expression of his belief in the importance of faith. For the Elves, the Valar and Ilúvatar are part of history; the Elves have experienced the Powers directly and are bound to them as they are bound to the world. For humans, however, Ilúvatar and the Valar are objects of a faith that will be rewarded with a release from the world, but not in any way that either they or the Elves can know. The Elves believe because they have seen; humans will be blessed if they believe without having seen. Sauron and Morgoth attempt to exploit the fear of death to subjugate humans; those who are willing to see death as a release rather than as a confinement preserve their own freedom in life, while those who are moved by fear to serve evil, as may be the case with Sam's fallen Haradrim soldier, end up enslaved by it.[41] Although Tolkien tends to categorize things into binary oppositions and notes the ability of evil to exploit ambiguity, he would also probably argue that uncertainty about death is a necessary part of life; without it, a free choice to trust in the afterlife is impossible. Strict binary categories may make life easier to deal with, but they cannot account for everything, and Tolkien shows that the same ambiguity that evil exploits for its ends also makes good possible. For Elves and humans, the awareness of their difference often causes strife, but the need to trust each other makes the occasion of doubt a *felix culpa*.

Tolkien's insistence on the separate categories of mortality and immortality, while probably based on the self–Other mindset of the medieval texts he knew and his conception of the natural and supernatural, nevertheless has led to criticism because racial issues are often presented by the dominant culture as a self–Other opposition, and modern scholarship on race, gender, and class often tends to begin by deconstructing such oppositions. While Tolkien abhorred racism and the denial of dignity to different races, he still had a tendency to create oppositions (dark and light, good and evil, beauty and ugliness, Elf and human, and so on) that might be interpreted as racism by readers trained to read against a text, and although Tolkien opposed racial discrimination in several of his letters, there are times when these oppositions cause problems of appearance for him.

Tolkien explicitly denounces claims of racial superiority several times in his letters. In 1938 Rütten and Loenig Verlag in Potsdam wished to publish a German edition of *The Hobbit*, but they sent a letter to Allen and Unwin asking if Tolkien were Aryan (*arisch*). Tolkien sent two letters to Allen and Unwin for forwarding, one of which was kept. The surviving letter suggests that Tolkien was polite but direct with the press. "I am not of *Aryan* extraction; that is, Indo-iranian. . . . But if I am to understand that you are enquiring whether or not I am of *Jewish* origin, I can only reply that I regret that I appear to have *no* ancestors of that gifted people. . . . I cannot, however, forbear to comment that if impertinent and irrelevant inquiries of this sort are to become the rule in matters of literature, then the time is not far distant when a German name will no longer be a source of pride" (*Letters*, 37–38).[42] When another correspondent asks about the Nordic element in his works, he responds, "Not *Nordic*, please! A word I personally dislike; it is associated. . .with racialist theories" (*Letters*, 375).[43] When discussing the abuse of the word "freedom" with his son Christopher, he notes that "at most, it would seem to imply that those who domineer over you should speak (natively) the same language—which in the last resort is all that the confused ideas of race or nation boil down to; or class for that matter, in England."[44] Later in the same letter, Tolkien denounces the dehumanizing tendencies of racism: "The Germans have just as much right to declare the Poles and Jews exterminable vermin, subhuman, as we have to select the Germans: in other words, no right, no matter what they have done" (*Letters*, 93). In another letter to Christopher, Tolkien also notes the racial implications of Allied involvement overseas, stating that he knows "nothing about British or American imperialism in the Far East that does not fill me with regret and disgust" (*Letters*, 115). The issues of race and class are certainly present in Tolkien's thinking, and he is able to recognize and reject explicit othering based on race.

As noted above, though, the implications of Tolkien's oppositions can leave him open to charges of sharing in the implicit racism of his time; although he recognizes the injustice of demonizing the Other, Tolkien occasionally slips into it himself, although with more qualification than many of his contemporaries. W.H. Auden once asked Tolkien if the race of Orcs, as totally irredeemable monsters, was heretical in Christianity, and Tolkien replied that he could not say: "I don't feel under any obligation to make my story fit with formalized Christian theology, though I actually intended it to be consonant with Christian thought and belief, which is asserted somewhere. . .where Frodo asserts that the orcs are not evil in origin. We believe that, I suppose, of all human kinds and sorts and breeds, though some *appear*, both as individuals and groups to be, by us at any rate, unredeemable" (*Letters*, 355; my emphasis). In a letter to Christopher, he again suggests that some are possibly irredeemable, and while including English people, he specifies the German and Japanese Others of World War II: "There are no genuine Uruks, that is folk made bad by the intention of their maker; and not many who are so corrupted as to be irredeemable (though I fear it must be admitted that there are human creatures that *seem* irredeemable short of a special miracle, and that there are probably abnormally many of such creatures in Deutschland and Nippon—but certainly these unhappy countries have no monopoly: I have met them, or thought so, in England's green and pleasant land)" (*Letters*, 90; my emphasis). Tolkien uses the words "appear" and "seem," implying the possibility of redemption and the danger of such apparent evil being a function of one's own biases; he also notes in the *Silmarillion* that "deep in their dark hearts the Orcs loathed the master whom they served in fear, the maker only of their misery" (*Silm*, 50).[45] However, the idea of the completely corrupted or overpowered free will is a subtle form of dehumanization and othering; Orcs and trolls can speak, which by medieval standards made them rational, mortal animals and "humane," to use Tolkien's term, but they appear to delight in evil and to be incapable of change. Tolkien's description of Orcs in a letter to Forrest Ackerman regarding an animated movie treatment is also unsettling: Orcs are "in fact degraded and repulsive versions of the (to Europeans) least lovely Mongol-types" (*Letters*, 274). Orcs are explicitly contrasted with European standards of beauty by being compared to Asian Others; whether Tolkien is commenting on European biases or acknowledging his own beliefs is unclear from the context. However, by describing Orcs in such terms Tolkien perpetuates a negative relation to non-European peoples, whether consciously or not, by equating evil with the Other. Despite acknowledging the evils of racism and recognizing the equality of the races, Tolkien may have inherited some of the implicit biases of his time toward others and does not seem to have questioned race itself as an intellectual category (which, to be fair, few others of his time did either).

Much of the criticism of Tolkien that Thomas Shippey has noted tends to attack the simplistic nature of Tolkien's worldview or some form of the binary oppositions noted throughout this essay.[46] However, the depiction of Middle-earth is to some extent conditioned by the literature Tolkien studied and adapted, which very often had the same kinds of binary oppositions behind it, and his experiences of war made him aware of the consequences of oversimplifying one's worldview.[47] Tolkien was a human being and would have admitted himself to be fallible; his society, also, had not yet become as self-aware or as self-critical with respect to colonialism and racism as it is today. However, one can perceive an awareness of the artificiality of dividing humans into races in Tolkien's work; the presence of the outsider is what allows a person to define him or herself against another but then to stand in the Other's place and see oneself as another,[48] and the presence of the Other in Tolkien's works allows humans to engage in a self-critique. Tolkien acknowledges the ambiguous treatment that the *sigelwara* receive in Anglo-Saxon literature, but the majority of texts emphasize only their difference, not their hostility to others; when encountered, they are quite human. Similarly, by depicting humanity from the perspectives of Hobbits and Elves, Tolkien allows his reader to empathize more with that which unites the "humane" beings than with that which divides them; we all must die, and the ways in which we isolate ourselves from the Other obscure the common being all humans share and rob us of the ability to perceive the beauty and wisdom to be gained by encountering the Other. Tolkien himself believed that the home of humans was not of this earth; his belief in the ultimate encounter with the Other shaped his fiction and allowed him—and us—to hope that we can find a way to overcome the divisions caused by exploitation of difference.

Notes

1. Lev Grossman, "Feeding on Fantasy," *Time*, December 2, 2002, 94.
2. See Jane Chance, *The Lord of the Rings: The Mythology of Power* (Lexington: University Press of Kentucky, 2001), 26–37; William Dowie, "The Gospel of Middle-earth according to J. R. R. Tolkien," in *J. R. R. Tolkien, Scholar and Storyteller: Essays in Memoriam*, ed. Mary Salu and Robert T. Farrell (Ithaca, NY: Cornell University Press, 1979), 269; Bradley J. Birzer, *J.R.R. Tolkien's Sanctifying Myth: Understanding Middle-Earth* (Wilmington, DE: ISI Books,

2002), 43, 109–10, 114–23; John Garth, *Tolkien and the Great War: The Threshold of Middle-Earth* (Boston: Houghton Mifflin, 2003), 301; and Humphrey Carpenter, *J. R. R. Tolkien: A Biography* (Boston: Houghton Mifflin, 1977), 13 (hereafter cited in text and notes as *Biography*).
3. Paul Ricoeur, *Oneself as Another*, trans. Kathleen Blamey (Chicago: University of Chicago Press, 1992), 125–39.
4. T.A. Shippey, *J. R. R. Tolkien: Author of the Century* (Boston: Houghton Mifflin, 2001), 327–28. See also Douglas A. Anderson, "Tolkien after All These Years," in *Meditations on Middle-Earth*, ed. Karen Haber (New York: St. Martin's, 2001), 136–41.
5. *Swerting* also occurs as a proper name in *Beowulf*; Tolkien probably knew Kemp Malone's article "Swerting," *Germanic Review* 14 (1939): 235–57.
6. Miranda Wilcox, "Exilic Imagining in *The Seafarer* and *The Lord of the Rings*," in *Tolkien the Medievalist*, ed. Jane Chance (London and New York: Routledge, 2003), 141–43.
7. Carpenter, *Biography*, 23–24.
8. See, for example, Shippey, *Author*, 130 ff.; Tolkien, *The Letters of J. R. R. Tolkien*, ed. Humphrey Carpenter with Christopher Tolkien (Boston: Houghton Mifflin, 1981), 84, hereafter cited in text and notes as *Letters*; Birzer, *Sanctifying Myth*, 46–49; Garth, *Great War*, 5, 48, 120–23.
9. All biblical citations are from *The Jerusalem Bible, Reader's Edition* (New York: Doubleday, 1968).
10. J.R.R. Tolkien, *The Silmarillion*, ed. by Christopher Tolkien, 2nd edn. (Boston: Houghton Mifflin, 2001), 129 (hereafter cited as *Silm* in text and notes).
11. Birzer, *Sanctifying Myth*, 95.
12. Tolkien, in "Sigelwara Land," *Medium Ævum* 1 (1932): 183–96 ("Sigelwara Land 1") and 3 (1934): 95–111, argues that the word for black beings in fiery surroundings draws more on Norse servants of Múspell than on Ethiopians, despite its use as a gloss for *Æthiopes*. See Frank Snowden, *Blacks in Antiquity: Ethiopians in the Greco-Roman Experience* (Cambridge, MA: Harvard University Press, 1970), 169–95; the association of demons with Ethiopians came when metaphoric discussions of color by Augustine and Isidore were misunderstood and literally applied by later Christian authors. See also Shippey, *Road to Middle-Earth* (Boston: Houghton Mifflin, 1983), 33–35.
13. Mary Clayton and Hugh Magennis, *The Old English Lives of St. Margaret* (Cambridge, UK: Cambridge University Press, 1994), 124, 162.
14. Tolkien gives a list of twenty-five occurrences of *sigelwara* in "Sigelwara Land 1," 184–90. In four of these occurrences, the Sigelwara are explicitly associated with evil or demons: Ælfric's homilies on St. Bartholomew (*ormæte silhearwa*, "a huge Ethiopian") and St. Simon and St. Jude (*twegen blace Silhearwan*, "two black Ethiopians"); in the *Old English Martyrology*, St. Bartholomew (*miclne Sigelhearwan*, "a great Ethiopian," i.e., in comparison to most Ethiopians); and Ælfric's *Lives of Saints*, St. Julian (*silhearwan atelices hiwes swa heage swa entes*, "an Ethiopian of terrible form, as tall as a giant").

The citations are from the following editions: Peter Clemoes, *Ælfric's Catholic Homilies: The First Series*, Early English Text Society s.s. 17 (Oxford: University Press for the Early English Text Society, 1997), 445; Malcolm Godden, *Ælfric's Catholic Homiles: The Second Series*, Early English Text Society s.s. 5 (Oxford: University Press for the Early English Text Society, 1979), 286; Günter Kotzor, *Das altenglische Martyrologium* (Munich: Bayerischen Akademie der Wissenschaften, 1981), 186–87; W.W. Skeat, *Ælfric's Lives of Saints, Being a Set of Sermons on Saints' Days Formerly Observed by the English Church*, Early English Text Society o.s. 76, 82 (London: Trübner for the Early English Text Society, 1881, 1900), 1:107.

15. Tolkien, "Sigelwara Land 1," 184–90; the twenty-one occurrences remaining are glosses and descriptions of the *sigelwara* themselves or of the places they live.
16. Andy Orchard, *Pride and Prodigies: Studies in the Monsters of the Beowulf-Manuscript* (Cambridge, UK: D. S. Brewer, 1995), 262–64: "Sunt enim Aethiopes toto corpore nigri, quos sol flagrans nimio ardore semper adurit, quia sub tertio zonarum feruentissimo et torrido mundi circulo demorantur, et a uapore ardentissimorum siderum terrarum defenduntur latebris."
17. Tolkien, "Sigelwara Land 1," 192.
18. Orchard, *Pride*, 202: "Ðær mannkynn is þæt syndan sweartes hiwes on ansyne, þa man hateð silhearwan."
19. *Exodus*, lines 69–71, in *The Junius Manuscript*, The Anglo-Saxon Poetic Records 1, ed. G.P. Krapp (New York: Columbia University Press, 1931), 93: "Wiston him be suðan Sigelwara land, / forbærned burhhleoðu, brune leode, / hatum heofoncolum." [They knew to be to the south of them the land of the Ethiopians, burned mountaintops, people brown from the heat of heaven's coals.]
20. Aelfric, *De temporibus anni*, ed. Heinrich Henel, Early English Text Society o.s. 213 (London: Oxford University Press for the Early English Text Society, 1942), 48: "Meroe hatte an igland. þæt is ðæra Silhearwena eard."
21. Ps. 86:3, in G.P. Krapp, *The Paris Psalter and the Meters of Boethius*, The Anglo-Saxon Poetic Records 5 (New York: Columbia University Press, 1932), 54.
22. *Fates of the Apostles*, line 64, in *The Vercelli Book*, ed. G.P. Krapp (New York: Columbia University Press, 1932), 53: "mid Sigelwarum soð yppe weard."
23. Orchard, *Pride*, 248: "Wæs he se bisceop .X. fota upheah, 7 eall him wæs se lichoma sweart."
24. Brian McFadden, "The Social Context of Narrative Disruption in *The Letter of Alexander to Aristotle*," *Anglo-Saxon England* 30 (2001): 102, 104, 106–07. Tolkien was familiar with Alexander's history; see *Letters*, p. 64. See also Garth, *Great War*, 98–100, for Elves as fearful of humans and vice versa.
25. McFadden, "Social Context," 104–05.
26. Cf. Augustine, *De civitate Dei* 16.8, ed. Emanuel Hoffmann, Corpus Scriptorum Ecclesiasticorum Latinorum 40 (Vienna: Tempsky, 1899–1900), 2:139: "homo, id est animal rationale mortale" [a man, that is, a rational mortal animal].
27. Tolkien, *The Lord of the Rings* (Boston: Houghton Mifflin, 1994), 6.5, 947, hereafter cited in text and notes as *LR*.

28. See Paul Ricoeur, *Time and Narrative*, trans. Kathleen McLaughlin and David Pellauer (Chicago: University of Chicago Press, 1984), 3:148–56, 184–92, and *Oneself*, 164, for the duty of a historical narrator to represent the narratives of the dead accurately.
29. See Garth, *Great War*, 124, 128, 218.
30. See Orchard for the elephant's Anglo-Latin and Old English occurrences in *Liber monstrorum* (*Pride*, 290), *Alexander to Aristotle* (*Pride*, 242), and *Wonders of the East* (*Pride*, 190). It should be noted that the text of *Wonders* in the *Beowulf* MS reads *olfenda* (camels); *ylpenda* (elephants) is found in the MS London, British Library, Cotton Tiberius B.v, and Oxford, Bodleian Library, Bodl. 614, versions, as well as in the Latin (*Pride*, 177). See J.E. Cross, "The Elephant to Alfred, Ælfric, Aldhelm, and Others," *Studia Neophilologica* 37 (1965): 373; *The Riddles of Aldhelm*, ed. J. H. Pitman (New Haven, CT: Yale, 1925), 58; and Garth, *Great War*, 97.
31. See, for example, Chance, *Mythology of Power*, 20–25; and Dowie, "Gospel," 278.
32. See Derek Brewer, "*The Lord of the Rings* as Romance," in *J. R. R. Tolkien, Scholar and Storyteller: Essays in Memoriam*, ed. Mary Salu and Robert T. Farrell (Ithaca, NY: Cornell University Press, 1979), 259–61.
33. See also Birzer, *Sanctifying Myth*, 47; and Garth, *Great War*, 110.
34. See Wilcox, "Exilic Imagining," 144–47.
35. David Williams, *Deformed Discourse: The Function of the Monster in Mediaeval Thought and Literature* (Montreal and Kingston: McGill-Queen's University Press, 1996), 23–60, especially 58–60.
36. See Jonathan Evans, "The Anthropology of Arda: Creation, Theology, and the Race of Men," in Chance, *Tolkien the Medievalist*, 216; both humans and Elves have experienced a fall that limits their vision and understanding to some degree.
37. Williams, *Deformed Discourse*, 61–103, especially 70–82.
38. Dowie, "Gospel," 281.
39. Tolkien, "On Fairy Stories," *The Tolkien Reader* (New York: Ballantine, 1966), 67–68.
40. Karen Jolly, "Father God and Mother Earth: Nature Mysticism in the Anglo-Saxon World," in *The Medieval World of Nature: A Book of Essays*, ed. Joyce Salisbury (New York: Garland, 1993), 224–25.
41. See Birzer, *Sanctifying Myth*, 84–85.
42. See also Garth, *Great War*, 96.
43. See Christine Chism, "Middle-earth, the Middle Ages, and the Aryan Nation: Myth and History in World War II," in Chance, *Tolkien the Medievalist*, 71–79.
44. See also Garth, *Great War*, 94–95.
45. See Birzer, *Sanctifying Myth*, 93–95.
46. Shippey, *Author*, xix–xxvi, 305–18; see also Orson Scott Card, "How Tolkien Means," in Haber, *Meditations*, 154–61.
47. Garth, *Great War*, 288–301.
48. Ricoeur, *Oneself*, 180–94.

CHAPTER 12

TOLKIEN AND THE OTHER: RACE AND GENDER IN MIDDLE-EARTH

Jane Chance

> *In this modern and postmodern analysis of alterity and difference, Tolkien in both his Anglo-Saxon scholarship and the fantasy of* The Lord of the Rings *reveals his abhorrence of the deliberate isolation of and prejudice against those who differ from the hegemonic norm, in race, nationality, culture, class, age, or gender.*

J.R.R. Tolkien's interest in the Middle Ages clearly shaped his scholarly writing, but it is not always as clear that this interest equally colored his fiction. That most readers fail to see this medievalness is not so strange: our assumptions about fantasy, like Tolkien's in "On Fairy-stories," depend upon the fantastic as an avenue of escape from reality. There is, therefore, no necessary correlation between fantasy and the historical medieval. Further, many readers look for entertainment instead of meaning in fantasy, especially Tolkien's.

Yet, as John Clute and John Grant aptly note, in *The Encyclopedia of Fantasy* (1997), fantasy *should be* subversive: "It could be argued that, if fantasy (and debatably the literature of the fantastic as a whole) has a purpose other than to entertain, it is to show readers *how to perceive*; an extension of the argument is that fantasy may try to alter readers' perception of reality.... Most full-fantasy texts have at their core the urge to *change* the reader; that is, full fantasy is by definition a subversive literary form."[1]

How does Tolkien subvert fantasy in *The Lord of the Rings*? In some respects, this is easy to answer. In the fantastic world of Middle-earth depicted in his modern epic-romance, Tolkien alters the nature of the questor and the purpose of the quest. Instead of a hero who participates in a contest or battle between adversaries from differing nations to settle an issue, often of a territorial as well as moral nature, Tolkien substitutes small middle-aged Hobbits unused to fighting—Frodo, Merry, Pippin, and Sam; a dirty Ranger who also emerges as the long-concealed King of Gondor—Aragorn; a shield-maiden from Rohan who is prohibited by her uncle-king from participating in the battle but who nevertheless in violation of that ban dons armor as the warrior Dernhelm to kill a Nazgûl lord—Éowyn; a second son of the Steward of Gondor who has been cast away to police outlying territory—Faramir; and walking tree-shepherds, who stand up to rampant wizards like Saruman. Tolkien similarly alters the quest to an anti-quest: a seemingly pedestrian mission to return a ring to the place where it was forged and destroy it. Meanwhile, epic battles do rage in the background, but Tolkien seems more interested in those who come to battle, if at all, in ways and forms and for reasons that differ from those in the conventional epic-romance.

His unconventional approach is one that valorizes the least heroic characters in the epic romance and thereby subverts its fantasy. This approach also deconstructs—unhinges—the medieval literary and heroic idealization of the epic romance. Not only in *The Lord of the Rings*, but in addition, as I argue in this essay, throughout his other fiction and his scholarly writing, Tolkien demonstrates that he dislikes most of all a very modern prejudice, segregation of the Other, and isolation of those who are different, whether by race, nationality, culture, class, age, or gender.

This idea may seem incongruent with previous Tolkien criticism that has argued for his conservative monarchism, Roman Catholicism, and even racism.[2] Exemplary of the assumption that Tolkien's personal commitments necessarily correlate with his creative practice, Fred Inglis, in an essay published over twenty years ago in England titled "Gentility and Powerlessness: Tolkien and the New Class," stated categorically that Tolkien is "ineffably English, with England's old and grim snobbery and stupidity, and England's excellent idealism and high-mindedness. . . . Tolkien is no Fascist, but his great myth may be said, as Wagner's was, to prefigure the genuine ideals and nobilities of which Fascism is the dark negation."[3]

Yet evidence from Tolkien's scholarship indicates that he is supremely conscious of precisely those individuals or groups or races who might be considered marginal within a Fascist system of exclusion, that is, who exist on the peripheries of society, often in exile, or as outcasts. Note the multicultural analogy the Southern African-born scholar constructs in his

"Valedictory Address," delivered when he retired from Oxford as Merton Professor of English Language and Literature: "I do not claim to be the most learned of those who have come hither from the far end of the Dark Continent. But I have the hatred of *apartheid* in my bones; and most of all I detest the segregation or separation of Language and Literature. I do not care which of them you think Whiter."[4] *Apartheid*, or "apartness," in South African dialect, according to *Webster's New World Dictionary*, refers to "the policy of strict racial segregation and discrimination against the nature of Negroes and other colored people as practiced in the Union of South Africa." But Tolkien means *apartheid* both literally and also more figuratively and generally. In British English Departments during much of the early twentieth century, the study of language (the early vernacular languages of Old and Middle English, for example) had been separated from the study of literature (modern literature from Chaucer to 1900). Over Tolkien's long career he sought means to connect both in the English Department curriculum. This desire was bolstered by his fiction writing, which grew out of his love of philology: he saw literature and philology as inextricably mixed.[5] Tolkien is also anti-*apartheid* in a more cosmic and multicultural sense: throughout his mythology he promotes the intermarriage of races—Maia, Elf, and Man—and the fellowship of species—Elf, Man, Dwarf, and Hobbit—in order to blend their strengths in governance and parliamentary representation. He even sees the three types of Hobbits—Harfoot, Fallohide, and Stoor—as separated unnecessarily by geography, so that much of the *Lord of the Rings* maps out the gradual acceptance of an obnoxious Stoor—Gollum—by a merciful and tolerant Harfoot-Fallohide, Frodo.

I would like to focus first on a few of Tolkien's scholarly ventures that demonstrate very specifically his broad interest in apartheid—that which separates one individual or race or nation or body of knowledge from another. In 1925, Tolkien published a long, two-part philological note, "Sigelwara Land,"[6] about those two words "Sigelwara" and "land" in the Old English poem *Exodus* (lines 69–71), which he later came to edit:

> Sigelwara land,
> forbærned burh-hleoðu, brune leode,
> hatum heofoncolum.[7]

In his later translation of the poem, Tolkien renders this epigraph to his published philological notes as "the Sundwellers' land, hill-slopes scorched and folk grown swart under the hot furnace of the skies" (*Exodus*, 21). The phrase "Sigelwara land" is an Anglo-Saxon appositive for the Ethiopians, whom he defines as classically graced initially because the Olympian gods had visited them. But in Old English, according to Tolkien, Ethiopia is usually referred to as "Sigelwara land" because of the color of its inhabitants' skin and its implied infernal landscape, that is, a fiery one that burned sinners black. "Their country," Tolkien notes, "was too like hell to escape the comparison, and the blackness of the inhabitants became more than skin-deep. A diabolic folk, yet worthy perhaps of a note, if not a visit."[8] For this reason the Old English compound *Sigelwara* usually appears in geographical descriptions or in descriptions of hell. In explanation, Tolkien notes that "Ethiopia was hot and its people black. That Hell was similar in both respects would occur to many."[9] The compound also appears in homilies (used like the "Weder-Geats" of a people) to refer to the Ethiopians as "devils, worshipped rather than worshippers."[10] Specifically, *Sigel* can mean "sun" or "jewel," most likely the sun: "Yet it cannot be ignored that Ethiopia was also a land of gems."[11]

For *hearwa*, in the *Sigelwara* compound (*Sigel* + *hearwa*), Tolkien finds some similar Old Norse words for "dusky" that apply to the wolf, the eagle, the raven (the topos for the beasts of battle) and also to a name for one of twelve sons of Praell and Pi'r, "who were with their twelve sisters the ancestors of all slaves."[12] Thus "*Sigelhearwa*," according to Tolkien, "would be made black by the sun."[13] Tolkien senses that "[g]limpses are caught, if dim and confused, of the background of English and northern tradition and imagination, which has colored the verse-treatment of Scripture, and determined the diction of poems."[14] He also likes words whose origins mirror their diverse cultures: "*Sigel* may be taken as a symbol of the intricate blending of the Latin and Northern which makes the study of Old English peculiarly interesting and controversial; *hearwa* of that large part of ancient English language and lore which has now vanished beyond recall, *swa hit no wære*."[15] The very marriage and interweaving of Latin with the northern and Anglo-Saxon is not just a matter of aesthetic appreciation for Tolkien: it anticipates many other forms of more explicit reconciliation he will celebrate in his writings.

These lines about "Sigelwara land" originate in one of Tolkien's posthumously published works, an edition and modern English translation of the Old English version of the biblical book of Exodus, which dramatizes the flight of the exiled Israelites from Egypt and their passage through the Red Sea. The very subject, although biblical and Old Testament, is *apartheid*—as understood through class (the protagonists are slaves), nation (they are Israelites in exile), and religion (their faith is Hebraic). Figuratively, their flight, according to the introduction to the translation in the commentary, signifies more generally the exile of the soul from God's grace: Tolkien describes it as "at once an historical poem about events of extreme importance, an account of the preservation of the chosen people and the fulfilment of the promises made to Abraham; and it is an allegory of the soul, or of the Church of militant souls, marching under the hand of God, pursued by the powers of darkness, until it attains to the promised land of Heaven."[16]

Additionally, in blending two distinct cultures, the scene in Tolkien's *Exodus* is imbued with Germanic heroic diction in order to valorize his protagonists, Moses and the Jews, the exiled peoples: the "chieftain" Moses, to whom God gives the "lives of his kinsmen," is "prince of his people, a leader of the host, sage and wise of heart, valiant captain of his folk" (*Exodus*, 20). The "enemies of God," Pharaoh's race, receives plagues and the "fall of their princes," so that "mirth was hushed in the halls bereft of treasure" (*Exodus*, 20). A poem thus reminiscent of *Beowulf* and the deadly visitation of the hall Heorot by the monster Grendel, *Exodus* describes how "far and wide the Slayer ranged grievously afflicting the people" (*Exodus*, 21). For the chieftain Moses, "high the heart of him who led the kindred" (*Exodus*, 21); the war scene, with the "gallant men" led by Moses, is elaborated with Germanic martial imagery and description of the brightness of the host and the flashing of the shields (*Exodus*, 22). Abraham, son of Noah, who follows as tenth in generations after Moses, is also described in the poem as in Germanic-like exile (*Exodus*, 28). And when Moses leads the Israelites in flight, they, too, are described as "Exiles from home, in mourning they possess this hall of passing guests, lamenting in their hearts" (*Exodus*, 31).

Thus far, the scholarly examples of *apartheid* and "apartness" involve ancient Africa. Tolkien the medievalist has identified racial difference as an expression of geographical and national difference and its concomitant marginalization in English, Northern, and Hebraic traditions; he has focused, in addition, on class differences—exiled peoples forced to live in foreign lands as wretched slaves. Tolkien was also fascinated by the figure of the Old English *wraecca*, the word from which modern "wretch" comes, but which refers to the exile in Old English. Given the comitatus nature of Old English society—one predicated upon the bond between the retainer and a goldlord, the retainer providing service and valor in battle when necessary, the goldlord providing food, a hall, and reward for valor in mead ceremonies— the man without a goldlord, in exile, was truly a man alone. The Old English elegy "The Wanderer" dramatizes the situation of a man who may be a *wraecca* because he has lost not only his goldlord but also his comitatus to some kind of calamity; it is clear he is a wanderer, in exile left to treasure only memories of his fellow warriors and his goldlord. "The Wanderer" is also cited in the "Valedictory Address" in which Tolkien expresses his loathing of *apartheid*. Additionally, Tolkien draws upon this poem to describe Rohan when Aragorn and his company stop there in *Two Towers*—Rohan itself constructed as a type of Old English society. In particular, Tolkien invokes the famous *ubi sunt* passage from "The Wanderer," in the words of

Tolkien expressed by Aragorn: "Where now the horse and rider? / Where is the horn that was blowing?" (*LR* 3.6, 497).[17] Tolkien the scholar, who translated *Beowulf* and then wrote the important essay about the epic that so changed its study in the twentieth-century academy,[18] also reveals an interest in the exile in that poem: Beowulf's own father, the Geat Ecgtheow, was an exile (and homicide) whom Danish Hrothgar took in. As a result, in recompense young Beowulf (whose early reputation suffered as a result of his father's ignominy) comes to Denmark at the time of greatest need to help Hrothgar by ridding his kingdom of Grendel after the aged king had failed to do so. But Beowulf also comes to earn his own fame, his *lof* (of which he is most desirous, as we learn from the last word in the epic, *lofgeornost*). Ironically, Grendel himself is described also as a wanderer, a monster of the race of Cain condemned to journey—homeless—over the earth.

But it is not just the stigma of racial, class, and national "apartness," difference, in the group or the individual that concerns scholar Tolkien; it is also that of class, age, and gender. For the Old English poem "The Battle of Maldon," about a battle recorded in the Anglo-Saxon chronicle entry for the year 991, Tolkien wrote a fictional verse-drama sequel in which the subordinate old warrior portrays the positive and heroic values of love and loyalty for his lord, as contrasted with the chief's negative and chivalric value of *ofermod*, or "pride."[19] In the Old English poem, the old (seemingly useless) retainer Beorhtwold, ready to lay down his life for his foolish lord, proclaims, when his lord has fallen and all seems to be lost, that

> Hige sceal þe heardra, heorte þe cenre,
> mod sceal þe mare þe ure mægen lytlað.
> [Will shall be the sterner, heart the bolder,
> spirit the greater as our strength lessens.][20]

In lines 89–90, the poet explains the reason for the loss of the battle (and with it, the disintegration of the comitatus): "Ða se eorl ongan for his ofermode/ alyfan landes to fela la þere ðeode," or, in Tolkien's translation in "Ofermod," "then the earl in his overmastering pride actually yielded ground to the enemy, as he should not have done."[21] Beorhtnoth gave the Danes an opportunity to fight on equal ground (cut off as they were by rising waters), but thereby lost the battle.

The reason for Beorhtnoth's pride—according to Tolkien in his essay, "Ofermod," which he appends to the sequel of "The Battle of Maldon," titled "The Homecoming of Beorhtnoth Beorhthelm's Son" (1953)—lies in the lamentable advent of chivalry: "Yet this element of pride, in the form of the desire for honor and glory, in life and after death, tends to grow, to become a chief motive, driving a man beyond the bleak heroic necessity to excess—to chivalry."[22] When a chief considers his men as a means to the end of self-glorification, he suffers, according to Tolkien, at least, from the pride characteristic of chivalry, which is not heroic. Not only does Beorhtnoth die in the Battle of Maldon as a result of his pride, but it is also left to retainer Beorhtwold to defend his lost lord in what has become a hopeless skirmish.

Why Tolkien sides with "the little guy," the ignominious exile, is clear from his own otherness in England as a southern African Catholic orphan with ties to the similarly marginalized western Midlands cities of Birmingham and Sheffield. An orphan like Frodo, he can also be described as in exile much of his life. Born in Bloemfontein in 1892, he was moved at the age of three to a town near Birmingham in England.[23] This traumatic journey existentially shaped much of his early perception of reality: he reveals, "quite by accident, I have a very vivid child's view, which was the result of being taken away from one country and put in another hemisphere—the place where I belonged but which was totally novel and strange. After the barren, arid heat a Christmas tree. But no, it was not an unhappy childhood. It was full of tragedies but it didn't tot up to an unhappy childhood."[24] These "tragedies" refer to his home life. He lost his father the year after the move from the south of Africa, when he was four; at the age of twelve (1904), he also lost his mother. Furthermore, as a Roman Catholic, he was definitely in the religious minority in a country wedded to the Church of England.

Feeling isolated in the academic community because of his professed field of Language (Old and Middle English), Tolkien also felt simultaneously called upon to do battle with critical adversaries—his colleagues in Literature (modern literature, every work up to 1900 other than the medieval). It is no accident that Tolkien quotes from "The Wanderer" in Old English on the page following his discussion of his hatred of *apartheid* in "Valedictory Address" (239). Identifying himself with the isolated speaker in the Old English dramatic monologue, Tolkien uses the famous *ubi sunt* passage from this poem ("Hwær cwóm mearh, hwær cwóm mago?" [Where is the horse gone, where the young rider?]) to point out his own apparent role as a lone exponent of Language, with new generations of scholars failing to understand its importance. He then follows the passage from "The Wanderer" in the address with an example of another language—his invented Elvish—to be understood, apparently, as another beleaguered and marginalized type of language. He felt that his colleagues at Oxford unfairly denigrated his fantastic fiction.[25]

Tolkien's very creation of the Hobbits as a species reflects his own sense of himself as displaced, marginal, exiled, queer, and different from other species and individuals. In letter 213 he confesses, "I am in fact a Hobbit," in that he smoked a pipe, liked gardens and trees and plain food, had a simple sense of humor, and did not travel much.[26] Aspects of his life also creep into the names in his fantasy: "Bag End" (the name of Bilbo's house) was named after his Aunt Jane's farm in Worcestershire.[27] "Hobbiton" with the mill on the river is actually outside Birmingham and can be identified with a village called Sarehole where Tolkien lived for four years as a child.

Given this context, it should come as no surprise that Tolkien's own comments about *The Lord of the Rings* reflect aspects of his own—and every Englishman's—day-to-day life during wartime as heroic, or that his Hobbit protagonist represents an unlikely antihero. Tolkien's definition of the hero in the twentieth century refers back to the ordinary man living on the small island of Great Britain during World War II: "I've always been impressed...that we are here, surviving, because of the indomitable courage of *quite small people* against impossible odds."[28] And in relation to *The Lord of the Rings*, he declares, in a draft letter to Michael Straits, written sometime in January or February 1956, that *The Lord of the Rings* is Hobbito-centric: it was planned primarily as "a study of the ennoblement (or sanctification) of the humble."[29] Put another way, the quest in the epic is an antiquest, and his hero, an antihero, one who fails, even if Tolkien exonerates him.[30] There are

> positions in which the "good" of the world depends on the behaviour of an individual in circumstances which demand of him suffering and endurance far beyond the normal—even, it may happen (or seem, humanly speaking), demand a strength of body and mind which he does not possess: he is in a sense doomed to failure, doomed to fall to temptation or be broken by pressure against his "will": that is against any choice he could make or would make unfettered, not under the duress. Frodo was in such a position.... The Quest therefore was bound to fail as a piece of world-plan, and also was bound to end in disaster as the story of humble Frodo's development to the "noble," his sanctification.... Fail it would and did as far as Frodo considered alone was concerned.[31]

We think of other antiheroes in *The Lord of the Rings*—Gollum, scarcely more than a shadow of a living thing, bites off the Ring still on Frodo's finger and incidentally also saves Middle-earth. And the very humble and insignificant gardener's son Sam himself aids Frodo in the fulfillment of his quest, selflessly spurns the Ring, and carries his master (when Frodo can no longer walk) up Mount Doom. Tolkien describes Sam as "a more representative hobbit than any others.... He did not think of himself as heroic or even brave, or in any way admirable—except in his service and loyalty to his master."[32] We are reminded of Beorhtwald, the old warrior in "The Battle of Maldon" who generously gives his life in support of his proud chief, Beorhtnoth.

Within this context of multicultural and multiracial difference, one of the major moral points of *The Lord of the Rings* is that all four of the Hobbit heroes (or antiheroes) are described as different from the other Hobbits. Of all these queer and unnatural Hobbits, Gollum is the most disgusting and least sympathetic. Both Sam and Frodo regard Gollum as queer and unnatural. For Frodo, Gollum is the Shire equivalent of a Brandybuck living across the river, so that the Ringbearer initially reacts to Gollum's strangeness—his "queerness"—as Sandyman did to him—with suspicion and indignation. Frodo himself wishes Gandalf had killed Gollum when he had had the chance. Yet it is because of Gollum that the quest is completed. Despite seeming initially different, Gollum remains a much diminished Hobbit. Descended from the wandering, matriarchal Stoor branch of the Gladden Fields, he is not a typical Harfoot Hobbit from the Shire or Bree or a fair, adventuresome Fallohide from the upper Anduin or Eriador (the branch of the Hobbits from which leaders often come, and the line from which the Tooks, Brandybucks, and Bolgars descended). In this sense Gollum represents a Hobbit alter ego for Bilbo–Frodo, both of the Bagginses so queer and different from others in the Shire because of their Fallohide–Harfoot mixed ancestry.

To explain: more than insignificant and ordinary, inadequate Frodo, like his first (and second) cousin Bilbo, comes from "queer folk."[33] One of the great inventions of Tolkien is to make his heroes marginal beings, ordinary and even antiheroic. Frodo is a Baggins, but half Brandybuck, that is, a family that hales from Buckland, where, as Old Noakes says, "folks are so queer" (*LR* 1.1, 22). Why are they queer, meaning "unnatural"? Because according to Daddy Twofoot they live "right agin the Old Forest. . .a dark bad place" (*LR* 1.1, 22). And also because, in an un-Hobbitlike way, these Hobbits use boats, also considered "unnatural" by the Gaffer. Indeed, Frodo's father, Drogo, married Primula Brandybuck, and then they both drowned, leaving Frodo an orphan, adopted by Bilbo, who makes him his heir. But Bilbo is also queer: according to the Miller, "Bag End's a queer place, and its folk are queerer" (*LR* 1.1, 24). This is so because of "the outlandish folk that visit [Bilbo]: dwarves coming at night, and that old wandering conjuror, Gandalf" (*LR* 1.1, 24),[34] "outlandish" meaning "queer and different," but also meaning "out of land." Personally, Bilbo is queer because he is perpetually young (from having borne the Ring) (unlike Jackson's film-version of Bilbo) and rich (because of his share of Smaug's treasure): the folk say, "It isn't natural, and trouble will come of it" (*LR* 1.1, 21).[35]

What exactly is Tolkien the scholar and fantasist trying to say about the Other? How is he trying to change his reader's understanding and behavior in relation to racial, national, and gender differences—which we have not yet discussed? One example of the latter, concerning the Ent Treebeard and his meeting with the Hobbits Merry and Pippin in *Two Towers*, within the larger epic dramatizes in miniature the ways that prejudice and intolerance develop and how the construction of alterity—when stereotyped as pejorative—can be halted.

Although in their different Hobbit ways Bildo, Frodo, Gollum, and Sam are all unnatural, or "queer," more dramatic are the differences among species (and genders) in *Two Towers*. Diversity and stereotyping dominate the second volume, one instance of which occurs in the early episode involving the Ents, the tree-shepherds, who are estranged both from other species (like the Hobbits) and from their own gendered counterparts, the Entwives. While the Ents, the leaders of trees who have been taught by the Elves (*LR* 3.4, 457),[36] are graced with movement—in fact, they have cut off Saruman's escape from Isengard—the trees of the Old Forest are rooted and envious of those creatures that can move. In addition, the Ent Treebeard explains to the Hobbits Merry and Pippin a gender difference within the Ent species that has nearly led to their extinction—the Ents have lost the Entwives because they are so self-absorbed (that is, Ents are interested in traveling and seeking out new trees, whereas Entwives like cultivating their gardens in one place) (*LR* 3.4, 464–65). Ents love the trees, woods, slopes, Elves, and Entwives like lesser trees, meads, sloe, wild apples (fruit), and herbs. When Treebeard sings a song of dialogue between an Ent and an Entwife, he therefore has to play both their parts: the Ent wants the Entwife to say his land is fair, but she wants a different kind of land; each wants the one to come to the other—but the Ent says he will come only in winter (*LR* 3.4, 466).[37] The Ents' lack of sensitivity to the Other has resulted in their mutual loss of one another through the Entwives' disappearance. How ironic that Treebeard's pushiness and insistence have led to the necessity of his singing both the parts, a necessity that might have educated him about their differences.

It is true that, within the larger context of Middle-earth, the agenda of both Maia Sauron and wizard Saruman is to erase not just gender difference but all difference, by installing one point of view—theirs. Yet, despite Treebeard's insensitivity, he is no tyrant. Treebeard at first proclaims his lack of interest in anyone else's perspective or cause, although his self-centeredness has not resulted in totalitarian domination over or manipulation of others: "I am not altogether on anybody's 'side,' because nobody is altogether on my 'side,' if you understand me: nobody cares for the woods as I care for them, not even Elves nowadays" (*LR* 3.4, 461).[38] His isolationism, however, has allowed the more aggressive Saruman to cut up the trees and leave them to rot. Treebeard confesses that "I have been idle. I have let things slip. It must stop!" (*LR* 3.4, 463).[39] So preoccupied with his own point of view, Treebeard has to learn how to understand others—including younger members of his own species and even the insignificant Hobbits—in order to rectify the situation. From Treebeard's point of view, for example, because Ents move so slowly, being hasty—presumably a trait of Hobbits—is bad (*LR* 3.4, 452).[40] Further, Treebeard has forgotten that, unlike the Ents, the Halflings do not stand to sleep (his forgetfulness once more demonstrates an insensitivity to the Other) (*LR* 3.4, 466).[41] Treebeard thinks he is talking to Entings, not to Merry and Pippin, who are not Orcs but a species new to him (*LR* 3.4, 463).[42]

The danger, then, of self-absorption is a lack of sensitivity to and respect for the differences of others that can develop into prejudice and intolerance. But Treebeard corrects his mistakes. Manifesting a new sensitivity to the Other, he introduces the Hobbits to a very appropriate Halfling companion, the Ent Bregalad, also known as Quickbeam for his hastiness, and therefore Treebeard is certain that they will "get along together." It is perhaps noteworthy that the un-Entlike Quickbeam might know of a tree that would please Entwives (although birds tore off the fruit and the Orcs cut the trees, which makes them silent and dead) (*LR* 3.4, 472).[43] Similarly, the Free Peoples' understanding of Sauron's intolerance for other viewpoints works to their advantage when the Dark Lord imagines the Free Peoples' motivations are identical to his: Sauron never realizes that they do not want war, that they do not have a new lord in mind to replace him, and that they wish to destroy the Ring (*LR* 3.4, 474).[44]

Even more important than the qualities of acceptance and understanding are those of forgiveness of and love for those who are different. Early on Gandalf reminds Frodo that forgiveness is the way to grace and peace of mind, because we simply do not know enough to judge others who are of different races or cultures. This reminder comes as a response at the moment early in *The Fellowship of the Ring* after Gandalf has explained the fact, history, and finding of the Ring, when Frodo, not understanding the mercy or pity that has stayed Bilbo's hand, wishes Gollum had been killed long ago (*LR* 1.2, 58).[45] That same mercy or pity toward Gollum will grow in Frodo and eventually save the Ring-bearer on the lip of Mount Doom. Even more ironically, Gollum's disobedience toward his "Master" Frodo at Mount Doom—only in a greater and providential sense to be construed as mercy or pity—saves Frodo when he betrays himself. And it is not that Gollum's (or Frodo's) *hand* is stayed—again, ironically, it is his finger that is bitten off, with the Ring still attached, that saves Frodo and also Middle-earth. As Tolkien himself says, in letter 181, to Michael Straits, about the end of the quest in *The Lord of the Rings*:

> [T]he "salvation" of the world and Frodo's own "salvation" is achieved by his previous pity and forgiveness of injury. At any point any prudent person would have told Frodo that Gollum would certainly betray him, and could rob him in the end. To "pity" him, to forbear to kill him, was a piece of folly, or a mystical belief in the ultimate value-in-itself of pity and generosity even if disastrous in the world of time. He did rob him and injure him in the end— but by a "grace," that last betrayal was at a precise juncture when the final evil deed was the most beneficial thing any one cd. have done for Frodo! By a situation created by his "forgiveness," [Frodo] was saved himself, and relieved of his burden.[46]

Finally, it is through such past and present love of other members of different species that the future of Middle-earth is guaranteed in the Fourth Age—the Age of Man. Throughout Tolkien's mythology, the linking of all families of Elves with the progeny of many different species—Maia, Elf, and Man—for Tolkien suggests the reconciliation of all social difference through peace and harmony. Modeling these intermarriages and mixed blood progeny on the classical prototype of the hero as half-god, half-human, Tolkien finds his ideal union in the seemingly tragic coupling of the ancestors of Aragorn, the lesser Man Beren and his superior, Elf Lúthien, in the *Silmarillion*.[47] Although the lovers suffer mutilation and even death, in Beren's case, in the quest to win her hand from her father, and although Lúthien will sacrifice her world-long stay in Valimar to share a possibly joyless mortality with Beren in Middle-earth, in Tolkienian terms their literal union is fruitful and symbolically expressive of their deep and loyal love for one another. In the last line of their tale Tolkien affirms that "in her choice the Two Kindreds have been joined; and she is the forerunner of many in whom the Eldar see yet, though all the world is changed, the likeness of Lúthien the beloved, whom they have lost."[48] This union of two kindred, one in which Tolkien saw himself and Edith, mirrors that of the Man Aragorn and Elf Arwen, which is only hinted at in the third volume of *The Lord of the Rings* (although more fully developed in the appendices).

Indeed, Aragorn and Arwen's ancestry, going back to Beren and Lúthien, explains the symbolic and political importance of their union. Arwen is the daughter of Elves Celebrían and Elrond and granddaughter of Elves Galadriel and Celeborn. However, Galadriel also represents the union of three Elf families, Noldo-Vanyar with Teleri through her mother, Eärwen, who was the daughter of Olwë of Alqualondë, of the Teleri.[49] What is significant here is not only the heroicization of the Man Aragorn through his Elven-Maian blood but also the fact that he is related to Arwen (not quite as cousins);[50] in her is mixed the blood of different families of Elves. Even more dramatic is Aragorn's descent ultimately from Elros, the brother of Arwen's father Elrond, both of these Elves the children of Earendil and Elwing and—not surprisingly—the grandchildren of Lúthien and Beren. But Lúthien's ancestry, before Aragorn's, is even more impressive in its symbolic importance in the uniting of differing species: Lúthien's mother was Melian the Maia (servant to the Valar), and her father, Thingol (or Elwë), the Elf brother of Olwë.

To conclude: In a review of *Lord of the Rings*, C.S. Lewis said about mythology that "[t]he value of the myth is that it takes all the things we know and restores to them the rich significance which has been hidden by the 'veil of familiarity.'. . .By putting bread, gold, horse, apple, or the very roads into a myth, we do not retreat from reality, we rediscover it."[51] What Tolkien has done, in his remaking of the Middle Ages, is to imbue his very modern fantasy with reality and its rediscovery—prejudice, discrimination, insensitivity toward those different from us, and selfishness. He then teaches us to understand how dangerous they can be as weapons and how healing, in contrast, it can be to reconcile and harmonize our differences through acceptance, understanding, forgiveness, and love.

Notes

This essay was originally delivered as an invited guest lecture at the following symposia: at the Bucknell University symposium, "More Than a Fantasy? Tolkien's Modern Middle Ages," Lewisburg, Pennsylvania, April 8, 2003; at the meeting of the Dallas Consortium of Medievalists, Southern Methodist University, Dallas, Texas, November 4, 2003; as the Annual McMichael Lecture at St. Paul's Episcopal Church, Fayetteville, Arkansas, January 25, 2004; as "Out of Africa: Tolkien's Anglo-Saxon Scholarship as a Window into/Gloss on Middle Earth," at the Symposium on "J. R. R. Tolkien, Fantasist and Medievalist," at University of Vermont, Burlington, Vermont, on March 6, 2004; as a plenary lecture at the Second Annual Tolkien Society conference at the University of Pécs, in Pécs, Hungary, April 24, 2004; in shortened form in a session on Neomedievalisms: Tolkien and Modern Fantasy, at the Thirty-Ninth International Congress on Medieval Studies, Medieval Institute, Western Michigan University, Kalamazoo, Michigan, May 7, 2004; at Ralph Woods's seminar on "Reading Tolkien and Living the Virtues" (June 4–July 2), sponsored by a Lilly Foundation Grant, at Baylor University, Waco, TX, on Thursday, June 22, 2004; as a guest lecture at the NEH Summer Institute for Teachers on "From *Beowulf* to Post-Modernism: J. R. R. Tolkien's *Lord of the Rings*," Texas A & M University-Commerce, June–July, 2004, on July 14, 2004; as "Out of Africa: Tolkien's Anglo-Saxon Scholarship as a Window into Middle-earth," for the University of New Mexico Institute for Medieval Studies Outreach Seminar for

High School Teachers on "Of Heroes and Hobbits in the Works of Tolkien and *Beowulf*," October 29, 2004; in a session on "Tolkien Our Contemporary" organized by Ralph Wood, Baylor University, for the Conference on Christianity and Literature, also in Philadelphia, PA, Dec. 27–30, 2004; and, finally, as a guest lecture for the Medieval Club and Arts and Lectures at California State University-San Marcos, April 22, 2005.

Thanks go to Theresa Munisteri, Rice University English Department editorial asistant, for her stylistic suggestions (and to the many members of the audience for their questions and points at lectures I have given who have helped me sharpen the focus and scope of the argument).

1. John Clute and John Grant, eds., *The Encyclopedia of Fantasy* (London: Orbit, 1997), s.v. "Perception" and "Fantasy," quotations which have been combined in this single citation.
2. See, for example, Clyde Kilby, *Tolkien and the Silmarillion* (Wheaton, Illinois: Harold Shaw Publishers, 1976); Joseph Pearce, *Tolkien: Man and Myth* (San Francisco: Ignatius Press, 1998); and questions about the dwarves as representing the Jews in the interview with Tolkien by Denys Gueroult, *Now Read On*, BBC Radio 4, December 16, 1970.
3. Fred Inglis, "Gentility and Powerlessness: Tolkien and the New Class," in *J.R.R. Tolkien: This Far Land*, ed. Robert Giddings (London and Totowa, New Jersey: Vision and Barnes and Noble Books, 1983), 39, 40.
4. J.R.R. Tolkien, "Valedictory Address," in *The Monsters and the Critics and Other Essays*, ed. Christopher Tolkien (London: Allen and Unwin, 1983; Boston, MA: Houghton Mifflin, 1984), 238.
5. See the groundbreaking book by Thomas A. Shippey, *The Road to Middle-Earth* (London: Allen and Unwin, 1982; Boston, MA: Houghton Mifflin, 1983; rev. edn. London: HarperCollins, Grafton, 1992; Boston MA: Houghton Mifflin, 2003), which documents Tolkien's love of philology as the foundation of his fiction and his mythology.
6. J.R.R. Tolkien, "Sigelwara Land," pts. 1 and 2, *Medium Aevum* 1 (1932): 183–96; 3 (1934): 1–70.
7. J.R.R. Tolkien, *The Old English Exodus: Text, Translation, and Commentary by J. R. R. Tolkien*, ed. Joan Turville-Petre (Oxford: Oxford University Press, 1981), my emphasis. Subsequent references to Tolkien's prose translation of the poem *Exodus* will appear in the text within parentheses and page number(s).
8. Tolkien, "Sigelwara Land," pt. 1, 183.
9. Tolkien, "Sigelwara Land," pt. 1, 192.
10. Tolkien, "Sigelwara Land," pt. 2, 108.
11. Tolkien, "Sigelwara Land," pt. 2, 106.
12. Tolkien, "Sigelwara Land," pt. 2, 110.
13. Tolkien, "Sigelwara Land," pt. 2, 109.
14. Tolkien, "Sigelwara Land," pt. 2, 111.
15. Tolkien, "Sigelwara Land," pt. 2, 111.
16. Tolkien, *Exodus*, 33.
17. For Rohan, see *The Lord of the Rings* (hereafter *LR*), 3 vols., 2nd edn. (London: Allen and Unwin, 1966; Boston, MA: Houghton Mifflin, 1967),

vol. 2, book 3, 132 (in "The King of the Golden Hall") (one-volume edn. *LR* 3.6, 497).
18. Tolkien, "Beowulf: The Monsters and the Critics," *Proceedings of the British Academy* 22 (1936): 245–95; reprinted in *An Anthology of "Beowulf" Criticism*, ed. Lewis E. Nicholson (Notre Dame, IN: University of Notre Dame Press, 1963); *The "Beowulf" Poet*, ed. Donald K. Fry (Englewood Cliffs, NJ: Prentice Hall, 1968); *Interpretations of "Beowulf": A Critical Anthology*, ed. R. Fulk (Bloomington and Indianapolis: Indiana University Press, 1991), 14–44; and, in abbreviated form, in *Readings on "Beowulf*," ed. Stephen P. Thompson, The Greenhaven Press Literary Companion to British Literature (San Diego, CA.: Greenhaven Press, 1998), 24–30. Most recently Tolkien's essay has introduced the other critical essays in a Norton Critical Edition, *"Beowulf": A Verse Translation*, trans. Seamus Heaney, ed. Daniel Donoghue, Norton Critical Editions (New York: W. W. Norton, 2002).
19. Tolkien, "The Homecoming of Beorhtnoth Beorhthelm's Son," in *Essays and Studies by Members of the English Association*, n.s., 6 (1953): 1–18; reprinted in *The Tolkien Reader* (New York: Ballantine, 1966). "The Homecoming" is preceded by a headnote by Tolkien, titled "Beorhtnoth's Death," and followed by his essay "Ofermod."
20. These lines from "The Battle of Maldon" are quoted and translated by Tolkien in "Beorhtnoth's Death," 5.
21. These lines from "The Battle of Maldon" are quoted and translated by Tolkien in "Ofermod," 21.
22. Tolkien, "Ofermod," 20.
23. See Humphrey Carpenter's chapter on Bloemfontein in *J. R. R. Tolkien: A Biography* (London, Boston, and Sydney: Allen and Unwin, 1977), 9–16, for the circumstances surrounding his parents' emigration to the Republic of the Orange Free State and the family's subsequent departure for Birmingham.
24. J.R.R. Tolkien, quoted by Philip Norman in "The Prevalence of Hobbits," *New York Times Magazine*, January 15 1967, 100.
25. See Humphrey Carpenter's comments in his interview in the film *Tolkien Remembered/Central Productions* (Princeton, NJ: Films for the Humanities and Sciences, 1993).
26. See Tolkien, Letter 213, in *The Letters of J. R. R. Tolkien: A Selection*, ed. Humphrey Carpenter with assistance from Christopher Tolkien (London: George Allen and Unwin, 1981; Boston and New York: Houghton Mifflin, 1981; London: HarperCollins, 1995), 288–89.
27. Carpenter, *Biography*, 176.
28. These lines from Tolkien's last radio interview, with Denys Gueroult, *Now Read On*, BBC Radio 4, December 16, 1970, are available in a rare cassette recording of the interview and are discussed in Carpenter, *Biography*, 176.
29. Tolkien, letter 181, in *Letters*, 237.
30. Tolkien, letter 181, in *Letters*, 233.
31. Tolkien, letter 181, in *Letters*, 234.
32. Tolkien, letter 246, to Mrs. Eileen Elgar, in *Letters*, 329.

33. Tolkien, *LR*, vol. 1, chap. 1, "A Long-Expected Party," where the term is used of various individuals and families considered strange by Shire rustics (*LR* 1.1, 22). See the longer discussion in Jane Chance, *The Lord of the Rings: The Mythology of Power* (New York: Twayne/Macmillan, 1992; rev. edn. Lexington: University Press of Kentucky, 2001), 26–37, " 'Queer' Hobbits: The Problem of Difference in the Shire."
34. Tolkien, *LR* 1.1, 24.
35. Tolkien, *LR* 1.1, 21.
36. Tolkien, *LR* 3.4, 457.
37. Tolkien, *LR* 3.4, 466.
38. Tolkien, *LR* 3.4, 461.
39. Tolkien, *LR* 3.4, 463.
40. Tolkien, *LR* 3.4, 452.
41. Tolkien, *LR* 3.4, 466.
42. Tolkien, *LR* 3.4, 453.
43. Tolkien, *LR* 3.4, 472.
44. Tolkien, *LR* 3.4, 474.
45. Tolkien, *LR* 1.2, 58.
46. Tolkien, letter 181, to Michael Straits, in *Letters*, 234.
47. See the important story in J.R.R. Tolkien *The Silmarillion*, ed. Christopher Tolkien (London: Allen and Unwin, 1976; Boston, MA: Houghton Mifflin, 1977), 195–228, chapter 19, "Of Beren and Lúthien." Richard C. West has written an excellent analysis of the story in "Real-World Myth in a Secondary World: Mythological Aspects in the Story of Beren and Lúthien," in *Tolkien the Medievalist*, ed. Jane Chance (London and New York: Routledge, 2002, 2003), 259–67; see also Jen Stevens's emphasis on another "real-world myth" in their tale, in "From Catastrophe to Eucatastrophe: J.R.R. Tolkien's Transformation of Ovid's Mythic Pyramus and Thisbe into Beren and Lúthien," in *Tolkien and the Invention of Myth: A Reader* ed. Jane Chance (Lexington: University Press of Kentucky, 2004), 119–32.
48. Tolkien, *The Silmarillion*, 187.
49. See the genealogical tables—for the Noldo Finwë, the Teleri brothers Olwë and Elwë, Bëor the Old, and the tribes of the Elves—that appear at the end of the text, in Tolkien, *The Silmarillion*, 379–83.
50. They are first cousins, but note that because Men—but not Elves—enjoy the gift of death, many more generations intervene between Elros and Aragorn than between Elros' brother Elrond and his daughter Arwen.
51. C.S. Lewis, "Tolkien's *Lord of the Rings* (Review)," in *On Stories, and Other Essays on Literature*, ed. Walter Hooper (New York and London: Harcourt Brace Jovanovich, 1982), 90. This review combines reviews by C.S. Lewis of Tolkien's epic trilogy originally published as "The Gods Return to Earth," in *Time and Tide*, August 14, 1954, and "The Dethronement of Power," in *Time and Tide*, October 22, 1955.

PART FOUR

VISUALIZING MEDIEVALISM: MIDDLE-EARTH IN ART AND FILM

CHAPTER 13

SIMILAR BUT NOT SIMILAR: APPROPRIATE ANACHRONISM IN MY PAINTINGS OF MIDDLE-EARTH

Ted Nasmith

This essay illustrates the relation between Tolkien's text and Nasmith's own award-winning visual images. The visual artist's creative reflections on Tolkien's fantasy text mirror the medieval and modern, namely, the creative and artistic reception of Tolkien's work in conjunction with modern concerns.

"Good Morning," said a famous Hobbit from his doorstep in the morning a long time ago. This seemingly innocent greeting belied the great adventure story about to be lived by young Bilbo Baggins, who quite sensibly balked at first at the suggestion made by his strange visitor, Gandalf the wizard. Gandalf had proclaimed that he wanted someone to go on an *adventure* but was having difficulty finding someone. "I should think so—in these parts! We are plain quiet folk and have no use for adventures. Nasty disturbing uncomfortable things! Make you late for dinner!" said Bilbo.[1] But Gandalf was a shrewd judge of character, and before he knew it, Bilbo's buried spirit of adventure was awakened and there was no turning back (see figure 13.1, Ted Nasmith, *An Unexpected Morning Visit* [detail, Gandalf by Bilbo's door], 1990).

Once upon a time, when I was a young art student, my sister suggested that I might like a book she and her friends were fans of: *The Lord of the Rings*. Until then, I was not aware that I had any particular interest in fairy tales or fantasy, or more accurately, I had mostly lost my early childhood fascinations

13.1 Ted Nasmith, *An Unexpected Morning Visit* [detail, Gandalf by Bilbo's door], 1990.

with such writing and imagery. Now I was more interested in cars, airplanes, space ships, and other shiny things and had discovered that I had a real gift for painting them, just as for years I had been filling blank pads with pencil drawings of them. Now there was something quite new to occupy my imagination, and like Bilbo, something passionate awoke in me before I really knew it. Had I not been captivated—like so many readers—by this fantastic, detailed work of fiction, I would very likely have joined the ranks of faceless technical illustrators who make an honorable and safe living supporting obscure industries with their talents.

Happily, this was not quite my fate, and yet, I did sensibly enter the field of architectural rendering, itself a decision that was almost completely spontaneous, given that I had studied in art school just about everything except perspective drawing (see figure 13.2, an architectural rendering by Ted Nasmith of a *Proposed Office-Hotel Complex, People's Republic of China*, ca. 1997). I was hired on the strength of my ability to capture high realism and soon mastered the skills of perspective and the other criteria applied to this special profession. It held me in good stead—and occasionally still does to this day, some thirty-odd years later.

The adventure with Tolkien developed slowly in the meantime, as I first drew and painted various landscapes, scenes, and characters from *The Lord of the Rings* and *The Hobbit* at home in my spare time. I began by experimenting stylistically, trying to imitate my impressions of simpler types of

13.2 Ted Nasmith, Proposed Hotel-Office-Commercial Complex, Peoples Republic of China, ca. 1997.

children's book illustrations, then other times indulging in obsessively detailed full color works. I had no certain idea what I was doing as far as illustration conventions, but I was trying to imagine the appropriate anachronistic "look" that seemed wanted.

The Unexpected Party (figure 13.3) was first painted in early 1972 as a school project, but it allowed me the chance to see if I could capture the feeling of fascination and intrigue the scene conveyed to me, as Gandalf unfurled the old map of the Lonely Mountain for the assembled Dwarves and the hapless Bilbo. (Maps, you will recall, were one of his weaknesses.) Notice the starry sky outside the window. I loved the idea that while others were asleep, the members of this company were busy plotting to travel into the wild in hopes of recovering their ancestors' lost gold, now hoarded by a great dragon. I believe some of my sentiment over such a situation may be linked to car trips our family would take when I was very young. It would still be dark outside as my mother roused us to get dressed and get in the car in order to drive several hours to Ottawa to visit my grandparents for Christmas. Such occasions meant a great pile of presents, under a heavily decorated tree, and cousins, uncles, aunts and a great Christmas feast with my grandfather solemnly saying grace. I sent photographs of this painting and its details to J.R.R. Tolkien at the time, along with a couple of other lesser works. I soon received a personal reply, dictated to his secretary, in which he pointed out that Bilbo ought to look less childish, but which was otherwise kindly. It was the one and only time I had any contact with the author, but it encouraged me considerably.

13.3 Ted Nasmith, *The Unexpected Party*, 1972.

During this period I also painted an early version of "Rivendell," a scene I drew using Tolkien's version as a guide. Despite the technical faults and idiosyncrasies of Tolkien's own illustrations, I was captivated by them because they were from the hand of the author and, at the very least, a useful guide to his mind visually. To me it was always important with Tolkien's art that I attempt to integrate my style and ideas with that unique flavor I felt on reading his fiction, and that there be a sense of continuity and natural, complementary quality.

Eventually, I came to recognize that since a work like *The Lord of the Rings* was basically anachronistic thematically (that is, set in a mythical past age), as well as stylistically related to nineteenth-century adventure novels and fairy tales, paintings that could capture its feeling and complement its grandeur ought to look back to what I saw as the corresponding golden era of detailed landscape painting. I was enamored of but largely uneducated in any depth about such art, but its great vividness and detail was very exciting to me. Here are a few examples of works inspired by the genre: see figure 13.4, Ted Nasmith, *Rivendell*, 1984; figure 13.5, *The Riders of Rohan*, 1998; and figure 13.6, *First Sight of Ithilien*, 2001.

13.4 Ted Nasmith, *Rivendell*, 1984.

13.5 Ted Nasmith, *The Riders of Rohan*, 1998.

13.6 Ted Nasmith, *First Sight of Ithilien*, 2001.

I was intrigued to discover recently that one of my favorite epic landscape painters, Frederick Church of the Hudson River School, was inspired by the work and writings of Alexander von Humboldt. Alex Lewis argues convincingly in his book *The Uncharted Realms of Tolkien* that Tolkien very likely was influenced in his own geographic creative work, which is famously well developed for a nonspecialist, by Humboldt's widely available work entitled *The Cosmos*, a comprehensive work of geographic scholarship in its day. The fact that the author's brother, Wilhelm von Humboldt, was considered "the father of modern philology" further tips the scale in his favor, argues Lewis.[2]

Increasingly, I came to recognize that I rightly felt at home in this era before realistic landscape painting became passé, replaced as it was by the fragmented, experimental, and often bleak visions of the mid-twentieth century. Those with a love of and a talent for realism were not valued in the fine arts anymore. It seemed I was born too late, I thought. Even the automotive illustration that inspired me before I discovered Tolkien was on its way out at just the point when I might have sought out a career in that field. It is one of the main reasons I accepted architectural rendering as a consolation (see figure 13.7, Ted Nasmith, *Portrait of Two Ferraris*, 1999).

Eventually, as I began to have my Tolkien art published in the annual calendars, I had a fairly strong notion of what I was aiming for. I had come to think of myself as someone who, if not necessarily the "official" illustrator of Tolkien (there has never been any such designation), might nonetheless *pretend* that was my job, to satisfy what it was internally that compelled me to express my creative faculties in this form. Works by other published Tolkien illustrators, such as the Hildebrandt brothers and Joan Wyatt, helped shape my own approach. The Hildebrandts, in particular, provided a template. Although in many ways I disagreed with their depictions, particularly those I now trace to their affinity for Disney, their full calendars of various scenes and the great vivid color they used gave me fuel for my own ideas. I felt they had missed the mark in many cases and I saw how I wanted to deal with the same and other subjects. I particularly disliked the ways by which they were clearly being too loose with the descriptions Tolkien gave.

Joan Wyatt, in her published amateur portfolio of *The Lord of the Rings* paintings, shows how an artist can delight in a great variety of scenes, both epic and intimate in turns; she captures some of the humor, sentiment and even pathos in Tolkien quite skillfully too.[3] These and other influences set me on a course to try to produce a large body of paintings, more or less comparable and consistent in quality, that explores the myriad aspects of Tolkien's Middle-earth and its tales. I had no idea whether I would or would not establish my presence

13.7 Ted Nasmith, *Portrait of Two Ferraris*, ca. 1999.

solidly enough to be commissioned for more than a few calendars, but I am very fortunate to have been able, through thick and thin, to continue the project and cultivate a very appreciative audience along the way.

Among the questions that arise in relation to paintings set in Middle-earth, I recognized the need to become as proficient in certain cultural details of Middle-earth as I could to convincingly depict such aspects as the architecture, costume and dress, and the other features that constitute the look I saw in my imagination. I would ask myself whether there ought to be regional or historical variations in architecture, costume, and so forth, depending on the culture, race, and era. It is not enough to simply imitate real-world medieval European castles. For one thing, the world of Tolkien is more archaic than that in general, picking up ideas spanning mythical prehistory through the Middle Ages and on down to the nineteenth century.

My general rule is that I want Tolkien's world in my depictions as much as possible to reflect the sense of "otherness" that he intended in his own work, and I take the trouble to find out what he said about a particular thing—like the aesthetics of Gondor, a culture comparable to ancient Egypt in certain respects, according to Tolkien.[4] I also bear in mind that Gondorians are descended from the surviving remnant of the great Atlantean empire of Numenor, with its maritime culture (see figure 13.8, Ted Nasmith, *Minas Tirith at Dawn*, 1989, and figure 13.9, *At the Court of the Fountain*, 1990).

13.8 Ted Nasmith, *Minas Tirith at Dawn*, 1989.

Yet the nearby peoples of Rohan might combine aspects of tenth-century Anglo-Saxons with some of the great nomadic horse cultures of Asia.

The Elves, with—ideally—variations sorted according to their heritages, suggested to me a strongly feminine, quasi-oriental elegance in their aesthetics. The emergence of the arts and crafts movement in the nineteenth century as well as the aesthetic explosion of art nouveau, with its various influences, would seem to provide models. The great variety of Celtic designs and knot work is obviously an important aspect to incorporate too—in fact, nearly anything that can contribute to the desired effect, including straight-out invention. I am not always fully consistent in this regard, but I do strive not just to transfer real-world aesthetic systems into Middle-earth but also to vary and alter them somewhat, just as Middle-earth is similar to our earth, but yet dissimilar and "other," in accordance with Tolkien's carefully articulated rules of Faërie, sub-creation, and fantasy (see figure 13.10, Ted Nasmith, *Eärendil Searches Tirion*, 1998).

An artist like me cannot hope to satisfy the nearly endless conceptual considerations that might apply, but it is certainly wonderful that, in illustrating a work like *The Lord of the Rings* or *The Silmarillion*, such development and refinement of ideas around specific elements like architecture or costume can be justified. One need only consider the stunningly elaborate invented languages and dialects at the heart of these two epic works to see

13.9 Ted Nasmith, *At the Court of the Fountain*, 1990.

13.10 Ted Nasmith, *Eärendil Searches Tirion*, 1998.

how fully they can support the development of other areas of cultural invention. Certainly, director Peter Jackson in his effort to bring *The Lord of the Rings* to the movie screen has marshaled the talents of a virtual army of artisans, as anyone who has sat through the credits can attest.

I would now like to return briefly to the matter of my own sense of vocation in illustrating Tolkien. Just what *did* send me on my adventures in Middle-earth? It would be understandable to question just why a teenager from middle-class suburban Toronto should discover such a powerful kinship with an English philologist who lived his adult life in academic Oxford and was reaching retirement age in the decade I was born. I have wondered the same thing, and it is one of the reasons that when I began attempting to illustrate *The Lord of the Rings* I assumed that it was merely a hobby.

Nonetheless, as I reflected on my early life, I began to see some interesting influences. Our family lived in France for three years while I was age two to five, because my father at the time was assigned duty under NATO as an electronics specialist in the Royal Canadian Air Force. Scenes from this extended time in Europe were captured in slides and shown repeatedly in the following years many times. Although most of the places we visited were very scenic or fascinating, an exception was the great cemetery and mausoleum at Verdun, France, commemorating the fallen of The Great War. I would have been about four years old at the time. The mausoleum struck

13.11 Anne Washington, War Mausoleum, Verdun, France, ca. 1958.

me as a frightening building that I only vaguely understood as having to do with the dead, but I found it disturbing in and of itself. That image unconsciously influenced my much later early conception of Barad-Dûr, which I remember thinking ought to look bleak, cold, and like a giant gravestone (see figure 13.11, Anne Washington, War Mausoleum, Verdun, France, ca. 1958; figure 13.12, Ted Nasmith, *Barad-Dûr*, 1975). According to my mother (I cannot recall this explicitly), we children at one point peered through a dusty basement window. Inside, human bones were stored, the unidentified remains of many of those who died!

In the bestseller *The Battle for God: A History of Fundamentalism*, author Karen Armstrong, as she articulates the consequences of the irreversible march toward the modern, "rational," and "logocentric" world we inhabit, says the following:

> After the Franco-Prussian war, the nations of Europe began a frantic arms race which led them inexorably to the First World War. They appeared to see war as a Darwinian necessity in which only the fittest would survive. A modern nation must have the most murderous weapons that science could provide, and Europeans dreamed of a war that would purify the nation's soul in a harrowing apotheosis. The British writer I.F. Clarke has shown that between 1871 and 1914 it was unusual to find a single year in which a novel or short story describing a horrific future war did not appear in some

13.12 Ted Nasmith, *Barad-Dûr*, 1975.

European country. The "Next Great War" was imagined as a terrible but inevitable ordeal: out of the destruction, the nation would arise to a new and enhanced life. At the very end of the nineteenth century, however, British novelist H.G. Wells punctured this Utopian dream in *The War of the Worlds* (1898) and showed where it was leading. There were terrifying images of London depopulated by biological warfare, and the roads of England crowded with refugees. He could see the dangers of a military technology that had been drawn into the field of the exact sciences. He was right. The arms race led to the Somme and when the Great War broke out in 1914, the people of Europe, who had been dreaming of the war to end all wars for over forty years, entered with enthusiasm upon this conflict, which could be seen as the collective suicide of Europe. Despite the achievements of modernity, there was a nihilistic death wish, as the nations of Europe cultivated a perverse fantasy of self-destruction.[5]

As a four-year-old, I was being gently exposed to the consequences of the convulsions of modernism, the result of *logos* becoming polarized from *mythos* in human civilization, as Armstrong argues. It is fascinating that a man like Tolkien came to recognize this essential imbalance surrounding him, and that he, because of his own terrible losses and the horrors he witnessed, turned his genius for language and invention into a lifelong creative outpouring, one in which, among other things, he attempted to reintegrate *mythos* and *logos* and demonstrate with exquisite poetic force his sense of the existential crisis we had unwittingly brought upon ourselves.

As mentioned, along with the somber image of Verdun, I also was exposed to much enchantment: European landscapes; the magical worlds of the Rotterdam Zoo; and the Miniature Village in The Hague, in Holland; camping trips in Switzerland; and a most memorable visit to a fairy-tale theme park in Luxembourg, Le Parc Merveilleux. Before the age of nine or ten, I did enjoy and love reading fairy tales, and seeing fairy-tale or adventure movies, as well as being taken into Canada's north country camping, so all in all, once I was introduced to *The Lord of the Rings*, these and other influences deeply resonated for me at a time when they had largely faded from my consciousness. As it has for millions of readers around the world, Tolkien's vast fictional world, like old Gandalf to Bilbo, arrived unexpectedly one day for me with a hearty "Good morning!"

Ted Nasmith Selected Pictography

1. *An Unexpected Morning Visit* (detail), 1990

APPROPRIATE ANACHRONISM IN MY PAINTINGS

Architectural Renderings (Dates and Other Details Unknown)
2. Proposed hotel-casino complex, Sydney, Nova Scotia
3. Proposed international airport expansion, Salt Lake City, Utah
4. Proposed new terminal facility, Zadar, Croatia
5. Proposed office-hotel complex, People's Republic of China
6. Proposed elevator lobby, commercial-office complex, Toronto, Canada
7. Proposed atrium, commercial-office complex, Toronto, Canada

Early Works
8. *Through the Forest*, 1971
9. *A Morning Visit*, 1972
10. *The Unexpected Party*, 1972
11. *Rivendell*, 1972
12. *Rivendell*, 1973
13. *The Riddle Game*, 1973
14. *The Unexpected Party* (detail), 1990

Landscapes
15. *Rivendell*, 1984
16. *Finduilas Is Led Past Túrin at the Sack of Nargothrond*, 1997
17. *The Ships of the Faithful*, 1997
18. *At Lake Cuivienen*, 1997
19. *The Lamp of the Valar*, 1997
20. *Beren and Lúthien Are Flown to Safety*, 1997
21. *The Incoming Sea at the Rainbow Cleft*, 1998
22. *Fangorn Forest*, 2001
23. *First Sight of Ithilien*, 2001
24. *Tarn Aeluin*, 2003
25. *Tuor and Voronwë See Túrin at the Pool of Ivrin*, 2003
26. *Saeros's Fatal Leap*, 2003
27. *White Ships from Valinor*, 2003
28. *Up the Rainy Stairs*, 2003

Automotive Art
29. 1973 Pontiac Le Mans, 1973
30. 1974 Pontiac Firebird, 1974
31. Portrait of two Ferraris, 1999
32. Portrait of Aston-Martin DB7 Vantage Volante, 2003

Examples of Architectural, Costume, Ship, and Other Middle-Earth Design

33. *Minas Tirith*, 1974
34. *Barad Dûr*, 1975
35. *Minas Tirith at Dawn*, 1989
36. *At the Court of the Fountain*, 1990
37. *At the Court of the Fountain*, 1990 (detail)
38. *An Unexpected Morning Visit*, 1990
39. *Tuor Reaches the Hidden City of Gondolin*, 1994
40. *Departure at the Grey Havens*, 1994
41. *Tuor and Voronwë are Presented to Turgon*, 1996
42. *Eärendil Searches Tirion*, 1998
43. *The Great Tree at Caras Galadhon*, 2000
44. *The Great Tree at Caras Galadhon*, 2000 (detail)
45. *The Betrothal of Arwen and Aragorn at Cerin Amroth*, 2000? (detail)
46. *The Wrath of the Ents*, 2001
47. *The Tower of the Moon* (detail), 2001
48. *White Ships from Valinor*, 2003
49. *Túrin Carries Gwindor to Safety*, 2003
50. *Orthanc*, 1998

Notes

1. J.R.R. Tolkien, *The Hobbit; or There and Back Again*. 2nd edn. (London: George Allen and Unwin, 1978; repr. Unwin Hyman, 1987).
2. Alex Lewis and Elizabeth Currie, *The Uncharted Realms of Tolkien: A Critical Study of Text, Context, and Subtext in the Works of J. R. R. Tolkien* (Weston Rhyn, Oswestry, UK: Medea Publishing, 2002), 18–20.
3. See Joan Wyatt, *A Middle-Earth Album: Paintings* (New York: Simon and Schuster, 1979).
4. See J.R.R. Tolkien, *Letters: A Selection*, ed. Humphrey Carpenter with assistance from Christopher Tolkien (London: George Allen and Unwin, 1981; Boston and New York: Houghton Mifflin, 1981; London: HarperCollins, 1995; New York: Houghton Mifflin, 2000), 281.
5. Karen Armstrong, *The Battle for God: A History of Fundamentalism* (New York: Ballantine, 2001), 136–37.

CHAPTER 14

TOLKIEN IN NEW ZEALAND: MAN, MYTH, AND MOVIE

Michael N. Stanton

> *Although Tolkien had no direct connection with New Zealand, the place proved both an excellent backdrop for Peter Jackson's films of* The Lord of the Rings *and the nexus of a meaningful literary coincidence. Another English writer who is associated with New Zealand, Samuel Butler (1835–1902), author of* Erewhon, *anticipated Tolkien in his dislike and fear of mechanical and technological progress.*

This essay is based on my recent experiences in New Zealand visiting sites where Peter Jackson's *The Lord of the Rings*[1] was filmed, on the peculiar juxtaposition of two very different authors that I became aware of there—namely J.R.R. Tolkien and Samuel Butler—and on the hatred both shared of a myth endemic in the modern world. It goes on to show how Peter Jackson failed to carry through the important implications of that myth in his film version of Tolkien's story, and thus did the story a disservice.

I am using "myth" here in the nonscholarly sense of a false or unproved collective belief that is used to justify social coercion or inaction—the myth in question here is the myth of progress, the comfortable (but when examined, somewhat silly) notion that our scientific and technological movements forward have improved our lives psychologically or spiritually in any significant way.

Tolkien as best I can tell had little or nothing to say about New Zealand; it was on the fringes of his consciousness at most. So far as one can deduce from his letters he loved England but not Great Britain and certainly not the British Commonwealth, or Empire, as it used to be called. He had little interest in travel per se; as Humphrey Carpenter observes, he did not need travel to stimulate his imagination.[2]

I dare not be presumptuous enough to say he would have loved New Zealand. I will say that (in my view) one of Peter Jackson's great accomplishments in making the film of *The Lord of the Rings* was in discovering that New Zealand was Middle-earth, or that it was eminently suitable for use as such. In its 100,000 square miles (just a fraction larger than Great Britain), it contains most of the landforms, landscapes, and terrains that we find in the 1,500,000 square miles of Middle-earth.

New Zealand lies within the South Temperate Zone, but its great length helps give it many microclimates. It is seagirt, like Great Britain. It has mountains like the mountains Tolkien loved in Switzerland and Wales. It has great rivers as well as plains, lakes, forests, and wetlands: all the varieties of beauty and sublimity in natural form that Middle-earth has. It has what Tolkien also loved: space, that is, spaciousness, open space. He wrote that in spite of loving "little lanes and hedges and rustling trees. . . .the thing that stirs me most and comes nearest to heart's satisfaction for me is space. . . .Indeed, I think I love barrenness itself, whenever I have seen it. My heart still lingers among the high stony wastes among the morains [*sic*] and mountain-wreckage, silent in spite of the sound of thin chill water."[3] These places are Eregion, or the Dimrill Dale, or the Emyn Muil as Jackson shows them to us.

What struck me as most like Middle-earth in New Zealand was its emptiness. New Zealand is a country of fewer than four million people, half of whom are concentrated in three largish cities (Auckland, Wellington, and Christchurch). It is an agricultural land with ten times as many sheep as people. Driving the sheep off would provide a landscape as deserted as Middle-earth's. And Tolkien emphasizes Middle-earth's emptiness. Sauron's hatred of life, especially free life, has led him to try to create conditions that depopulate Middle-earth and that isolate the populations it still has.

The village of Bree, for instance, with its people "stands like an island in the empty lands round about." Tolkien adds that "the Northern lands had long been desolate, and the North Road [running through Bree] was now seldom used."[4] When the Fellowship leaves Rivendell they head south, and we are told that "the spies of Sauron had hitherto seldom been seen in this empty country" (*LR* 2.3, 274); "hitherto" should be emphasized, because *crebain* and Wargs and other such vile creatures are about to beset the company. When Aragorn wonders about pipe tobacco being found at Isengard, he thinks about "the empty countries that lie between Rohan and the Shire" (*LR* 3.9, 560).

Examples need not be multiplied. And New Zealand, for quite different reasons, gives a similar sense of both high stony wastes among the mountains and great unused tracts of empty territory. So New Zealand can be seen as an eminently suitable country, physically and demographically, in which to film *The Lord of the Rings*. The next question is, what did Peter Jackson do with it? In a number of interviews, he said, in a variety of expressions, that in spite of changes and adaptations he tried to preserve and embody Tolkien's *themes* as faithfully as possible.

That he did so is doubtful. If theme is ever embodied in a character, for instance, and the nature of the character is changed, then theme is changed: Faramir comes to mind in that connection. But I want to focus on a theme being abandoned, not just altered. It is clearly and forcefully presented in Jackson's *Fellowship* and *Two Towers*, but disappears in *Return*. It is the pervasive theme that mechanical or industrial progress, as it may be dubiously termed, is part of the encroachment of evil in Middle-earth.

Back in New Zealand again: if you stand on Mt. Sunday in the Canterbury region of the South Island, you are standing where Peter Jackson chose to site Edoras, the capital of Rohan, and Meduseld, the hall of Théoden, Rohan's king. If you turn 180 degrees you are looking directly across the Rangitata River at what they call Mesopotamia ("between the rivers"), which was where Samuel Butler, the author of the Victorian fantasy novel *Erewhon*, had a prosperous sheep run between 1860 and 1864.

The satiric/dystopian *Erewhon* is perhaps the best known of the varied works of Samuel Butler (1835–1902), but his quasi-autobiographical *The Way of All Flesh* (1902) is equally an attack on Victorian morality, hypocrisy, and wavering social standards. Butler was also a painter, a scholar, and a scientist, who both attacked and defended Darwin's theory of evolution. He was an iconoclast and a controversialist who loved few things better than a good quarrel.

Quite apart from their different centuries, it is hard to imagine two men more unlike than Samuel Butler and J.R.R. Tolkien. Butler was rich (his sheep farming venture had made him wealthy); Tolkien was comparatively poor for most of his working life. Butler was a lifelong bachelor; Tolkien, a confirmed family man. Butler was an eccentric, even among the great array of Victorian eccentrics (he wrote a book proving, to his own satisfaction anyway, that Homer was a woman); Tolkien, outwardly at least, was thoroughly conventional. Most of all, Butler was antireligious, an atheist, while Tolkien was deeply religious, a Roman Catholic.

Living in New Zealand, however, living in that great empty land, that land so suitable to play the role of Middle-earth decades later, gave Samuel Butler the opportunity to shake off the conventional pieties of middle-class Victorian England and to think on his own for the first time in his young life.

One result was *Erewhon*, his fantasy of an imaginary society in the hinterlands of a suppositious New Zealand—a book that Tolkien clearly knew and to whose ideas he subscribed in part.

Writing to his son Christopher in the middle of World War II, Tolkien said, "Labour saving machinery only creates endless and worse labour. And in addition to this fundamental disability of a creature, is added the Fall, which makes our devices not only fail of their desire but turn to new and horrible evil. So we come inevitably from Daedalus and Icarus to the Great Bomber. It is not an advance in wisdom! This terrible truth, glimpsed long ago by Sam Butler, sticks out so plainly and is so horrifyingly exhibited in our time, with its even worse menace for the future, that it seems almost a world-wide mental disease that only a tiny minority perceive it" (*Letters*, 88).

The truth Samuel Butler glimpsed in *Erewhon* and other writings is that machines will/and can take over the world. He had been reading Charles Darwin and he postulated that machines could evolve and achieve consciousness ("artificial intelligence," in today's parlance). Butler may have been half-serious and half-playful (it is not always easy to tell with him—sometimes his satire tips over into burlesque), but his real concern was not with what would happen to machines if they started to think but with what would happen to human beings if human beings became helplessly dependent on machines: "Day by day," Butler writes, "we are becoming more subservient to [machines]; more men are daily bound down as slaves to tend them, more men are daily devoting the energies of their whole lives to the development of mechanical life. . .the time will come when the machines will hold the real supremacy over the world and its inhabitants."[5] The writer into whose mouth Butler puts these words advocates total war against the machine. (This, by the way, is where Frank Herbert got the term for what he calls the Butlerian jihad against machines in his classic science-fiction novel *Dune*.)

As the quotation from his letter already cited suggests, this was a point of view with which Tolkien sympathized very strongly, especially in the middle of a war in which machines such as tanks and airplanes had an unprecedented capacity to destroy the human world. Tolkien's dislike of the modern world, especially of its machinery, was well-nigh notorious. To exclude the more vulgar productions of modern industrial "progress" such as electric street lights from one's stories is not escape in the bad sense, Tolkien says in "On Fairy-Stories"; that exclusion proceeds rather "from a considered disgust for so typical a product of the Robot Age, that combines elaboration and ingenuity of means with ugliness, and (often) with inferiority of result." It is possible, he goes on, to see that the so-called escapist literature, by its silence about them, condemns "progressive things like factories, or the machine-guns and bombs that appear to be their most natural and inevitable, dare we say 'inexorable,' products."[6] On a less ominous note, we know that Tolkien gave up early up on the automobile and distrusted modern household appliances; when confronted by a wire recorder into which he was to read parts of *The Hobbit* and *The Lord of the Rings*, he playfully exorcised the devils from it by reciting the Lord's Prayer in Gothic.

But his citation of Butler is not playful. Tolkien certainly did not learn from Butler that machinery is hateful, but he seems to have found his abomination of it reinforced at some early point in life by reading *Erewhon*. The context of Tolkien's letter to Christopher, along with his remarks in "On Fairy-Stories," suggests that he was not particularly interested in Butler's rather odd notion that machinery could develop consciousness, but in the broader idea that we are more and more becoming, or in fact have become, dependent on machinery to our disadvantage and indeed to our peril. Tolkien speaking in a wartime context is thinking how ingeniously we have created machinery for wholesale destruction of human property and human life.

How does this work out in *The Lord of the Rings*, in the text and in the film? Primarily, of course, in the character and work of Saruman, who is seen as enacting a vision of a mechanized and inorganic future. Saruman is the modernist, the man of today who tells Gandalf that "a new Power is rising. Against it the old policies and allies will not avail us at all" (*LR* 2.2, 253). As Gandalf well knows, Saruman is speaking of Sauron, not a new power at all, but a very old and evil power in a seemingly new guise.

In the film as in the book this new mechanized world of Saruman is excellently portrayed by the conversion of Isengard from a garden into an iron-girt circle (a Ring, in fact), not only on the surface, but also down below, where forges and fires burn and where unspecified machines hammer out unspecified implements. And Saruman's new technology has enabled him to breed a new kind of Orc called the Uruk-Hai. (They are not strictly speaking robots, but they do, typically of the Robot Age, combine "elaboration and ingenuity of means with ugliness.") The film graphically depicts these new forms being dug up in Saruman's underground chambers, even as Christopher Lee (playing Saruman with great verve, even though dressed quite inappropriately in white) speaks of the might of industry as the wave of the future.

At the Battle of Helm's Deep, Saruman's Orcs light the "fire of Orthanc," as it is called, "a devilry...a blasting fire" (*LR* 3.7, 525, 526), some new invention from the arsenal of Isengard that threatens to carry the day until Gandalf, and Erkenbrand, and finally the Huorns appear, these latter manifesting a power far older than wizardry, as Gandalf says.

It is similarly appropriate that the power of Isengard and its ingenious mechanical world is eventually destroyed by the forces of unadulterated nature: tree against rock, clean water of the River Isen against the lurid fires of perverse industry. Saruman apparently sees himself as the embodiment of this theme of mechanical progress, the visionary bringer of an ironbound future, but he is only an agent: he thinks he is using Orcs and others to augment his power, but he is only *being* used, as Tolkien tells us in that wonderful paragraph from the chapter "The Road to Isengard":

> A strong place and wonderful was Isengard, and long it had been beautiful. . . . But Saruman had slowly shaped it to his shifting purposes, and made it better, as he thought, being deceived—for all those arts and subtle devices, for which he forsook his former wisdom, and which fondly he imagined were his own, came but from Mordor, so that what he made was naught, only a little copy, a child's model or a slave's flattery, of that vast fortress, armoury, prison, furnace of great power, Barad-dûr, the Dark Tower. (*LR* 3.9, 542)

But that—as far as the film is concerned—is the end of the theme of the defeat of the progressive and mechanical. Jackson drops the idea, and Saruman disappears from our ken just when you would expect his fate—and the theme it exemplifies—to be dealt with decisively in the third segment. (It seems doubly unfortunate that Christopher Lee, the only one of the major actors who knew and loved Tolkien's work, who had actually met Tolkien once upon a time, should be given such short shrift.)

Still, more important than following Saruman the individual in carrying through this theme of the power of machinery and modernity, and the need to resist such power, would have been portraying on-screen the Scouring of the Shire. Actually, the theme at this point becomes not just industrial progress, represented by the spoiling of the Shire, with ugly factories being built and streams being polluted, but the general persistence of evil. What has happened to the Shire in the absence of the Hobbits, and the condition in which they find it when they return, tells us that just destroying a Ring will not drive evil out of the world.

And that seems to be an important statement on Tolkien's part. Five chapters and nearly one hundred pages of text ensue after the Ring falls into the Cracks of Doom with Gollum attached, and they all suggest that much remains to be done; evil may have been defeated, but it has certainly not been destroyed. Whatever the dramatic or cinematic difficulties of bringing that important idea to the screen might have been, it would have been worth the effort. It would have been true to a major theme of Tolkien's, as Peter Jackson said he intended it to be.

The omission of Saruman's downfall also slights another important theme in *The Lord of the Rings*, the antiwar theme. Tolkien's hatred of war is well known; it is stated emphatically in his foreword and is based on the experience, not only of his own generation of young men and women, but of the next also. It was the foundation of those remarks on false progress in which he alluded to Samuel Butler. Saruman's industry and technology, misguided and derivative as it is, is essentially a military technology. He is attempting to create superior devices of war as well as superior warriors. We need to see those attempts as crushed completely if we are to see Tolkien's theme carried through.

It is thus richly ironical that, besides short-circuiting the argument against technology by dropping Saruman, Peter Jackson has been able to produce the movie he did only by employing the most sophisticated and marvelous technology in the whole film industry. The helicopter, the blue screen, the studio wizardry, and the motion capture work are all part of an advanced technology about whose implications Tolkien, I suspect, would have had more than vague misgivings.

Still, Tolkien was no Luddite. He was resigned to the fact that we are living in the Fourth Age, the Age of Men, and little can be done to subvert or avert Man's devilish and self-destructive ingenuity. What each individual must do, he seems to suggest, is forego his pride in human achievement and thereby preserve his freedom from human enslavement.

Notes

1. *The Lord of the Rings: The Fellowship of the Ring, The Two Towers; The Return of the King*, film, directed by Peter Jackson (Hollywood, CA: New Line Cinema, 2001–2003).
2. Humphrey Carpenter, *Tolkien: A Biography* (Boston: Houghton Mifflin, 1977), 124.
3. *The Letters of J. R. R. Tolkien*, ed. Humphrey Carpenter (Boston: Houghton Mifflin, 1981), 91 (hereafer cited in text and notes as *Letters*).
4. J.R.R. Tolkien, *The Lord of the Rings* (London: HarperCollins, 1995), 1.9, 147 (hereafter cited in text and notes as *LR*).
5. Samuel Butler, "Darwin among the Machines," in *The Shrewsbury Edition of the Works of Samuel Butler*, ed. Henry Festing Jones and A.T. Bartholomew (1923; repr. New York: AMS Press, 1968), I: 212.
6. "On Fairy-Stories," in *The Tolkien Reader* (New York: Ballantine, 1966), 61, 63.

WORKS CITED

Writings of J.R.R. Tolkien

"Philology: General Works." *The Year's Work in English Studies* 5 (1924): 26–65.

"Sigelwara Land." Pts. 1 and 2. *Medium Aevum* 1 (1932): 183–96; 3 (1934): 1–70.

"Chaucer as a Philologist: The Reeve's Tale." *Transactions of the Philological Society* (1934): 1–70.

"Beowulf: The Monsters and the Critics." *Proceedings of the British Academy* 22 (1936): 245–95. Repr. in *An Anthology of "Beowulf" Criticism*. Ed. Lewis E. Nicholson. Notre Dame, IN: University of Notre Dame Press, 1963; *The "Beowulf" Poet*. Ed. Donald K. Fry. Englewood Cliffs, NJ: Prentice Hall, 1968; *The Monsters and the Critics and Other Essays*, 5–48; *Modern Critical Interpretations: "Beowulf."* Ed. Harold Bloom, 5–31. New York and Philadelphia: Chelsea House, 1987; *Interpretations of "Beowulf": A Critical Anthology*. Ed. R. Fulk, 14–44. Bloomington and Indianapolis: Indiana University Press, 1991; *"Beowulf": A Verse Translation*. Tran. Seamus Heaney. Ed. Daniel Donoghue, 103–30. Norton Critical Editions. New York: W.W. Norton, 2002.

The Hobbit; or, There and Back Again. London: George Allen and Unwin, 1937; Boston: Houghton Mifflin, 1938. 2nd edn. London: George Allen and Unwin, 1951; Boston: Houghton Mifflin, 1958; New York: Ballantine, 1965. Rev. edn. New York: Ballantine, 1966; repr. 1974. London: George Allen and Unwin, 1978. Reprint, Unwin Hyman, 1987.

Letter to the editor. *Observer*, February 20, 1938, 9.

"On Fairy-Stories." In *Essays Presented to Charles Williams*. Ed. C.S. Lewis, 38–89. London: Oxford University Press, 1947. Repr., Grand Rapids, Mich: William B. Eerdmans, 1966. Rev. and repr. in *Tree and Leaf*. London: Allen and Unwin, 1964; Boston: Houghton Mifflin, 1965. Repr. in *The Tolkien Reader*, 3–73; and in *Tree and Leaf Including the Poem "Mythopoeia."* London: Unwin Hyman, 1988; Boston: Houghton Mifflin, 1989. Repr., HarperCollins, 2001. *The Monsters and the Critics and Other Essays*, 109–61.

Farmer Giles of Ham. London: George Allen & Unwin, 1949.

"The Homecoming of Beorhtnoth Beorhthelm's Son." *Essays and Studies by Members of the English Association*, n.s., 6 (1953): 1–18. Repr. in *The Tolkien Reader*, 1–28.

The Lord of the Rings. 3 vols.: *The Fellowship of the Ring*, *The Two Towers*, and *The Return of the King*. London: George Allen and Unwin, 1954, 1955; Boston: Houghton

Mifflin, 1954, 1955, 1956. Rev. edn. New York: Ballantine Books, 1965, 1966. 2nd edn. London: George Allen and Unwin, 1966; Boston: Houghton Mifflin, 1967. One-volume edn. London: George Allen and Unwin, 1968; London: HarperCollins, 1993. Reset edn., HarperCollins, 1994; Boston: Houghton Mifflin, 1994.

"English and Welsh." In *Angles and Britons*. Ed. J.R.R. Tolkien et al., 1–41. Cardiff: University of Wales Press, 1963. Repr. in *The Monsters and the Critics and Other Essays*.

Tree and Leaf. London: Allen and Unwin, 1964; Boston: Houghton Mifflin, 1965. Rev. edn., *Tree and Leaf Including the Poem Mythopoeia*. London: Unwin Hyman, 1988; Boston: Houghton Mifflin, 1989.

The Tolkien Reader. New York: Ballantine, 1966.

Smith of Wootton Major. London: George Allen and Unwin, 1967; Boston: Houghton Mifflin Company, 1978.

Interview with Denys Gueroult. *Now Read On*. BBC Radio 4, December 16, 1970. Cassette recording.

"Guide to the Names in *The Lord of the Rings*." Rev. for publication by Christopher Tolkien. In *A Tolkien Compass*. Ed. Jared Lobdell, 155–201. LaSalle, IL: The Open Court Publishing Company, 1975.

The Silmarillion. Ed. Christopher Tolkien. London: George Allen and Unwin, 1977; Boston, New York: Houghton Mifflin, 1977. Repr., New York: Ballantine, 1981, and London: HarperCollins, 1994. 2nd edn. Boston: Houghton Mifflin, 2001.

The Letters of J. R. R. Tolkien: A Selection. Ed. Humphrey Carpenter with assistance from Christopher Tolkien. London: George Allen and Unwin, 1981; Boston and New York: Houghton Mifflin, 1981; London: HarperCollins, 1995; New York: Houghton Mifflin, 2000.

The Old English "Exodus": Text, Translation, and Commentary by J. R. R. Tolkien. Ed. Joan Turville-Petre. Oxford: Oxford University Press, 1981.

The Monsters and the Critics and Other Essays. Ed. Christopher Tolkien. London: George Allen and Unwin, 1983. Repr., Boston: Houghton Mifflin, 1984; London: HarperCollins, 1997.

The Lays of Beleriand. Vol. 3 of *The History of Middle-Earth*. Ed. Christopher Tolkien. Boston: Houghton Mifflin, 1985; London: George Allen and Unwin, 1985; New York: Ballantine, 1994.

The Annotated Hobbit. Annotated by Douglas Anderson. Boston: Houghton Mifflin, 1988; London: George Allen and Unwin, 1988; London: Unwin Hyman, 1989. 2nd edn. Boston: Houghton Mifflin, 2002; London: HarperCollins, 2003.

Sauron Defeated: The End of the Third Age [part 4 of *The History of* The Lord of the Rings]. Vol. 9 of *The History of Middle-Earth*. Ed. Christopher Tolkien. Boston: Houghton Mifflin, 1992.

Translated. *"Sir Gawain and the Green Knight," "Pearl," and "Sir Orfeo."* Ed. Christopher Tolkien. Boston: Houghton Mifflin, 1975; London: Grafton, 1975. Repr., London: HarperCollins, 1995.

Beowulf and the Critics. Edited by Michael D.C. Drout. Medieval and Renaissance Texts and Studies 248. Arizona Center for Medieval and Renaissance Studies: Tempe, Arizona, 2002.

Other Works

Ælfric. *Ælfric's Lives of Saints, Being a Set of Sermons on Saints' Days Formerly Observed by the English Church.* Ed. W. W. Skeat. 4 vols. Early English Text Society, o.s. 76, 82, 94, 114. London: Trübner, 1881–1900.

———. *De temporibus anni.* Ed. by Heinrich Henel. Early English Text Society, o.s. 213. London: Oxford University Press, 1942.

———. *Ælfric's Catholic Homilies: The Second Series.* Ed. Malcolm Godden. Early English Text Society, s.s. 5. Oxford: Oxford University Press, 1979.

———. *Ælfric's Catholic Homilies: The First Series.* Ed. Peter Clemoes. Early English Text Society, s.s. 17. Oxford: Oxford University Press, 1997.

Aers, David. *Chaucer, Langland, and the Creative Imagination.* London: Routledge, 1980.

Aldhelm. *The Riddles of Aldhelm.* Ed. James Hall Pitman. New Haven: Yale University Press, 1925.

———. "Tolkien after All These Years." In *Meditations on Middle-Earth.* Ed. Karen Haber, 129–51, New York: St. Martin's, 2001.

Anderson, Douglas A. *The Annotated Hobbit.* Boston: Houghton Mifflin, 2002.

Armstrong, Karen. *The Battle for God: A History of Fundamentalism.* New York: Ballantine, 2001.

Athanasius. *The Life of St. Antony and the Letter to Marcellinus/Athanasius.* Trans. Robert Gregg. New York: Paulist Press, 1980.

Attebery, Brian. *Strategies of Fantasy.* Bloomington: Indiana University Press, 1992.

Auden, W. H. "The Quest Hero." In *Tolkien and the Critics: Essays on J. R. R. Tolkien's "The Lord of the Rings."* Ed. Neil D. Isaacs and Rose A. Zimbardo, 40–61. South Bend, IN: University of Notre Dame Press, 1968.

Augustine. *Sancti Aurelii Avgustini episcopi De civitate Dei libri XXII.* Ed. Emanuel Hoffmann. Corpus Scriptorum Ecclesiasticorum Latinorum 40. 2 vols. Vienna: Tempsky, 1899–1900.

Barthes, Roland. *S/Z.* Trans. Richard Miller. New York: Hill and Wang, 1974.

———. "From Work to Text." Trans. S. Heath. In *Modern Literary Theory: A Reader.* Ed. Philip Rice and Patricia Waugh, 166–72. London: Edward Arnold, 1992.

———. "The Death of the Author." Trans. S. Heath. In *Modern Literary Theory.* Ed. Philip Rice and Patricia Waugh, 114–18. 2nd edn. London: Edward Arnold, 1992.

Basil, Saint, of Caesarea. *Hexaemeron.* In *Basil: Letters and Select Works.* Nicene and Post-Nicene Fathers, 2nd series, vol. 8. Trans. Blomfield Jackson, 52–107. 1895. Repr., Peabody, MA: Hendrickson, 1999.

Basney, Lionel. "Myth, History, and Time in *The Lord of the Rings.*" In *Tolkien: New Critical Perspectives.* Ed. Neil D. Isaacs and Rose A. Zimbardo, 8–18. Lexington: University Press of Kentucky, 1981.

Battarbee, K. J., ed. *Scholarship and Fantasy: Proceedings of the Tolkien Phenomenon, May 1992, Turku, Finland. Anglicana Turkuensia* no. 12. Turku: University of Turku, 1993.

Bauschatz, Paul. *The Well and the Tree: World and Time in Early Germanic Culture.* Amherst: The University of Massachusetts Press, 1982.

Benson, Larry, ed. *The Riverside Chaucer.* Boston: Houghton Mifflin, 1987.

Beowulf. Trans. Howell Chickering. New York: Doubleday, 1977.
Beowulf. Ed., with an introduction, notes, and new prose trans. Richard Hamer. Manchester: Manchester University Press, 1978.
Beowulf. Ed. and trans. Michael Swanton. Manchester: Manchester University Press, 1978.
Bellamy, Edward. *Looking Backward: 2000–1887.* 1887. Ed. Heywood Broun. New York: Modern Library, 1931.
Birzer, Bradley, J. *J.R.R. Tolkien's Sanctifying Myth: Understanding Middle-Earth.* Wilmington, DE: ISI Books, 2002.
Blair, Hugh. "A Critical Dissertation on the Poems of Ossian, the Son of Fingal." 1763. In James Macpherson, *The Poems of Ossian and Related Works.* Ed. Howard Gaskill, 342–99. Edinburgh: Edinburgh University Press, 1996.
Blamires, David. *David Jones: Artist and Writer.* Toronto: University of Toronto Press, 1972.
Bolintineanu, Alexandra. "'On the Borders of Old Stories': Enacting the Past in *Beowulf* and *The Lord of the Rings.*" In *Tolkien and the Invention of Myth.* Ed. Jane Chance, 263–73. London and New York: Routledge, 2002–03.
Brandl, Alois. "Venantius Fortunatus und die angelsächsischen Elegien *Wanderer* und *Ruine.*" *Archiv* 139 (1919): 84.
Brewer, Derek. "*The Lord of the Rings* as Romance." In *J.R.R. Tolkien, Scholar and Storyteller: Essays in Memoriam.* Ed. Mary Salu and Robert T. Farrell, 249–64. Ithaca, NY: Cornell University Press, 1979.
Brewer, Elizabeth, and Beverly Taylor. *The Return of King Arthur.* Cambridge, UK: D.S. Brewer, 1983.
Brogan, Hugh. "Tolkien's Great War." In *Children and Their Books: A Celebration of the Work of Iona and Peter Opie.* Ed. Gillian Avery and Julia Briggs, 351–67. Oxford: Clarendon Press, 1989.
Browning, Robert. "Love Among the Ruins." 1855. Repr. in *Robert Browning, The Poems.* Ed. John Pettigrew and Thomas J. Collins, 525–29. Harmondsworth: Penguin, 1981.
Buell, Lawrence. *The Environmental Imagination.* Cambridge, MA: Belknap Press, 1995.
Butler, Marilyn. *Romantics, Rebels, and Reactionaries: English Literature and Its Background, 1760–1830.* Oxford: Oxford University Press, 1981.
Butler, Samuel. *The Shrewsbury Edition of Samuel Butler's Works.* Ed. Henry Festing Jones and A.T. Bartholemew, 1923. Repr., New York: AMS Press, 1968.
Calabrese, John A. "Continuity with the Past: Mythic Time in Tolkien's *The Lord of the Rings.*" In *The Fantastic in World Literature and the Arts: Selected Essays from the Fifth International Conference on the Fantastic in the Arts.* Ed. Donald E. Morse, 31–45. Contributions to the Study of Science Fiction and Fantasy 28. New York: Greenwood Press, 1987.
Cantor, Norman F. *The Civilization of the Middle Ages.* Rev. and expanded edn. New York: Harper Perennial, 1994.
Card, Orson Scott. "How Tolkien Means." In *Meditations on Middle-Earth.* Ed. Karen Haber, 153–73.
Carey, John "The Irish 'Otherworld': Hiberno-Latin Perspectives." *Éigse* 25 (1991): 154–59.

---. "Lament of the Old Woman of Beare." *Celtica* 23 (1999): 30–37.

---. *A Single Ray of the Sun: Religious Speculation in Early Ireland*. Andover, MA, and Aberystwyth, UK: Celtic Studies Publications, 1999.

---. "The Location of the Otherworld in Irish Tradition." In *The Otherworld Voyage in Early Irish Literature*. Ed. Jonathan Wooding, 113–17. Dublin: Four Courts Press, 2000.

---. "Etymology and Time." *Temenos Academy Review* 5 (2002): 85–100.

---. "The Lough Foyle Colloquy Texts: *Immacaldam Choluim Chille ₇ ind Óclaig oc Carraic Eolairg* and *Immacaldam in Druad Brain ₇ inna Banfátho Febuil ós Loch Febuil.*" *Ériu*, 52 (2002): 53–87.

---. "The Encounter at the Ford: Warriors, Water and Women." *Éigse* 34 (2004): 10–24.

Carpenter, Humphrey. *The Inklings: C. S. Lewis, J. R. R. Tolkien, Charles Williams, and Their Friends*. London: George Allen and Unwin, 1978; Boston: Houghton Mifflin, 1979.

---. *J. R. R. Tolkien: A Biography*. London: George Allen and Unwin, 1977; Boston: Houghton Mifflin, 1977. Rev. edn., London: Unwin Paperbacks, 1982. Repr., Boston: Houghton Mifflin, 2000.

Cecil, Hugh. *The Flower of Battle*. Vermont: Steerforth Press, 1996.

Cerquiglini, Bernard. *In Praise of the Variant: A Critical History of Philology*. Trans. Betsy Wing. Baltimore, MD: Johns Hopkins University Press, 1999.

Chance, Jane. *Tolkien's Art: A Mythology for England*. London: Macmillan, 1979; New York: St. Martin's, 1980. Rev. edn. Lexington: University Press of Kentucky, 2001.

---. *The Lord of the Rings: The Mythology of Power*. New York: Twayne/Macmillan, 1992. Rev. edn., Lexington: University Press of Kentucky, 2001.

---, ed. *Tolkien the Medievalist*. London and New York: Routledge, 2002–03.

---, ed. *Tolkien and the Invention of Myth: A Reader*. Lexington: University of Kentucky Press, 2004.

---. "Subversive Fantasist: Tolkien on Class Difference." In *Proceedings of the Conference on "The Lord of the Rings, 1954–2004: Scholarship in Honor of Richard E. Blackwelder," October 21–23, 2004*. Ed. Wayne Hammond and Christina Scull, Milwaukee: Marquette University Press, 2005.

Chaucer, Geoffrey. *The Riverside Chaucer*. Ed. Larry Benson. Boston: Houghton Mifflin, 1987.

Chism, Christine. "Middle-earth, the Middle Ages, and the Aryan Nation: Myth and History in World War II." In *Tolkien the Medievalist*. Ed. Jane Chance, 63–92. London New York: Routledge, 2002–03.

A Choice of Anglo-Saxon Verse. Selected with an introduction and a parallel verse translation by Richard Hamer. London: Faber, 1970.

Christensen, Bonniejean. "Gollum's Character Transformation in *The Hobbit*." In *A Tolkien Compass*. Ed. Jared Lobdell, 7–26. 2nd edn. Chicago and La Salle: Open Court, 2003.

Clayton, Mary, and Hugh Magennis. *The Old English Lives of St. Margaret*. Cambridge Studies in Anglo-Saxon England, vol. 9. Cambridge, UK: Cambridge University Press, 1994.

Clopper, Lawrence. "The Engaged Spectator: Langland and Chaucer on Civic Spectacle and the *Theatrum*." *Studies in the Age of Chaucer* 22 (2000): 115–39.
Clute, John, and John Grant, eds. *The Encyclopedia of Fantasy*. New York: St. Martin's Griffin, 1997.
Clute, John, and David Langford. *The Encyclopedia of Fantasy*. London: Orbit, 1997.
Cochran, B. Barnett. "Robert Wallace and Rousseau in the Republic of Virtue." In *Scotland and France in the Enlightenment*. Ed. Deidre Dawson and Pierre Morère, 284–304. Lewisburg: Bucknell University Press, 2004.
Coleman, Janet. *Ancient and Medieval Memories: Studies in the Reconstruction of the Past*. Cambridge: Cambridge University Press, 1992.
Conybeare, John Josias. *Illustrations of Anglo-Saxon Poetry*. Ed. William Daniel Conybeare. London: Harding and Lepard, 1826.
Cook, Raymond A. *Thomas Dixon*. New York: Twayne, 1974.
Cox, Jeffrey, and Larry J. Reynolds, eds. *New Historical Literary Study: Essays on Reproducing Texts*. Princeton, NJ: Princeton University Press, 1993.
Cross, J.E. "The Elephant to Alfred, Ælfric, Aldhelm, and Others." *Studia Neophilologica* 37 (1965): 367–73.
Curry, Patrick. *Defending Middle-Earth: Tolkien, Myth and Modernity*. New York: St. Martin's, 1997.
Dargan, E. Preston. "Scott and the French Romantics." *PMLA* 49 (1934): 599–629.
Dawes, James. *The Language of War*. Cambridge, MA: Harvard University Press, 2002.
deGategno, Paul J. *James Macpherson*. Boston: Twayne Publishers, 1989.
Delveaux, Martin. "From Pastoral Arcadia to Stable-State Mini-Cities: Morris's *News from Nowhere* and Callenbach's *Ecotopia*." *Journal of the William Morris Society* 14, no. 1 (2000): 76–81.
Derrida, Jacques. "Freud and the Scene of Writing." *Yale French Studies* 48 (1972): 74–117.
Devine, T.M. *The Scottish Nation: A History, 1700–2000*. New York: Viking Penguin, 1999.
Dietrich, F. "Die Räthsel des Exeterbuchs." *Zeitschrift für deutsches Altertum und deutsche Literatur* 11 (1859), 452–53.
Dilworth, Thomas. *The Shape of Meaning in the Poetry of David Jones*. Toronto: University of Toronto Press, 1988.
Dobson, R.B. *The Peasants' Revolt of 1381*. London: Macmillan, 1970.
Dowie, William. "The Gospel of Middle-Earth According to J.R.R. Tolkien." In *J. R. R. Tolkien, Scholar and Storyteller: Essays in Memoriam*. Ed. Mary Salu and Robert T. Farrell, 265–85.
Dundes, Alan. "Nationalistic Inferiority Complexes and the Fabrication of Fakelore: A Reconsideration of Ossian, the *Kinder- und Hausmärchen*, the *Kalevala*, and Paul Bunyan." In *Papers of the 8th Congress for the International Society for Folk Narrative Research, Bergen, June 12–17, 1984*, vol. 1. Ed. Reimund Kvideland and Torunn Selberg, 155–71. Bergen, Norway: International Society for Folk Narrative Research, 1984.
Duriez, Colin. *Tolkien and C. S. Lewis: The Gift of Friendship*. Mahwah, NJ: Paulist Press, Hidden Spring, 2003.

Elias, Amy J. *Sublime Desire: History and Post-1960s Fiction*. Baltimore, MD: Johns Hopkins University Press, 2001.
Ellis, John M. *One Fairy Story Too Many: The Brothers Grimm and Their Tales*. Chicago, IL: University of Chicago Press, 1983.
Esty, Jed. *A Shrinking Island: Modernism and National Culture in England*. Princeton, NJ: Princeton University Press, 2004.
Evans, Jonathan. "The Anthropology of Arda: Creation, Theology, and the Race of Men." In *Tolkien the Medievalist*. Ed. Jane Chance, 194–224. London and New York: Routledge, 2002–03.
Exodus. In *The Junius Manuscript*. Ed. G.P. Krapp. The Anglo-Saxon Poetic Records, vol. 1. New York: Columbia University Press, 1936.
Farrell, Joseph P. *Free Choice in St. Maximus the Confessor*. South Canaan, PA: St. Tikhon's Seminary Press, 1989.
Fates of the Apostles. In *The Vercelli Book*. Ed. G.P. Krapp, 51–54. The Anglo-Saxon Poetic Records, vol. 2. New York: Columbia University Press, 1932.
Feldman, Burton R. and Robert D. Richardson. *The Rise of Modern Mythology, 1680–1860*. Bloomington: Indiana University Press, 1972.
Fellman, Michael. "Bloody Sunday and *News from Nowhere*." *Journal of the William Morris Society* 8, no. 4 (1990): 9–18.
Flieger, Verlyn. *A Question of Time: J. R. R. Tolkien's Road to Faërie*. Kent, OH: Kent State University Press, 1997.
———. "J. R. R. Tolkien and the Matter of Britain." *Mythlore* 87, 23, no. 1 (2000): 47–59.
———. *Splintered Light: Logos and Language in Tolkien's World*. Rev. edn. Kent, OH: Kent State University Press, 2002.
Ford, George H. "Alfred Lord Tennyson." In *The Norton Anthology of English Literature*. 6th edn. Vol. 2. Ed. M.H. Abrams, et al., 1056. New York: W.W. Norton, 1993.
Ford, Patrick. *The Mabinogi*. Berkeley: University of California Press, 1977.
Foucault, Michel. "What Is an Author?" Trans. Josue V. Harari. In *Contemporary Literary Criticism: Literary and Cultural Studies*. Ed. Robert Con Davis and Ronald Schleifer, 262–75. 2nd edn. New York: Longman, 1989.
Fowles, John. *The French Lieutenant's Woman*. Boston: Little, Brown and Company, 1969.
Frantzen, Allen. *Bloody Good: Chivalry, Sacrifice, and the Great War*. Chicago: University of Chicago Press, 2004.
Friedman, Barton R. "Fabricating History: Narrative Strategy in *The Lord of the Rings*." *Clio* 2 (1973): 123–44.
———. "Tolkien and David Jones: The Great War and the War of the Ring." *Clio* 11, no. 2 (1982): 115–36.
Frye, Northrop. "The Argument of Comedy." In *Shakespeare, Modern Essays in Criticism*. Ed. Leonard F. Dean, 79–89. London: Oxford University Press, 1967.
Fussell, Paul. *The Great War and Modern Memory*. London: Oxford University Press, 1975.
Gallatin, A.E. *Art and the Great War*. New York: E. P. Dutton, 1919.
Gardner, John. *Grendel*. New York: Alfred A. Knopf, 1971.
Garth, John. *Tolkien and the Great War: The Threshold of Middle-Earth*. London: HarperCollins; Boston: Houghton Mifflin, 2003.

Gaskill, Howard, ed. *Ossian Revisited*. Edinburgh: Edinburgh University Press, 1991.

———. "Ossian in Europe." *Canadian Review of Comparative Literature* 21, no. 4 (1994): 643–78.

Gemmill, Janet. "*In Parenthesis*: A Study of Narrative Technique." *Journal of Modern Literature* 1 (1971): 311–30.

Gibbon, Edward. *The Decline and Fall of the Roman Empire*, vol. 2. New York: Modern Library, n.d.

Giddings, Robert, ed. *J.R.R. Tolkien: This Far Land*. London: Vision Press; Totowa, NJ: Barnes & Noble Books, 1983.

Girard, René. *Violence and the Sacred*. Trans. Patrick Gregory. Baltimore: Johns Hopkins University Press, 1977.

Gordon, R.K., trans. *Anglo-Saxon Poetry*. London: J.M. Dent, 1926.

Graves, Robert. *The White Goddess: A Historical Grammar of Poetic Myth*. New York: Farrar, Straus and Giroux, 1966.

Grein, Christian W.M. *Bibliothek der angelsächsichen Poesie*. Vol. 1. Göttingen: Georg H. Wigand, 1857.

Grossman, Lev. "Feeding on Fantasy." *Time*, December 2, 2002, 90–94.

Hammond, Wayne G. and Christina Scull. "The History of Middle-Earth." *Seven* 12 (1995): 105–25.

Haycock, Marged. "The Significance of the 'Cad Goddeu' Tree-List in the Book of Taliesin." *Current Issues in Linguistic Theory* 68 (1990): 297–331.

Herbert, Máire. "The Legend of St. Cothíne: Perspectives from Early Christian Ireland." *Studia Hibernica* 31 (2000): 27–35.

Hicketier, F. "*Klage der Frau, Botschaft des Gemahls, und Ruine*." *Anglia* 11 (1889): 363–68.

Holmes, John. "Tolkien and the Nineteenth Century." Paper, International Medieval Congress, Kalamazoo, MI, May 6, 2004.

Hughes, Peter. "Narrative, Scene, and the Fictions of History." In *Contemporary Approaches to Narrative*. Ed. Anthony Mortimer, 73–87. Tübingen: Gunter Narr, 1984.

Irenaeus. *Against Heresies*. 1885. In *Ante-Nicene Fathers* 1. Trans. Alexander Roberts and James Donaldson, 309–567. Repr., Peabody, MA: Hendrickson, 1999.

Jackson, Kenneth. "The British Languages and Their Evolution." In *The Mediaeval World*, Ed. by D. Daiches and A. Thorlby, 113–26. London: Aldus Books, 1973.

Jackson, Peter. *The Lord of the Rings: The Fellowship of the Ring*. Platinum Series, extended edition DVD. New Line Home Entertainment, 2002.

Jameson, Fredric. *Postmodernism, or, The Cultural Logic of Late Capitalism*. Durham, NC: Duke University Press, 1991.

The Jerusalem Bible, Reader's Edition. New York: Doubleday, 1968.

John Scottus Eriugena. *The Periphyseon*. Trans. Myra L. Uhlfelder. Indianapolis: Bobbs Merrill, 1976.

Jolly, Karen. "Father God and Mother Earth: Nature Mysticism in the Anglo-Saxon World." In *The Medieval World of Nature: A Book of Essays*. Ed. Joyce Salisbury, 221–52. New York: Garland, 1993.

Jones, David. *In Parenthesis*. New York: New York Review of Books, 2003.
Keegan, John. *The First World War*. New York: Alfred A. Knopf, 1999.
Kerr, Douglas. *Wilfred Owen's Voices: Language and Community*. Oxford: Clarendon, 1993.
Kinzer, Stephen. "Movie on Armenians Rekindles Flame over Turkish Past." *New York Times*, January 20, 2004, sec. E.
Kirkland, J.H. "A Passage in the Anglo-Saxon Poem *The Ruin*." *American Journal of Philology* 7 (1886): 367–69.
Klaeber, Fr[iedrich]. *Beowulf* and *The Fight at Finnsburgh*. 3rd edn. New York: D.C. Heath, 1950.
Kocher, Paul H. "Middle-Earth: Imaginary World?" In *Tolkien: New Critical Perspectives*. Ed. Neil D. Isaacs and Rose A. Zimbardo, 121–32. Lexington: University Press of Kentucky, 1981.
Kolve, V.A. *Chaucer and the Imagery of Narrative*. Stanford, CA: Stanford University Press, 1984.
Kotzor, Gunter, ed. *Das altenglische Martyrologium*. 2 vols. Munich: Bayerischen Akademie der Wissenschaften, 1981.
Kristeva, Julia. "Dostoevsky, the Writing of Suffering, and Forgiveness." In *Black Sun*. Trans. Leon Roudiez, 173–218. New York: Columbia University Press, 1987.
Kurath, Hans et al., eds. *The Middle English Dictionary*. Ann Arbor: University of Michigan Press, 1952–2001.
Layard, A.H. *Nineveh and Its Remains: With an Account of a Visit to the Chaldaean Christians of Kurdistan, and the Yezidis, or Devil Worshippers*. 2 vols. New York: G. P. Putnam, 1849.
Leslie, R.F. *Three Old English Elegies*. Manchester: Manchester University Press, 1961.
Letcher, Andy. "The Scouring of the Shire: Fairies, Trolls and Pixies in Eco-Protest Culture." *Folklore* 112 (2001): 147–61.
Levenson, Michael, ed. *The Cambridge Guide to Modernism*. Cambridge: Cambridge University Press, 1999.
Lewis, Alex, and Elizabeth Currie. *The Uncharted Realms of Tolkien: A Critical Study of Text, Context, and Subtext in the Works of J. R. R. Tolkien*. Weston Rhyn, Oswestry, UK: Medea Publishing, 2002.
Lewis, C.S. "The Gods Return to Earth." *Time and Tide*, August 14, 1954.
———. "The Dethronement of Power." *Time and Tide*, October 22, 1955.
———. "Tolkien's *Lord of the Rings* (Review)." In *On Stories and Other Essays on Literature*. Ed. Walter Hooper, 83–90. New York and London: Harcourt Brace Jovanovich, 1982.
Lewis, Roger C. "*News from Nowhere*: Arcadia or Utopia?" *Journal of the William Morris Society* 7, no. 2 (1987): 15–25.
Lincoln, Bruce. *Theorizing Myth: Narrative, Ideology, and Scholarship*. Chicago: University of Chicago Press, 1999.
Lobdell, Jared. *A Tolkien Compass*. LaSalle, IL: The Open Court Publishing Company, 1975.
Lotman, Yuri. "Problems in the Typology of Culture." In *Soviet Semiotics: An Anthology*. Ed. Daniel P. Lucid, 213–21. Baltimore, MD: Johns Hopkins University Press, 1977.

Louth, Andrew. "The Body in Western Catholic Christianity." In *Religion and the Body*. Ed. Sarah Coakley, 113–30. Cambridge, UK: Cambridge University Press, 1997.

Lukács, Georg. *The Historical Novel*. Trans. by Hannah Mitchell and Stanley Mitchell. Harmondsworth, UK: Penguin, 1969.

MacCarthy, Fiona. *William Morris: A Life for Our Time*. London, UK: Faber and Faber, 1994.

Machen, Arthur. "The Coming of the Terror." In *Tales before Tolkien*. Ed. Douglas A. Anderson, 264–301. New York: Ballantine, 2003.

Macpherson, James. "A Dissertation." 1765. In *The Poems of Ossian and Related Works*. Ed. Howard Gaskill, 216–17.

———. "A Dissertation Concerning the Antiquity &c. of the Poems of Ossian the Son of Fingal." 1765. In *The Poems of Ossian and Related Works*. Ed. Howard Gaskill, 43–52.

Mahaffey, Vicki. "Modernist Theory and Criticism." In *The Johns Hopkins Guide to Literary Theory and Criticism*. Ed. Michael Groden and Martin Kreiswirth. Baltimore and London: Johns Hopkins University Press, 1994.

Mallet, M. *Northern Antiquities; or, An Historical Account of the Manners, Customs, Religion, and Laws, Maritime Expeditions and Discoveries, Language and Literature of the Ancient Scandinavians (Danes, Swedes, Norwegians, and Icelanders.) With Incidental Notices Respecting Our Saxon Ancestors*. Translated by Bishop Percy. Ed. I.A. Blackwell. 2nd edn. London: Henry G. Bohn, 1847.

Malone, Kemp. "Swerting." *Germanic Review* 14 (1939): 235–57.

"The Marion E. Wade Center." http://www.wheaton.edu/learnres/wade/.

Marx, Karl. *Capital*. 1867. Trans. Ernest Untermann. New York: Modern Library, 1906.

Marx, Karl and Friedrich Engels. *Manifesto of the Communist Party*. English edn., 1888. In *The Marx-Engels Reader*. Ed. Robert C. Tucker, 331–62. New York: Norton, 1972.

McFadden, Brian. "The Social Context of Narrative Disruption in *The Letter of Alexander to Aristotle*." *Anglo-Saxon England* 30 (2001): 91–114.

Meek, Donald. "The Gaelic Ballads of Scotland: Creativity and Adaptation." In *Ossian Revisited*. Ed. Howard Gaskill, 19–48. Edinburgh: Edinburgh University Press, 1991.

Meyendorff, John. *Christ in Eastern Thought*. Crestwood, NY: St. Vladimir's Seminary Press, 1969.

Middlebro', Tom. "Brief Thoughts on *News from Nowhere*." *Journal of the William Morris Society* 2, no. 4 (1970): 8–13.

Mill, J.S. Review of Tennyson, *Poems, Chiefly Lyrical* [1830] and *Poems* [1833]. In *Tennyson: The Critical Heritage*. Ed. John D. Jump, 84–97. London: Routledge, 1967.

Minnis, Alastair J. *Medieval Theory of Authorship: Scholastic Literary Attitudes in the Later Middle Ages*. 2nd edn. Aldershot: Wildwood House, 1988.

Mitchell, Bruce and Fred C. Robinson. *A Guide to Old English*. 6th edn. Oxford: Blackwell Publishers, 2001.

Morris, May. *William Morris: Artist, Writer, Socialist.* 2 vols. 1936. Repr., New York: Russell and Russell, 1966.

Morris, Richard, ed., *The Blickling Homilies, with a Translation and Index of Words Together with the Blickling Glosses.* Oxford: N. Trübner and Co. for the Early English Text Society, 1880.

Morris, William. *The Well at the World's End.* 1896. Ed. Lin Carter. 2 vols. New York: Ballantine, 1970.

———. "How I Became a Socialist." 1894. Repr. in *Political Writings of William Morris.* Ed. A.L. Morton, 240–45. New York: International Publishers, 1973.

———. *News from Nowhere and Other Writings.* New York: Penguin, 1993.

———. *The Water of the Wondrous Isles.* Ed. May Morris. 1913. Repr. with introduction by Norman Talbot. Bristol: Thoemmes Press, 1994.

———. "Socialism from the Root Up." 1886. In *William Morris on History.* Ed. Nicholas Salmon, 143–76. Sheffield, UK: Sheffield Academic Press, 1996.

———. *The Collected Letters of William Morris.* Vol. 3, *1889–1892.* Ed. Norman Kelvin. Princeton, NJ: Princeton University Press, 1996.

———. *The Earthly Paradise.* 1868–70. Ed. Florence S. Boos. 2 vols. New York and London: Routledge, 2002.

———. *News from Nowhere; or, An Epoch of Rest: Being Some Chapters from a Utopian Romance.* 1890. Ed. David Leopold. Oxford: Oxford University Press, 2003.

Morus, Iwan Rhys. " 'Uprooting the Golden Bough': J. R. R. Tolkien's Response to Nineteenth-Century Folklore and Comparative Mythology." *Mallorn* 27 (1990): 5–9.

Muhr, Kay. "Water Imagery in Early Irish." *Celtica* 23 (1999): 193–210.

Nagy, Gergely. "The Great Chain of Reading: (Inter-)Textual Relations and the Technique of Mythopoesis in the Túrin Story." In *Tolkien the Medievalist.* Ed. Jane Chance, 239–58. London and New York: Routledge, 2002–03.

———. "Samu és a szilmarilok" [Sam and the Silmarils]. *Lassi Laurië* (Hungarian Tolkien Society) 2, no. 2 (2003): 8–10.

———. "Sauron and the Sign: from Mythological Sign to Mythological Subject." Paper read at the 6th conference of the Hungarian Society for the Study of English. HUSSE 6, Debrecen, Hungary, January 2003.

———. "The Adapted Text: The Lost Poetry of Beleriand." *Tolkien Studies* 1 (2004): 21–41.

———. "Saving the Myths: The Re-creation of Mythology in Plato and Tolkien." In *Tolkien and the Invention of Myth: A Reader.* Ed. Jane Chance, 81–100. Lexington: University Press of Kentucky, 2004.

———. "The 'Lost' Subject of Middle-Earth: Elements and Motifs of Subject Constitution in the Figure of Gollum in J.R.R. Tolkien's *The Lord of the Rings*." Forthcoming.

Natoli, Joseph and Linda Hutcheon, eds. *A Postmodern Reader.* Albany: State University of New York Press, 1993.

Norman, Philip. "The Prevalence of Hobbits." *New York Times Magazine*, January 15, 1967, 100.

Oleksa, Michael. *Alaskan Missionary Spirituality.* New York: Paulist Press, 1987.

Orchard, Andy. *Pride and Prodigies: Studies in the Monsters of the Beowulf Manuscript*. Cambridge, UK: D. S. Brewer, 1995.

Ó Riain, Pádraig. "A Study of the Irish Legend of the Wild Man." *Éigse* 14 (1971–72): 179–206.

Owen, Wilfred. "Strange Meeting." In *Wilfred Owen: The Complete Poems and Fragments*. Ed. Jon Stallworthy, 125–26. New York: Norton, 1986.

"Ossianic." *Oxford Universal Dictionary on Historical Principles*. 3rd edn. 1933. Repr., London: Oxford University Press, 1964.

The Paris Psalter and the Meters of Boethius. Ed. G.P. Krapp. The Anglo-Saxon Poetic Records, vol. 5. New York: Columbia University Press, 1932.

Partridge, Brenda. "No Sex Please We're Hobbits: The Construction of Female Sexuality in *The Lord of the Rings*." In *J.R.R. Tolkien: This Far Land*, Ed. Robert Giddings, 179–98. London: Vision Press; Totowa, NJ: Barnest Noble, 1983.

Patterson, Lee. "The Knight's Tale and the Crisis of Chivalric Identity." In *Chaucer and the Subject of History*, 165–230. Madison: University of Wisconsin Press, 1991.

Pearce, Joseph. *Tolkien: Man and Myth*. San Francisco: Ignatius Press, 1998. Repr., London: HarperCollins, 2001.

———. *Small is Still Beautiful*. New York and London: HarperCollins, 2001.

Pevear, Richard. "Foreword." In *Notes from Underground* by Fyodor Dostoevsky. Trans. Pevear and Larissa Volokhonsky, vii–xxiii. New York: Vintage Books, 1993.

Prebble, John. *The Highland Clearances*. London: Secker and Warburg, 1963. Repr., Harmondsworth, NY: Penguin, 1969.

Reynolds, Patricia and Glen H. Goodknight, eds. *Proceedings of the J.R.R. Tolkien Centenary Conference, Keble College, Oxford, 1992*. Combined issue of *Mythlore* 80; *Mallorn* 30. Milton Keynes, UK: Tolkien Society; Altadena, CA: Mythopoeic Press, 1995.

Ricks, Christopher. *Tennyson*. 2nd ed. Basingstoke, UK: Macmillan, 1989.

Ricoeur, Paul. *Time and Narrative*. Trans. Kathleen McLaughlin and David Pellauer. 3 vols. Chicago: University of Chicago Press, 1984.

———. *Oneself as Another*. Trans. Kathleen Blamey. Chicago: University of Chicago Press, 1992.

Robson, W.W. *A Prologue to English Literature*. Totowa, NJ: Barnes & Noble, 1986.

Roeder, Fritz. *Die Familie bei den Angelsachsen*: Erster Haupteil: *Mann und Frau*. Halle: Niemeyer, 1899.

Rogers, Deborah Webster and Ivor A. Rogers. *J. R. R. Tolkien*. Boston: Twayne Publishers, 1980.

Rosebury, Brian. *Tolkien. A Critical Assessment*. New York: St. Martin's Press, 1992. Rev. edn., as *Tolkien: A Cultural Phenomenon*. London and New York: Palgrave Macmillan, 2003.

Rousseau, Jean-Jacques. "Discourse on the Sciences and Arts." In *The First and Second Discourses Together with the Replies to Critics and Essay on the Origin of Languages*. Ed. and trans. Victor Gourevitch. New York: Perennial, 1986.

Sale, Roge. "Tolkien as Translator." *Parnassus: Poetry in Review* 4, no. 2 (1976): 183–91.

Salter, Elizabeth. *Chaucer: "The Knight's Tale" and "The Clerk's Tale"*. London: E. Arnold; New York: Barrons, 1962.

Scala, Elizabeth. *Absent Narratives, Manuscript Textuality, and Literary Structure in Late Medieval England*. New Middle Ages. New York: Palgrave/Macmillan, 2002.

Schmidt, Karl Horst. "Insular Celtic: P and Q Celtic." In *The Celtic Languages*. Ed. Martin J. Ball, 64–98. London: Routledge, 1993.

Schumacher, E.F. *Small is Beautiful: Economics as if People Mattered*. London: Blond and Briggs, 1973.

———. *A Guide for the Perplexed*. New York: Harper and Row, 1979.

Scott, Sir Walter. "Review of Report of the Committee of the Highland Society of Scotland and *The Poems of Ossian*." *Edinburgh Quarterly* 6 (1805): 429–62.

———. "An Essay on Romance." In *Essays on Chivalry, Romance, and the Drama*. 1834. Repr., Freeport, NY: Books for Libraries Press, 1972.

———. *Ivanhoe*. 1819. Ed. Graham Tulloch. London: Penguin, 2000.

Shippey, T[homas] A. "Tolkien as a Post-War Writer." *Mythlore: A Journal of J. R. R. Tolkien, C.S. Lewis, Charles Williams, and the Genres of Myth and Fantasy Studies* (1996): 84–93.

———. *J. R. R. Tolkien, Author of the Century*. London: HarperCollins, 2000; Boston: Houghton Mifflin, 2001.

———. *The Road to Middle-Earth*. London: Allen and Unwin, 1982; Boston: Houghton Mifflin, 1983. Rev. edn. London: HarperCollins, Grafton, 1992; Boston: Houghton Mifflin, 2003.

———. "Light-elves, Dark-elves and Others: Tolkien's Elvish Problem." *Tolkien Studies* 1 (2004): 1–15.

Sieper, Ernst. *Die altenglische Elegie*. Strassburg: K. J. Trübner, 1915.

Siewers, Alfred. "Landscapes of Conversion: Guthlac's Mound and Grendel's Mere as Expressions of Anglo-Saxon Nation-Building," *Viator* 34 (2003): 1–39.

———. "How Green Was My Martyrdom? Ec(o)centricity in Early Irish Cosmology." Paper, International Medieval Congress, Kalamazoo, MI, May 6, 2004; revised as "Colours of the Winds, Colours of Martyrdom: Iconographic Landscape in Early Irish Texts," Early Irish Seminar, University College Cork, November 10, 2004.

Sims-Williams, Patrick. "The Visionary Celt: The Construction of an Ethnic Preconception." *Cambridge Medieval Celtic Studies* 2 (1986): 71–96.

———. "The Invention of Celtic Nature Poetry." In *Celticism*. Ed. Terence Brown, 97–124. Amsterdam: Rodopi, 1996.

S[mith], G[eoffrey] B[ache]. "Roman Roads." In *Oxford Poetry*. Ed. G.D.H.C. and T.W.E. Oxford: B. H. Blackwell, 1915.

Smollett, Tobias. *Humphrey Clinker*. 1771. Ed. Lewis M. Knapp. London: Oxford University Press, 1966.

Snowden, Frank. *Blacks in Antiquity: Ethiopians in the Greco-Roman Experience*. Cambridge, MA: Harvard University Press, 1970.

Snyder, Christopher A. *The Britons*. Oxford: Blackwell Publishing, 2003.

Sontag, Susan. *Regarding the Pain of Others*. New York: Farrar, Straus, and Giroux, 2003.

de Staël, Germaine Necker, baronne de Staël-Holstein. *De la littérature considérée dans ses rapports avec les institutions sociales*. 1800 [An 9]. In *Oeuvres Complètes de Madame la Baronne de Staël*, vol. 4, 245–46. Paris: Treuttel et Würtz, 1820.

Stafford, Fiona. *The Sublime Savage: A Study of James Macpherson and The Poems of Ossian*. Edinburgh: Edinburgh University Press, 1988.

———. Introduction. "The Ossianic Poems of James Macpherson." In *The Poems of Ossian and Related Works*. Ed. Howard Gaskill, v–xxi.

Stenstrom, Anders. "A Mythology? For England?" *Mythlore* 80 (1996): 310–14.

Stewart, Susan. *On Longing*. Durham, NC: Duke University Press, 1993.

Talbot, Norman. Introduction to W. Morris, *The Water of the Wondrous Isle*, v–xxvi.

Tennyson, Alfred, Lord. "Locksley Hall" In *Poetry of the Victorian Period*, Ed. Jerome Hamilton Buckley and George Benjamin Woods. 3rd edn. Glenview, Illinois: Scott, Foresman, and Company, 1965.

———. *The Poems of Tennyson*. Ed. Christopher Ricks. London: Longman, 1969.

———. "Locksley Hall." 1842. *In Tennyson: A Selected Edition*. Ed. Christopher Ricks, 181–93. Berkley: University of California Press, 1989.

Thompson, E.P. *William Morris: Romantic to Revolutionary*. London: Lawrence and Wishart, 1955.

Timmer, B.J. "The Elegiac Mood in Old English Poetry." *English Studies* 24 (1942): 34–36.

Tolkien Remembered/Central Productions. Princeton, NJ: Films for the Humanities and Sciences, 1993.

Tolkien Society. "Tolkien Country Park Proposal." Accessed on June 1, 2004. http://www.tolkiensociety.org/t_park/proposal_tolkienpark_2000.html.

Trumpener, Katie. *Bardic Nationalism: The Romantic Novel and the British Empire*. Princeton, NJ: Princeton University Press, 1997.

van Tieghem, Paul. *Le Préromantisme: Études d'histoire littéraire européenne*. Paris: F. Rieder, 1924.

Ware, Kalistos. "The Body in Greek Christianity." In *Religion and the Body*. Ed. Sarah Coakley, 90–110. Cambridge: Cambridge University Press, 1997.

———. *The Orthodox Way*. Crestwood, NY: St. Vladimir's Seminary Press, 1999.

Weatherby, Harold. "Greek Fathers." In *The Spenser Encyclopedia*. Ed. A.C. Hamilton et al. Toronto: University of Toronto Press, 1990.

Weinbrot, Howard D. *Britannia's Issue: The Rise of British Literature from Dryden to Ossian*. Cambridge, UK: Cambridge University Press, 1993.

Wells, Robin Headlam, Glenn Burgess, and Rowland Wymer, eds. *Neo-Historicism: Studies in Renaissance Literature, History, and Politics*. Cambridge, UK: Brewer, 2000.

Wesseling, Elisabeth. *Writing History as a Prophet: Postmodernist Innovations of the Historical Novel*. Philadelphia: John Benjamins, 1991.

West, Richard C. "Real-World Myth in a Secondary World: Mythological Aspects in the Story of Beren and Lúthien." In *Tolkien the Medievalist*. Ed. Jane Chance, 259–67. London and New York: Routledge, 2002–03.

White, Hayden. *Metahistory: The Historical Imagination in Nineteenth-Century Europe*. Baltimore: Johns Hopkins University Press, 1973.

———. *The Content of the Form: Narrative Discourse and Historical Representation*. Baltimore: Johns Hopkins, 1987.

Wilcox, Miranda. "Exilic Imagining in *The Seafarer* and *The Lord of the Rings*." In *Tolkien the Medievalist*. Ed. Jane Chance, 133–54. London and New York: Routledge, 2002–03.

Williams, David. *Deformed Discourse: The Function of the Monster in Mediaeval Thought and Literature*. Montreal and Kingston: McGill-Queen's University Press, 1996.

Wilson, Edmund. "Oo Those Awful Orcs!" *Nation* 182 (April 14, 1956): 12–13.

Winter, Jay. *Sites of Memory, Sites of Mourning: The Great War in European Cultural History*. Cambridge, UK: Cambridge University Press, 1995.

Woolf, Virginia. *The Common Reader*. London: Hogarth Press, 1925.

Wülker, Richard Paul. "Aus englischen Bibliotheken." *Anglia* 2 (1879): 374–87.

Wyatt, Joan. *A Middle-Earth Album: Paintings*. New York: Simon and Schuster, 1979.

Yeats, W.B. "The Happiest of the Poets." In W.B. Yeats, *Essays and Introductions*, 53–64. New York: Macmillan, 1961.

Yonge, Charlotte M. *The Long Vacation*. London: Macmillan, 1895.

LIST OF CONTRIBUTORS

Jane Chance, professor of English at Rice University, has taught a Tolkien course since 1976. Among her twenty other books are revised editions of *Tolkien's Art: A Mythology for England* (1979, 2001) and *The Lord of the Rings: The Mythology of Power* (1992, 2001), the latter translated into Japanese in 2003. She has also edited two collections, *Tolkien the Medievalist* (2002) (a finalist for the 2004 and 2005 Mythopoeic Award for Scholarship on the Inklings) and *Tolkien and the Invention of Myth: A Reader* (2004), and two issues of *Studies in Medievalism*, on the twentieth century (1982) and the Inklings (1991). Her essay on Tolkien on *Beowulf*—"The Structural Unity of *Beowulf*: The Problem of Grendel's Mother" (1981)—has been published or reprinted seven times.

Deidre Dawson comes to Tolkien Studies from the perspective of eighteenth-century Scottish and French studies. Author of a book on Voltaire's correspondence and coeditor of two volumes of comparative cultural studies, *Scotland and France in the Enlightenment* (2004) and *Progrès et violence dans les lumières* (2001), Dawson is now returning to her original interest in medieval studies. Dawson is currently associate professor of French at Michigan State University.

Verlyn Flieger is professor of English at the University of Maryland, where she teaches courses in medieval literature, comparative mythology, and Tolkien studies. Her works on Tolkien include *Splintered Light: Logos and Language in Tolkien's World*, *A Question of Time: Tolkien's Road to Faerie*, and (as coeditor with Carl Hostetter) *Tolkien's Legendarium: Essays on the History of Middle-Earth*. Her latest book is *Interrupted Music: Tolkien's Making of a Mythology*. She is also the author of two works of fiction related to medieval traditions, *Pig Tale*, and "Avilion," a novella in *The Doom of Camelot*.

John R. Holmes is professor of English at Franciscan University in Steubenville, where since 1985 he has taught, among other things, medieval literature, Old English language, and Tolkien. Most of his published articles have been in the field of early American literature (he is currently editing the letters of Charles Brockden Brown), but his recent discovery of the delightful fellowship of Tolkien scholars has encouraged him to write more on J.R.R. Tolkien.

John Hunter is the Christian A. Johnson Endeavor chair in Comparative Humanities at Bucknell University, where he teaches in the humanities program and its affiliated residential college. A coeditor of the recent Blackwell anthology of Renaissance literature, his teaching and research centers on ways in which classical culture and influences helped shape Western modernity, examining in particular authors such as Ovid—and Tolkien—whose writings easily cross time periods and cultures.

Rebekah Long is a PhD candidate at Duke University, where she specializes in medieval literature and has taught Tolkien's fantasy writings in relation to modern ethical issues. Her essay in this volume in earlier conference-paper form won the Outstanding Graduate Student Paper award at the 25th annual International Conference on the Fantastic in the Arts in Florida, March 2004. Rebekah is currently completing work on another Tolkien essay that draws on the final chapter of her dissertation, which deals with the fourteenth-century *Pearl* poem and Tolkien's treatment of loss in fantasy.

Andrew Lynch teaches in English, Communication, and Cultural Studies at the University of Western Australia. Among his publications are *Malory's Book of Arms* (1997) and articles on the medieval English tradition of war and peace. He also writes on the modern reception of medieval literature, including a chapter on *Le Morte Darthur* in *Adapting the Arthurian Legends for Children*, edited by Barbara Tepa Lupack (2004).

Brian McFadden, assistant professor of English at Texas Tech University, has taught graduate and undergraduate Old and Middle English literature, medieval and Renaissance surveys, the history of the English language, and *Beowulf*. In addition, he has recently taught a Tolkien seminar. He has published articles on marvel texts and miracle stories in Old English and Anglo-Latin prose; his current project is a book on the *Beowulf* manuscript in the social context of the tenth century.

Gergely Nagy is a junior assistant professor at the Institute of English and American Studies at the University of Szeged, Hungary. He is working on a dissertation on Tolkien and poststructuralist theory, with an especial focus on processes of cultural history. He is also involved in the study of medieval English romances and Arthurian literature, more specifically with the works of Sir Thomas Malory. He has published essays on both Tolkien and Malory and serves as vice president of the Hungarian Tolkien Society.

Ted Nasmith is an illustrator who lives in Toronto, Canada. He has illustrated Tolkien calendars from 1987 onward, as an adjunct to a career in architectural rendering. Over the years his reputation for highly detailed paintings has earned high praise and critical renown. Among notable successes is the commission to illustrate Tolkien's *The Silmarillion*.

Chester N. Scoville has taught Chaucer, Shakespeare, and Tolkien at the University of Toronto at Mississauga. Active in medieval drama productions as well as in Tolkien studies, his research has included work in late-medieval drama and ways in which it reconstructed earlier traditions in a bridge to the modern. He is the author of *Saints and the Audience in Middle English Biblical Drama* (2004).

Alfred K. Siewers, assistant professor of medieval English literature at Bucknell University, wrote the first comparative ecocritical approach to *Beowulf*, "Landscapes of Conversion: Guthlac's Mound and Grendel's Mere as Expressions of Anglo-Saxon Nation-building," in the 2003 issue of *Viator*. He also is the author of a project integrating the study of cultural and literary landscapes at Glastonbury, "Gildas and Glastonbury," in *Via Crucis*, edited by Thomas N. Hall (2002). A veteran teacher of Tolkien, he penned the foreword to *The Origins of Tolkien's Middle-Earth for Dummies* by Greg Harvey (2003).

Michael N. Stanton retired in 2001 after teaching in the English Department at the University of Vermont for thirty years. He is the author of *Hobbits, Elves, and Wizards: Exploring the Wonders and Worlds of J. R. R. Tolkien's "The Lord of the Rings"* (2001).

INDEX

Note: In subheadings the titles *The Lord of the Rings* and *Silmarillion* are abbreviated as *LR* and *Silm*, respectively. Illustrations are indicated with *italic* page numbers.

Ackerman, Forrest, 165
Aers, David, 129
allegory
   and Aragorn as Victorian allegoric hero, 88
   moral, as reaction to war, 86–87
   political allegory, *LR* as, 68, 78, 115
   of postwar industrialism, in *LR*, 130–31
   WWII, allegorical readings of, in *LR*, 68, 78, 115
alliterative verse, 20–21, 80
allusion
   modernism and, 4, 6
   source criticism and Tolkien's works, 44, 63, 71
Anderson, Douglas, 93–94
Andrew Lang lecture, "On Fairy Stories" (Tolkien, 1939), 20, 30–33, 44
Anglo-Saxon language and culture
   dustsceawung and, 46–47
   freedom or liberty as Saxon heritage in, 68
   Nordic Renaissance and, 65
   polychronic time sense revealed in, 53
   Rohan and, 18, 20, 106
animals, Tolkien and, 114–15, 141, 143–44

Annotated Hobbit, The (Anderson), 93–94
antiquest in *LR*, 172, 178
anti-Semitism, 3, 164
apartheid, 172–73, 175, 177
Aragorn
   Alexander compared with, 158–59
   Arwen and, 21, 34, 182–83
   as unlikely hero, 172
   as Victorian allegoric icon, 88
Arcadian pastoral tradition, 97–100
archaeology, and Victorian consciousness of time, 47–48
archaism, 81, 84–85, 88, 108
Armstrong, Karen, 200–1
Arthurian legend, 21, 44, 77–78, 146
Attebery, Brian, 124
At the Court of the Fountain (Nasmith), *198*
Auden, W[ystan] H., 160
audience
   broad appeal of Tolkien's works to, 1, 4, 23–24, 139–40
   implied through use of language, 36
   Macpherson's popular, 111
   political marginalization and appeal to, 4–5, 96
   postmodern, 1–2
   postmodernism and, 4–5

authenticity
   of Anglo-Saxons as English people, 65
   Jackson on film design of
      Middle-earth, 70
   of *Kalevala*, 64
   linguistic, of Tolkien's invented
      languages, 107–8
   of *LR*, 83
   of Macpherson's Ossian poems,
      65–66, 109, 111
   of myth and engagement with the
      real world, 183
   narrative, 6
   originality and medieval manuscript
      culture, 32–33
   style and, 108–9
   of Tolkien's fictional world, 62–63
authorship
   and author as reader, 34
   compilation and, 33–38
   and fictional characters as author,
      33–34, 61–62
   of history, 38
   interpretation and, 31, 34, 36–37, 39
   medieval manuscript culture and,
      32–33, 36
   postmodern theories of, 36–37
   and theological codedness of
      representation, 38

Baggins, Bilbo, *see* Bilbo Baggins
Baggins, Frodo, *see* Frodo Baggins
Bakhtin, Mikhail, 5, 12, 144
Barad-Dûr (Nasmith), *201*
Barthes, Roland, 36, 37
Battle of Brunanburh, 44
Battle of Maldon, The, 46, 48, 81, 83, 88;
   see also Homecoming of
   Beorhtnoth Beorhthelm's Son
   (Tolkien)
"Battle of Pelennor Fields, The," 52–53,
   80, 115–16
Baynes, Pauline, 20
Beare, Rhona, correspondence with,
   18, 20

Beowulf
   critics on historical nature of, 51
   dustsceawung in, 49–50
   exile as theme in, 176
   Exodus compared with, 175
   Gardner's *Grendel* and, 26
   gnomic tense in, 55
   as heroic-elegiac poem, 46
   as historical document, 51
   polychronic time-sense and, 53–54
   as self-reflexive, self-referential
      text, 25
   as source or shadow text for *LR*,
      52–53, 142
   as stylistic influence, 80–81
   theory of Northern courage in,
      48–50
   time consciousness in, 48–49
   Tolkien and, 101
   Tolkien's scholarship, 20, 30–33, 48,
      52, 78, 82–83, 90n4
"Beowulf: Monsters and the Critics"
   British Academy lecture
   (Tolkien, 1936), 48
Beren and Lúthien, 34, 163, 182–83; *see
   also Silmarillion, The* (Tolkien)
Bilbo Baggins
   depictions of, 179, 192
   as marginalized "queer" Hobbit, 179
   as translator/editor, 33–35, 61
binary oppositions in Tolkien's works,
   9, 44, 125, 155–58, 162–64, 166
Birth of a Nation (film), 70
Blackburn, Francis, 49
Blair, Hugh, 109
Blickling homilies, 46–47, 51
*Bloody Good: Chivalry, Sacrifice, and the
   Great War (Frantzen)*, 126; *see also*
   Frantzen, Allen
Boethius, Anicius Manlius Severinus
   (480–524), 45, 47, 48
Bolintineanu, Alexandra, 34
Bratt, Edith, 21, 182
Brogan, Hugh, 78–79, 108
Buell, Lawrence, 142

Butler, Marilyn, 68
Butler, Samuel, 11, 205, 207–11

Calabrese, John A., 34
Carey, John, 145, 148, 149
Carpenter, Humphrey, 94, 206
Catholicism, *see* Roman Catholicism
Celticism
  and bardic traditions, 7, 115
  Celtic as problematic term, 150n5
  and imagery shared by pagan and Christian, 145
  and linguistic heritage of Britain, 106–7
  LR compared with Celtic texts, 18, 143–44
  and Macpherson's Ossian poems, 8–9, 105, 109–11
  and monasticism, 148
  Nasmith on Celtic elements in works, 197
  and Otherworld narratives, 9–10, 140–41, 143
  and overlay landscape in Otherworld texts, 141, 143
  Tolkien on Celtic art, 105, 146–47
Celtic languages, 106–7
Cerquiglini, Bernard, 33, 36
Chance, Jane, 4, 52
  contributor's note, 229
  on gender, race, and the Other in Middle-earth, 171–83
  introductory essay, 1–12
Chaucer, Geoffrey, 5, 9, 129–30
chivalry
  in Chaucer's "Knights Tale," 129–30
  in *Ivanhoe*, 68–69
  pride and, 176–77
  propagandic use of, 128, 131
  symbolic war and, 8, 77–78
  Tennyson and, 77
  WWI and, 128, 134n16
Christianity
  Beowulf and, 49–50
  centrality of religion for Tolkien, 101

  conservative traditionalists as audience for *LR*, 139
  cosmological traditions of and environmental consciousness, 140–41, 147–49
  Germanic mythology contrasted with, 49
  hierarchy of as theologically coded, 30
  imagery of shared with pagan Celtic traditions, 145
  imperfectability in and Tolkien's pastoral ideal, 8
  monastic tradition of, 9–10, 148
  pagan traditions and syncretism of, 143–47
  representation of, as theologically coded, 30, 37–38
  sin and fear in, of the Other, 156–57
  Tolkien on *LR* and theology, 165
  Tolkien on myth and, 142–43
  Tolkien's engagement with the Other shaped by value system, 5
  transformation in, and information of the tragic, 49
  see also Roman Catholicism
Christopher, Joe R., 47
Church, Frederick, 195
Civil War (United States), 69
Clansman, The (Dixon), 69–70
class, social, 164, 172, 175–76
classicism
  elegy in and Anglo-Saxon *dustsceawung* "contemplation of the dust," 44–45
  models and sources as "classical," 29
  Northern tradition and, 49
Clute, John, 171
Coleman, Janet, 37
commemoration of the dead, 126, 129, 199–200
Common Speech, 22, 117–18, 159
compilation and authorship, 33–38
conservatism, 2, 95–96, 139–40, 172

consumerism, 139–40
Conybeare, William Daniel, 45, 47
correspondence, 181–82
  with A. Ronald, 49
  with Christopher Tolkien, 51–52, 95, 165, 208
  with H. Schiro, 160
  with M. Straits, 178
  with N. Mitchinson, 125
  with publisher, 114, 164
  with R. Beare, 18, 20
  with T. Nasmith, 192
courage
  elegy and, 46
  heroic will, 83–84
  in *LR*, 79
  Northern, 31, 46, 47, 48–49
  Shippey on Hobbit, 79
Cranshaw, Edward, 105
critical reception of Tolkien's works, 105, 125, 134n10, 160, 172
  and collegues' denigration of Tolkien's fiction, 177
Culhwch ac Olwen, 144
culture
  authorship and, 33–34
  "culture wars," Tolkien as common ground in, 9–11
  see also Recovery
Curry, Patrick, 4–5

Dawes, James, 125, 130, 133–34n7
Dawson, Deidre
  contributor's note, 229
  on cultural recovery and language, 9, 105–18
death
  as barrier to communication, 159
  difference defined by mortality and, 162
  as equalizing, 129, 160
  faith as response to uncertainty of, 163–64
  fear of, 156, 160
  mortality as shared experience of, 156

deGategno, Paul J., 110
demons
  darkness associated with, 14, 157–58, 167nn12, 164
  exorcised from appliances, 209
Devine, Thomas M., 112–13
difference, *see* Other
diversity, 2
  cultural difference and modernist authors, 3
  England as culturally and linguistically diverse, 118
  erasure of difference linked to evil, 180–81
  forgiveness and acceptance of difference, 181–82
  racial difference in *LR*, 10, 118
  Tolkien and engagement with the Other, 5
  see also Other; race
Dixon, Thomas, Jr., 69
Dostoevsky, Fyodor, 12
Dream of John Ball, A (Morris), 127
dustsceawung "contemplation of the dust," 6–7
  Anglo-Saxon reflection on, 46–47
  artifacts or heirlooms and, 52–53
  in *Beowulf*, 49–50, 52–53, 57n32
  classical elegy and, 44–45
  eternity and, 47
  impulse to write linked to, 50–51
  poetry and philology united in, 50
  polychronic time-sense and, 53
  time and, 44
  Tolkien's dust-mote apperception, Holmes on, 47, 51–52
Dwarves, 19, 117–18, 184n2

eagles, 143–44, 151n18
Eärendil Searches Tirion (Nasmith), *199*
ecocentrism in *LR*, 139–50
Eddas, 20, 64–65
Egypt and Egyptian culture, 18–19
elegy and elegiac mode, 7
  Beowulf as heroic-elegiac poem, 46

Germanic tradition, 46
Greek elegiac tradition, 45–46
LR and, 83
memory and consolation as function of, 115–16
Northern courage linked to, 46
in Old English poetry, 45, 47
see also dustsceawung "contemplation of the dust"
Eliot, Thomas Stearns, 4, 127
Elves
  ancestry of, 161
  depictions of, 197
  division and ancestry of, 182–83
  divisions among races and languages, 55, 117, 157
  as exiles, 148, 157
  immortality of, 161–62
  otherworldly light and, 144
  Tolkien's use of term "elf," 146
  see also Elvish languages
Elvish languages
  and audience implied through use of language, 36
  and Celtic and Finnish, 8
  and cultural and linguistic separation of Elvish races, 117, 157
  and marginalization of language studies, 177–78
  Quenya, 117
  Sindarin, 107, 117, 118, 157
  and Welsh, 58n39, 107
embodiment
  body as interpreter, 140–41
  characters as embodiment of themes, 207
  Eucharistic contemplation of dust mote, 51–52
  incarnation of spirit in Christian cosmology, 9–10, 142–43, 146, 147, 149
England
  as culturally and linguistically diverse, 118
  lost cultural heritage of, 9, 62, 114
  as Middle-earth, 206
  "English and Welsh" (Tolkien, Cardiff lecture, 1963), 53–54, 107
Ents, 114, 116, 140, 143–44, 149
  as isolated and insensitive to the Other, 180–81
  Old English origin of term, 50
Entwives, 180
environmental issues
  and Christian cosmology and nature, 140
  ecological activism, 4–5
  good kingship, 86
  Green politics, 96, 97, 140, 141
  Morris's *News from Nowhere* and ecological consciousness, 96–98
  Orcs as polluting, 86
  as politically unifying, 96
  rural destruction and *LR*, 78
  "The Scouring of the Shire" and, 8, 86, 130–31
  the "spirit of Isengard" and destruction of nature, 115
  Victorian utopianism and, 96
  war and restoration of natural order, 86
  see also nature
Éowyn, 106, 172
epic mode
  LR as subversive to convention, 172
  style issues, 21–22
Erewhon (Butler), 11, 207–11
escapism, 62, 71
  vs. empowerment of reader, 1
  fantasy genre and, 7
  literature as escape from civilization's progress, 111
  Macpherson's works as escapist, 69
  progress and, 208–9
  social or political criticism mistaken for, 3
Ever-new Tongue, The, 149
Everyman, 10, 178

evil, 54, 88
  complexity and ambiguity in
    Tolkien's treatment of good and
    evil, 9, 70–71, 125, 163–64
  erasure of difference and, 180–81
  mechanical or industrial progress as
    evil, 207–10
  Other as, 156–57, 160, 165–66,
    167n14
  persistence of, 71, 101, 210
exile, 84, 148, 157, 172, 173–75, 176,
  177–78
Exodus, Old English (Tolkien's
  translation), 174–75

Faerie Queene, The (Spenser), 146
fairy stories, 17, 27, 30–33, 44
faith, 163
  Tolkien's personal faith, 51–52, 140,
    149–50, 155–56, 163
Fall (biblical), the
  fear of the Other linked to, 156–57
  freedom and original sin, 101
  human imperfection and, 8, 100
  in *LR*, 157
  and paradise lost after original
    sin, 147
  and separation of humans from
    nature as a result, 147–48, 149
  and Tolkien on technology as failed
    creation, 208
"Fall of Arthur" (Tolkien), 20
fantasy
  "generic duality" and, 7
  LR as, 17
  Morris and invention of novel, 93
  mythos and logos in, 5
  open-ended language and, 124–25
  social or political criticism in, 10
  as sphere for exploring the self and
    the Other, 155–56
  subversive nature of, 10, 171–72
  Tolkien's use of, 126
  Victorian reimagining of medieval
    tradition as, 7

Farmer Giles of Ham (Tolkien), 20
Fascism, 172
film (*Lord of the Rings*), 11, 210
  fantasized history and, 69–70
  New Zealand as setting of, 11, 142,
    205, 206
Finland, 64
First Sight of Ithilien (Nasmith), *194*
Flieger, Verlyn
  contributor's note, 229
  on Elvish and human perception
    of time, 54
  on eternity and *dustceawung*, 47
  on Tolkien as postmodern
    medievalist, 5–6, 171–83
  works of, 4
Ford, George H., 47
forgiveness and acceptance of
  difference, 181–83
Foucault, Michel, 36
Fowles, John, 23, 25
Frantzen, Allen, 123–24, 126, 128,
  134n16
freedom
  Anglo-Saxon culture and, 68
  Arcadian tradition and, 98–99
  Mallet and Northern Europe as
    cradle of, 64–65
  Marx on, 99
  original sin and, 101
  respect for the Other linked
    to, 118
  Tolkien on abuse of word, 164
  of will, lack of as dehumanizing, 165
French Lieutenant's Woman, The
  (Fowles), 23
Friedman, Barton, 133n4
Frodo Baggins
  as author or historian, 33–34,
    61–62
  as hero, 18, 21, 24–25, 34, 89,
    130–31, 172, 178, 181–82
  as queer Hobbit, 179–80
Frye, Northrop, 146
Fussell, Paul, 131, 133n4

INDEX

Gallatin, Albert E., 123, 124
Gamgee, Samwise, *see* Samwise Gamgee
Gandalf the Grey, 18, 62, 86–87, 89, 101, 143, 181, *191*, *192*, 209
Gardner, John, 26
Garth, John, 79, 82, 95, 125
Gaskill, Howard, 63
gender, 10
  Entwives as Other, 180–81
  Éowyn as Boudicca figure, 106
Germanic tradition, mythology contrasted with Christianity, 49
Gibbon, Edward, 45
Giddings, Robert, 4
Gilson, Rob, 50
globalization, 1, 9, 140
gnomes, 55
gnomic tense, 6–7, 55
Gollum, 26, 129, 173, 178–79, 181–82
Gone with the Wind (film), 70
Gone with the Wind (Mitchell), 69
good and evil, 9, 70–71, 80, 87, 125, 163–64
grammar (English)
  future tense, 54–55, 58n36
  gnomic tense (Anglo-Saxon), 6–7, 55
  "grammar" of violence, 9
  inversion, 80–82
  modal verbs, 58n36
  Old English grammar, 54–55
  parataxis, 21–22, 80–82
  polychronic time sense in Old English tenses, 53
  present tense, 7
Grant, John, 171
"Green" politics, 96, 97, 140, 141
Grendel (Gardner), 26
Grossman, Lev, 155

Heisenberg's indeterminacy principle, 25
hero, heroes
  Aragorn as Victorian allegoric, 88
  archaic heroism in *LR*, 84, 88
  artist as, 52
  dustsceawung as heroic trait, 52
  everyman as heroic, 178
  Gollum as, 26
  Hobbits as, 79, 80, 87, 172, 178
  interpretation of stories by, 34
  as outcast or unconventional in *LR*, 10, 172, 178
  symbolic heroism and chivalry in Victorian medievalist literature, 77–78
Highland culture, loss of, 112–13
high style, 21–22, 80–82, 86, 89
Hildebrandt brothers, 195
historical fiction
  European historical novel tradition, 67
  fantasized history, 69–70
  fantasy and reimaging of history, 7
  LR as, 30, 61–62
  Scott and, 66–69
historicity
  of text, 31–32, 37
  textuality and, 6, 29–39
  "timeless present" in postmodern works, 36–37
  Tolkien as ahistorical, 2, 6
history
  Beowulf as document of, 51
  as discourse, 38
  dustsceawung and, 51
  as fragmentary knowledge, 62
  historical emergence in *LR*, 63
  postmodern Western culture and historical change, 71–72
  present rescued by knowledge of the past, 62
  remembrance and history, 35
  role of knowledge of, in *LR*, 61–62
  Shire and neglect of history, 101
  Tolkien on, as a "long defeat," 49
  see also historical fiction
Hobbits
  ancestry and types of, 173, 179
  depiction of, 192

Hobbits—*continued*
  as heroes, 79, 80, 87, 172, 178
  industrialization of the Shire and, 100–1
  as marginalized characters, 179
  Shippey on courage of, 79
  Tolkien's self-identification as, 177–78
Holmes, John R.
  contributor's note, 229–30
  on *dustsceawung* in Tolkien's works, 6–7, 43–56
Homecoming of Beorhtnoth Beorhthelm's Son (Tolkien), 83–84, 176–77
Hugo, Victor, 67–68
Hulme, Thomas E., 3
Humphrey Clinker (Smollett), 113
Hunter, John
  contributor's note, 230
  on historical fiction, 61–72

identity, 82
  of England and loss of cultural heritage, 114, 116–17
  modernism and gender and racial, 3
  national, 110, 116, 118
  the Other and, 5, 144, 166
Idylls of the King (Tennyson), 44
  warfare as symbolic in, 77–78
imperialism, 8–9, 165, 206
indeterminacy, 25
industrialism, 2, 6
  "appropriate technology" of E. F. Schumacher and, 13n11
  development of rural countryside and, 142
  Hobbits as complicit in, of the Shire, 100–1
  Isengard and, 209–10
  the mechanization of war, 8, 19, 87, 125, 208
  Morris's *News from Nowhere* and rejection of capitalism in, 96–99
  myth of progress and, 205
  "The Scouring of the Shire" as allegory of postwar, 130–31
  social change and destruction of traditional ways of life in, 112–13
  the "spirit of Isengard" and, 115
  Victorian tradition and resistance to, 4
  see also mechanization
Inglis, Fred, 172
Inklings, 96
In Parenthesis (Jones), 9, 126–28, 132–33n4
interpretation, authorship and, 31, 34, 36–37, 39
Ireland, 105; *see also* Celticism
Isengard, 18, 87, 115, 118, 141, 208–9
isolation, empty lands in Middle-earth, 113, 206
isolationism, 180–81
Ivanhoe (Scott), 67–69

J. R. R. Tolkien, This Far Land (Giddings), 4
J. R. R. Tolkien: Author of the Century (Shippey), 4, 125; *see also* Shippey, Thomas
Jackson, Kenneth, 106–7
Jackson, Peter S., 11, 70; *see also Lord of the Rings, The* (films)
James, David, 126–28
Jameson, Fredric, 71
John Scottus Eriugena (ca. 800–877), 147, 148
Johnson, Samuel, 65, 111
Jones, David, 9, 123, 132–33n4
  Tolkien compared with, 128, 133n4

Kalevala (Lönnrot), 64, 143, 151n18
kingship and the "true king," *see* monarchy
Kittridge, George Lyman, 49
"Knight's Tale" (Chaucer), 9, 123–29, 136n26
Kristeva, Julia, 149

landscape(s), 82
  illustrations of Middle-earth, 193–95
  as memorial, 115

overlay, 140–41, 143–44
psychological and moral analysis and
  description of, 85
solitude and empty, 113, 206
of war, 87, 114, 135n23
Lang, Andrew, 44
language, 82
  audience implied through, 36
  as central in Tolkien's fantasy, 8–9
  Common Speech and cooperative
    communication in, 22,
    117–18, 159
  culture and, 117
  fantasy and open-endedess of,
    124–25
  as immanent (cosmic language), 149
  invented languages in *LR*, 58n39; *see
    also* Elvish languages
  Jones's use of, 126–27
  language studies as marginalized,
    177–78
  linguistic heritages of Britain,
    106–7
  meaning as essential to vitality
    of, 117
  memorial function of, 117
  national identity and, 110, 116, 118
  open-ended language and meaning,
    124–25
  of Orcs, 22, 117
  postmodern distrust of, 39
  primacy of philology in creation of
    LR, 109, 118
  recuperative power of, 116–17
  temporal signals in, 53–54
  Tower of Babel, 157
  violence and, 9, 125, 126–27, 128,
    130, 131, 133–34n7
  see also style; *specific languages*
Language of War, The (Dawes), 125, 130,
  133–34n7
Latin, 106
Le Morte Darthur (Malory), 80
Leopold, Aldo, 140
Leslie, Roy F., 45
Letcher, Andy, 139

Letters (Tolkien)
  on Celtic culture, 105
  on Elvish languages, 107
  on good and evil, 87
  on imperialism, 165
  on mortality and immortality, 160
  on Orcs, 165
  on peoples of Middle-earth, 18–19,
    20, 165
  on progress and the destruction of
    nature, 208
  on progress as destructive, 114–15,
    208
  on racial prejudice, 160, 164–65, 165
  on reductive critical readings of
    LR, 125
  on restoration of English epic
    tradition, 65, 114
  on *Silm* as "already 'there'," 112
  on style, 81–82, 108–9
  on theology and *LR*, 208
  on Utopianism, 101
  on war, 79, 87, 90n3, 113–14
  see also correspondence
Lewis, Alex, 195
Lewis, Clive Staples, 54, 58n37, 94,
  142–43, 183
liberty, *see* freedom
light
  and darkness, 157–58, 164
  Elves and otherworldly light, 144
Lincoln, Bruce, 66
logoi, 149, 152n22, 202
Lombard, Peter, 37–38
Long, Rebekah
  contributor's note, 230
  on World War I as context for works
    of Jones and Tolkien, 9, 123–32
Lönnrot, Elias, 64
Lord of the Rings, The (films)
  ecocentric imagery and scenes in
    film, 141
  as fantasized history, 70
  "Scouring" omitted from, 11, 151n9,
    205, 210
  visual design of, 70, 199

Lord of the Rings, The (Tolkien)
   biographical details linked to, 21, 177–78, 182
   contexts for writing, 18, 64–65, 66, 68, 78, 82, 125, 200–2
   European historical novel tradition and, 67
   historical emergence as theme in, 63
   as historical fiction, 70–71
   Ivanhoe compared with, 68–69
   Nordic Renaissance and, 64–65
   as postmodern work, 71–72
   primacy of philology and creation of, 109, 118
   romance elements in, 21
   style in, 21–22, 80–82, 86, 108
   as subversive text, 22–23, 172
   Victorian medievalism and, 78
   see also specific chapters by title
Lord of the Rings: The Mythology of Power, The (Chance), 4
Lotman, Yuri, 38
Louth, Andrew, 140–41, 144
love
   forgiveness and acceptance of difference, 181–82
   romantic love in Tolkien's works, 21, 34, 182–83
Lukács, Georg, 69
Lúthien, Beren and, 34, 163, 182–83
Lynch, Andrew, 7–8
   contributor's note, 230
   on war discourse in *LR*, 43–56

Mabinogi, 143–44, 151n18
machines, *see* mechanization
Macpherson, James, 3–4, 7, 8–9, 108
   and authenticity of Ossian poems, 65–66, 109, 111
   Ossian poems of, as "recovery" project, 63–66, 109–13
   Scott compared with, 67
   Tolkien compared with, 71, 109–10, 113
   works of, as pseudohistories, 63–66
Mahaffrey, Vicki, 3

Mallet, Paul Henri, 64, 66
Malory, Sir Thomas, 18, 21–22, 80
marginalization, 62
   apartheid and racial, 172–73, 175, 177
   of Hobbit characters, 179
   of language studies, 177–78
   political, 96
   "queerness" of characters, 179
   Tolkien as marginalized, 177–78
   Tolkien's heroes as outcast or unconventional, 172, 179
Marx, Karl, 2, 99
Marxism, 95, 99
Maximus the Confessor (ca. 580–662), 147, 148–49
McFadden, Brian
   contributor's note, 230
   on racial difference in Tolkien's works, 155–66
mechanization
   Saruman and, 100, 141, 151n9, 209–10
   state socialism and, 98
   Tolkien on machines and, 208
   warfare as mechanized, 8, 19, 87, 125, 208
medieval, use of term, 17, 25
medievalism
   adaptation of medieval themes, 1–2
   "medieval" as construct, 2
   themes in *LR*, 19
   Victorian literary tradition and, 3–4
medieval manuscript culture, 30, 34, 36, 37–38
memory
   commemoration of the dead, 126, 129, 199–200
   Dead Marshes as war memorial, 128–29
   elegiac form and, 115–16
   exile and, 84
   as function of written history, 62
   history and, 35, 62, 78
   Tolkien on *LR* and, 125–26
   war and memorialization, 82, 125–26, 199–200

Mercia, 20
mercy, 181
Merwin, William Stanley, 132–33n4
metanarratives, 23
Metres of Boethius (Alfred), 45, 47, 48
Middlebro', Thomas, 98, 100
Middle-earth
  as empty landscape, 206–7
  as England, 206
  as integration of mythical and physical, 142
  New Zealand cast as, 206–7
  as Other, 196–97
  sources of name, 142
Midsummer Night's Dream (Shakespeare), 146
Mill, John Stuart, 85
Minas Tirith at Dawn (Nasmith), 197
Mitchell, Bruce, 46–47
Mitchell, Margaret, 69
Mitchison, Naomi, 101, 125
modernism
  allusion in, 6
  classicism and, 3
  as defined literary style, 3–4
  "modern" as construct in, 2
  "mythical method" and, 4
  narrative unity and, 4
  Nasmith on, 202
  time consciousness of Tolkien and, 55–56
  Tolkien as modernist writer, 44n37
  and Victorian resistance to modernization, 4
  World War I and emergence of, 82
monarchy, 85–86, 89, 95, 158–59, 172
monsters, 158, 160, 161–62, 163
Morris, William, 3–4, 7, 8, 19
  A Dream of John Ball, 127
  as influence on Tolkien, 93–94
  as socialist, 95, 98
  Tolkien's knowledge of works, 94–95
mortality and immortality
  as central to *LR*, 160–61
  in Christian theology, 162

and death as common experience, 156
Northern Theory of Courage and mortality, 48–49
in *Silm*, 161–62, 163
and uncertainty, 163–64
Morte d'Arthur (Tennyson), 84–85
Morus, Iwan Rhys, 32
Muhr, Kay, 145
"mythical method," 4
mythology
  England's lack of legend and literature and, 67–68
  Lewis on, 183
  mythological discourse, 38
  Northern Renaissance and recovery of, 64–65
  Tolkien on, 142–43

Nagy, Gergely
  contributor's note, 230
  on textuality and historicity, 6, 29–39
names
  Anglo-Saxon linked to, in *LR*, 106
  linked to personal biographical details, 178
  as literary allusion to Morris's works, 94
  Middle-earth, sources of name, 142
  of swords, 52
Nasmith, Ted
  contributor's note, 231
  on his work as illustrator, 189–202
  works by pictured, *190*, *191*, *192*, *193*, *194*, *196*, *197*, *198*, *199*, *201*
nationalism
  literary nationalism, 63–66, 142
  national identity and language, 110, 116, 118
nature
  agency of, 143–44
  Augustinian perspective on, 147
  Christian cosmology and, 9–10, 143, 146, 147–49

nature—*continued*
  Christian theology and, 147
  Christian traditions and environmental consciousness, 140–41
  in Macpherson's Ossian poems, 116
  Morris on objectification of nature, 98
  objectification of (incarnational views), 9–10
  objectification of the Other, 141
  as polyphonic text, 144
  psychological and moral analysis and description of, 85
  Tolkien on progress and the destruction of, 114–15
  Tolkien's affection for animals and trees, 114
  Tolkien's ecocentric view of nature, 139–50
Nazism, 18, 164–65
News from Nowhere (Morris), 96–99
New Zealand, 11, 142, 205, 206
Nordic Renaissance, 64–67
Norse language and tradition, 18, 49, 64–65, 82, 88, 142, 167n12
Northern courage, 31, 46, 47, 48–49
nostalgia, 7, 78, 82–83, 86, 88, 98–99, 126, 151n9

obituary of Tolkien written by C. S. Lewis, 58n37
O'Donnell lecture "English and Welsh" (Tolkien, 1963), 53–54, 107
Old English, 6–7, 53–55, 80, 83–84
  Rohan as Old English society, 175–76
  Siglewara (Ethiopians) in, 10, 156–59
  see also dustsceawung "contemplation of the dust"; *specific works*
"On Fairy Stories," Andrew Lang lecture (Tolkien, 1939), 20, 30–33, 44, 208
On Longing (Stewart), 83, 133n6
orality, 55, 61–62, 111–12
Orcs
  language of, 22, 117
  modern warfare and, 87
  Old English origin of term, 50
  as pollution, 86
  redemption of, 165
  as robot-like, 209
  Tolkien on nature of, 165
original sin, *see under* Fall (biblical), the
Ossian Poems (Macpherson), 8–9, 63–66, 109–13
  Blair on authentic tone of, 109
  Brogan on "Ossianic" style in *LR*, 108
  critical reception of, 111
  nature in, 116
Other
  apartheid or segregation, 172–73, 175, 177
  Catholic as, in England, 156, 177
  as distant and unknown, 158–59
  engagement with, 5, 158–60
  Ethopians as, 158, 173–74
  as evil, 156–57, 160, 165–66, 167n14
  the Fall and fear of difference, 156–57
  fantasy as sphere for exploring the self and, 155–56
  forgiveness and acceptance of difference of, 181–82
  Gollum as, 181
  identity of, alternatives to definition in opposition to, 144
  immortal Elf as, 161
  intermarriage and love of, 173, 182
  language and communication with, 118
  medieval violence as, 78
  Middle-earth as, 196–97
  mortality and recognition of commonality with, 166
  objectification of nature of, 141
  Orcs as, 165
  prejudice and intolerance linked to insensitivity, 180–81
  racial differences in *LR* and, 10, 118, 157–58
  redemption of the, 165
  repetition and otherness of narrated experience, 83–84

INDEX

Samwise and recognition of
humanity of, 10, 135n23,
158–60
Tolkien as, 177
Otherworld
in Celtic narrative, 9–10, 140–41, 143
water associated with, 137n36,
144–46
overlay landscape
Christian cosmology and, 148–49
in *LR*, 143–44
syncretism of pagan and Christian
beliefs and, 148
Owen, Wilfred, 123–24

paganism, 31, 44, 142, 145
eco-pagans and, 139
syncretism of, with early Christian
traditions, 31, 49, 140, 141,
145, 148
paradise
Elves as exiles from, 148, 157
Fall and loss of, 147
imperfectability and earthly, 8,
101–2, 146
paratactic constructions, 21–22,
80–82
"Passage of the Marshes, The," 113–14,
128–29, 135n23
pastoralism, 8, 11, 97, 98–99, 100–2
Pearl, The, 136–37n35
Pelennor Fields, 52–53, 80, 115–16
perfectability, Christianity and earthly
paradise, 8, 100–2, 146–47
philology, 37, 109, 118, 173–74
place, sense of, 145–46
politics
appropriation of art for political
agendas, 3
broad audience appeal, 96, 139–40
ecocentrism as politically unifying, 5,
139–40, 150
"Green" politics, 96, 97, 140, 141
LR as political allegory, 78
socialism or Marxism, 95, 98
subtexts of works, 4

Tolkien as apolitical, 95–96, 101
"true king" as central in Tolkien's
LR, 85–86
polychronic viewpoint, 7
polyphony, 144
Pope, Alexander, 55
popular culture
audience for *LR*, 23–24
Giddings and Tolkien's popular
appeal, 4
Portrait of Two Ferraris (Nasmith),
195, *196*
postmodernism
historical change as preoccupation of
Western culture, 71
medieval texts as similar to
postmodern hypertext, 32
subversive tone and, 23
"timeless present" and historicity of
postmodern texts, 36–37
Tolkien as postmodern author,
22–23
poststructural theory, 4
power, 30, 161
Prebble, John, 113
prejudice, 10
Pre-Raphaelites, 3, 93–94
pride, 176–77, 211
progress, myth of, 205
propaganda, 79, 128, 131, 132n1,
135n22
proverbs, as "survival" equipment, 55

"queerness" of characters, 179
Quenya, 117, 157
Question of Time, A (Flieger), 54
quests, 21, 70
antiquest in *LR*, 172, 178

race
apartheid and racial marginalization,
172–73, 175, 177
binary oppositions mistaken for
racism, 164
depictions of people of color in *LR*,
155–66

race—*continued*
  distrust between Dwarves and Elves, 118
  Elvish races, 55, 117, 157
  Ethopians as Other, 158, 173–74
  fantasy as subversive of racial constructs, 10
  intermarriage and racial blending in *LR*, 173, 182
  light/darkness in *LR*, 157–58
  medieval texts and portrayal of racial difference, 10, 158, 173–74
  modernism and racial identity, 3
  Nazism and racialist theories, 164–65
  racial difference in *LR*, 10, 118
  racism, 164, 172
  Sigelwara (Ethopians), 10, 14, 156–59, 166, 167n12, 167n14, 173–74
  Swertings and Haradrim in *LR*, 156
  Tolkien's rejection of racial prejudice, 164–65, 172–73
Radagast the Brown, 141
realism, 123–24
  fantasy and, 7, 124–25
  historical fiction and, 69
  Nasmith on realism in works, 190, 195
Recovery
  Christian cosmology and *LR* as, 149–50
  of ecocentric literary traditions, 9–10, 142
  as effort to restore cultural continuity, 82–83
  England's national identity and, 116–17
  language and cultural, 105–18
  of language and culture as resistance to imperialism, 8–9
  linguistic authenticity of Tolkien's invented languages, 107–8
  LR as recovered history rather than invention, 33, 62, 112
  Macpherson's Ossian poems as "recovery" project, 63–66, 109–13
  Nordic Renaissance and, 64–67
  recuperative power of language and, 116–17
  Tolkien on, 27, 62
  Yeat's works as projects of cultural, 142
religion
  eco-paganism, 139
  Morris on Middle Ages and, 95, 101
  paganism, 31, 44, 142, 145
  syncretism between paganism and Christian traditions, 31, 49, 140, 141, 145, 148
  theological discourse in Tolkien's fiction, 31, 38
  see also Christianity; Roman Catholicism
representation, 30, 33, 37–38
revision, Tolkien's writing process, 26, 130–31, 146–47
Riders of Rohan, The (Nasmith), *194*
Rivendell (Nasmith), 193, *193*
Robinson, Fred C., 46–47
Rohan and Rohirrim
  Anglo-Saxon culture and, 18, 20, 106
  depictions of, 197
  Éowyn as Boudicca figure, 106
  as medieval culture, 6
  Old English society as, 175–76
  The Wanderer and, 175–76
Roman Catholicism
  Catholic as Other in England, 156, 177
  critics and Tolkien's faith, 172
  mortality and immortality in theology, 162
  Tolkien on *LR* as religious work, 146–47
  Tolkien's personal faith, 51–52, 140, 149–50, 155–56, 163
  see also Christianity
romance (genre)
  Aragorn/Arwen love story as, 21, 34, 182–83
  LR and, 17, 87–88
  medieval literature as, 17

Scott on history and, 67
  subversion of convention of,
    in *LR*, 172
Roman roads, 50–51
Romanticism, 43, 47
Ronald, Amy, 49
Root, Jerry, 139–40
Rosebury, Brian, 2, 71, 79, 82
Rosenberg, John D., 85
Ruskin, John, 2, 96

sagas, 20, 64–65, 94
salvation, 181–82
Samwise Gamgee
  identification with the Other, 10, 135n23, 158–60
  as left behind, 88–89
  proverbial knowledge as survival equipment, 55
  as representative Hobbit, 178–79
  as storyteller or historian, 24–25, 34, 36, 62
sarcwiðe (sorrow speech), 47
Saruman, 18, 100, 101, 141, 151n9, 180, 209–10
Scala, Elizabeth, 32
Schumacher, Ernest F., 11, 13n11
Scott, Sir Walter, 3–4, 7, 66
  historical fiction and, 66–69
  Macpherson compared with, 67
  Nordic Renaissance and, 67
  Tolkien compared with, 68–69, 71
"Scouring of the Shire, The," 8
  as exploration of violence, 130
  good kingship and, 86
  Hobbits as complicit in industrialization of the Shire in, 100–1
  omitted in film, 11, 151n9, 205, 210
  self-reflection and, 131
Scoville, Chester N.
  contributor's note, 231
  on Morris and Tolkien, 8, 93–102
sea, *see* water
self-projection, 52
self-reflexivity, 24–25, 34

self-sacrifice, 178–79
Sentences (Lombard), 37–38
Shakespeare, William, 146
Shelley, Mary, 3–4
Shippey, Thomas
  as critic, 62, 71, 94, 106, 156, 166
  on Hobbit courage, 79
  on Lönnrot's *Kalevala*, 64
  on "The Scouring of the Shire," 129
  on Tolkien's depictions of Elves, 44
  on Tolkien's relationship with language, 50, 136n35
  works cited, 4
Shire, the
  as eco-topia, 151n9
  as imperfect, 8, 100–1
  see also "Scouring of the Shire, The"
Sieper, Ernest, 45
Siewers, Alfred K.
  contributor's note, 231
  on ecocentric views of nature and Tolkien's works, 139–50
  introductory essay, 1–12
Sigelwara (Ethopians), 10, 14, 156–59, 166, 167n12, 167n14, 173–74
Silmarillion, The (Tolkien), 24, 33, 36, 38, 148
  as "already 'there'," 112
  creation in, 149
  critics on Celtic qualities of, 105
  Elves as immortal Other in, 161–63, 182
  fear in, 160, 165
  as historical text, 35
  modernist "mythical method" and, 4
  mortality and immortality in, 161–63, 182
  nature in, 148
  Orcs in, 165
  parallels to biblical stories, 157
Sindarin, 117, 118, 157
  Welsh and, 58n39, 107
Sir Gawain and the Green Knight, 20
Sméagol, *see* Gollum
Smith, Geoffrey B., 50
Smith of Wootton Major (Tolkien), 21

Smollett, Tobias, 113
socialism, 95, 98
Somme, the, 128–29, 132–33n4, 135n23
Sontag, Susan, 136n24
source criticism, 63
  Beowulf as source or shadow text for *LR*, 52–53
  "classical" sources for Tolkien's works, 29
  LR's literary tradition obscured by, 71
Spenser, Edmund, 146
spirituality, self-reflection and "The Scouring of the Shire," 131
Splintered Light: Logos and Language in Tolkien's World (Flieger), 4
Stafford, Fiona, 111, 112
"Stairs of Cirith Ungol," 23–25, 26, 34
Stanton, Michael N.
  on Butler and Tolkien, 11, 205–11
  contributor's note, 231
St. Augustine (354–430), 147, 149
St. Basil of Caesarea (329–79), 152n22
St. Columba (d. 597), 144–45, 148
Stewart, Susan, 83–84, 133n6
St. Maximus the Confessor (ca. 580–662), 147, 148–49
Straits, Michael, 178, 181–82
"Strange Meeting" (Owen), 123–24
style
  alliterative verse, 20–21, 80
  as archaic, 30, 108
  archaisms and high, 81–82
  authenticity and, 108–9
  Brogan on "Ossianic," 108
  "Common Speech," 22
  "high" or epic, 21–22, 80–82, 86, 89
  "low" or common, 22
  in *LR*, 21–22, 80–82, 86, 108
  modernism as literary, 3–4
  paratactic constructions in, 21–22, 80–82
  stylistic influences on and comparisons with, 80–81, 85
  Tolkien on, 81, 108
  tone and, 81

subversion
  fantasy as subversive, 10, 171–72
  medieval texts and subversive meaning, 5
  political and social, 2
  tone as, 22–23
  traditions as subversive, 11–12
suffering
  as redemptive, 162, 178, 182
  as witnessing the pain of others, 129, 136n24
swords, 18, 52–53, 79, 89–90

Táin Bo Cuailnge, 143
Tea Club-Barrovian Society (TCBS), 94
technology, *see* mechanization
Tennyson, Alfred, Lord, 7–8, 47–48
  as influence, 82
  Morris and, 44
  as poetic model, 82, 84–85
  Tolkien compared and contrasted with, 84–86, 88–89
textuality
  edition as rewriting, 33
  historical complexity of texts, 31–32
  historicity and, 6, 29–39
  medieval manuscript culture, 30
  "originality" and history of text, 32–33
  plurality and fluidity of text, 32–33
  Tolkien's emphasis on, 33
  "textuary modernity," 33
The Hobbit (Tolkien), 26, 55, 61, 94, 101, 112, 164, 191–92
Thompson, Edward P., 99
time
  Elf-land and discrepancies of, 44
  Elvish and human perception of, 54
  eternity and *dustsceawung*, 47
  Northern theory of, 48–49, 53
  primeval vs. old, 48
  temporal signals in language, 53–55
  Tolkien's consciousness of as modern, 55–56
  Victorian consciousness of, 47–48

INDEX

timelessness, 6, 36–37
Tolkien, Christopher, 164
   correspondence with father, 51–52, 95, 165, 208
   on "The Scouring of the Shire," 131
   Silm edited by, 33, 35
Tolkien, Edith Bratt, 21, 182
Tolkien, John Ronald Reuel
   as antimodernist, 81, 140, 141
   as apolitical, 95–96, 101
   biography linked to content of works, 21, 177–78, 182
   Butler compared with, 205, 207–11
   on Celtic influences, 146–47
   childhood of, 177
   E. Bratt and, 21, 182
   as Hobbit, 177–78
   on "King-Arthurish" Middle Ages, 20
   on *LR* and Christian theology, 165
   Macpherson compared with, 71, 109–10, 113
   Malory compared with, 21–22
   Morris compared and contrasted with, 96–97, 100–2
   primacy of philology and creation of *LR*, 109, 118
   Scott compared with, 68–69, 71
   on Shire as Utopian, 101
   on study of language separated from study of literature, 177
   Tennyson compared with, 84–86, 88–89
   on Welsh language, 107
Tolkien and the Great War (Garth), 114
Tolkien the Medievalist (Chance), 4
Tom Bombadil, 48, 52, 140–44, 149
tone, 22–23, 81, 109
translation
   and authorship, 35
   of medieval themes, 1
Tree and Leaf (Tolkien), 52
"Tree of Tales" (Tolkien), 32
trees
   agency of, 143
   as image, 94
   Tolkien's affection for, 114
   see also Ents

Uncharted Realms of Tolkien, The (Lewis), 195
Unexpected Morning Visit, An (Nasmith), 189–90
Unexpected Party, An (Nasmith), 192
Unwin, Stanley, 105
utopianism, 3
   vs. Arcadian pastoralism, 98–99
   Marx on, 99
   Morris and, 95, 96–99
   nostalgia and, 83
   pastoral ideals in, 8, 11
   Shire as utopian, 101

"Valedictory Address" (Tolkien), 172–73, 175, 177
Victorian literary tradition
   archeology and, 47
   dustsceawung "contemplation of the dust" and, 44
   fairy stories in, 44
   medievalist fantasy and, 7
   medieval sources and, 44
   time consciousness of Victorians, 47–48
   Tolkien and, 2–3, 44
   war reduced to symbolic heroism and chivalry in, 8, 77–78, 131
   see also specific authors
victory, Tolkien on, 132
violence
   chivalric war and, 129–30
   language and, 9, 125, 126–27, 128, 130, 131, 133–34n7
   medieval violence as Other, 78
   "Scouring of the Shire" as exploration of, 130
visual arts, 10–11
   Nasmith on Middle-earth as subject of works, 189–202
   Tolkien's own illustrations, 193
von Humboldt, Alexander, 195

Wagner, Richard, 3
Wain, John, 96
Waldman, Milton, 112
Wanderer, The, 45, 83, 175–76, 177
war, 2
   antiwar theme in *LR*, 210–11
   art as propaganda during, 123, 124
   as ennobling or heroic, 79, 84
   "high style" and descriptions of, in *LR*, 80–82, 86
   inspirations for depictions of, 90n3
   landscape of, in *LR*, 87, 114
   Macpherson and, 113
   mechanized warfare, 8, 19, 87, 125, 208
   medieval warfare and *LR*, 79–80, 87
   as moralized combat in Victorian medievalist literature, 8, 77–78, 131
   restoration of natural order and, 86
   as spectatorial or demanding witness, 129–30, 136n24
   as symbolized, 128
   Tolkien on, in *LR*, 125
   Tolkien on victory, 132
   Tolkien's experiences of, 7–8, 50, 78–79, 87, 90n3, 113–14, 125, 128–29, 135n23
   violence and linguistic confrontation, 9, 125, 126–27, 128, 130, 131, 133–34n7
   WWII, *LR* as allegory for, 78, 115, 125–26
   see also chivalry; war discourse
war discourse, 89–90
   cultural factors as context for, 79
   in *LR*, 77–90
   Owen's "Strange Meeting" as, 123–24
   realism and allegory blended in, 87
Ware, Kallistos, 141, 144

War Mausoleum, Verdun, 200
water
   Christian imagery and, 145–46
   as environ of the dead, 114
   Otherworld associated with, 137n36, 144–46
Weatherby, Harold, 147, 148
Welsh, 53–54, 146
   as inspiration for Sindarin, 58n39, 107
   Tolkien on, 107
   see also Celticism
West, the (in Middle-earth), 88–89
White, Hayden, 38, 72
will
   heroic will (courage), 83–84
   see also courage
Williams, David, 163
Wilson, Edmund, 23
Winter, Jay, 82
Woolf, Virginia, 81
World War I
   as context for art and literature, 200–2
   post-war nationalism as context for writing, 66
   propaganda during, 128, 131, 132n1
   Tolkien's personal experiences and *LR*, 7–8, 50, 78–79, 87, 90n3, 125, 128–29, 135n23
World War II
   as context for writing, 18, 82, 125
   efforts to read *LR* as allegory for, 78, 115, 125–26
   racism and Nazism during, 164–65
Woses, 18, 62, 86, 159
Wyatt, Joan, 195–96

Yeats, William Butler, 4, 142
Yonge, Charlotte, 77–78

Printed in Great Britain
by Amazon